RUSSIA

A SHORT HISTORY

Also by Abraham Ascher

Stalin: A Beginner's Guide
The Russian Revolution: A Beginner's Guide

RUSSIA

A SHORT HISTORY

ABRAHAM ASCHER

ONEWORLD

A Oneworld Book

First published by Oneworld Publications 2002
Second edition published 2009
This revised third edition published 2017
Reprinted, 2020, 2022

ISBN 978-1-78607-142-2
eISBN 978-1-78607-143-9

Typeset by Jayvee, Trivandrum, India
Printed and bound in Great Britain by Clays Ltd, Elcograf S.p.A.

Oneworld Publications
10 Bloomsbury Street
London WC1B 3SR
England

Stay up to date with the latest books,
special offers, and exclusive content from
Oneworld with our newsletter

Sign up on our website
oneworld-publications.com

MIX
Paper from
responsible sources
FSC
www.fsc.org   FSC® C018072

CONTENTS

PREFACE TO THE THIRD EDITION

Writing a book is always difficult, but to write a history of Russia in about ninety thousand words, from its beginnings in the ninth century to the most recent events under President Putin, proved to be far more challenging than I ever imagined. Important events and developments that deserve several pages had often to be compressed into a few sentences, and some subjects, most notably cultural and intellectual trends, had to be accorded much less space than I would have liked. I am painfully aware that these are shortcomings of the book, but I hope that I have succeeded in my main goal, which is to present a coherent account of Russia's political, social, and economic institutions as they evolved over one thousand years, so as to enable the reader to gain a better understanding of contemporary Russia.

It was in this spirit that I agreed to update the book that I had already brought up to date once before, in 2009. At that time I added a section that outlined the main features of Russian history during the first eight years of Vladimir Putin's presidency. Now, it seems to me important to evaluate the changes that have occurred since the last update because this year marks a milestone in Russian history. One hundred years have passed since the tsarist regime was overthrown and the Bolsheviks under Lenin's leadership took control of the country with the aim of creating a socialist economy. The means of production were to be owned by the government and there would be only minor discrepancies in income. The Bolsheviks never came close to achieving the goal of an egalitarian society, and it could be argued that since the Soviet Union was an economically backward country it would take time to achieve the final goals. But since the collapse of communism in 1991, the country has drifted further away from Lenin's aims. And Russia's leaders now do not even pretend to be socialists. Putin has nurtured what is generally known as a market economy heavily controlled by the state, an economy that favors the rich and that is riddled with corruption.

Moreover, President Putin has increasingly made the restoration of Russia as a great world power the focus of his rule. The clearest example of this is his pursuit of an aggressive policy towards Ukraine, a large state that gained independence in 1991. The Baltic countries Estonia, Latvia, and Lithuania – which also became independent in 1991 – are now fearful that Russia may have designs on bringing them under its control. The West eyes these potential developments with much anxiety and there is a danger of continuing tension between the West and Russia. It is to be hoped that a revival of what was known as the Cold War, which lasted from 1946 until 1991, can be avoided.

There are some difficult questions that readers of this book may wish to ponder: were the revolutionaries such as Lenin, Trotsky, and Stalin, who engineered the revolution of 1917, deluding themselves in believing that they could create an egalitarian society? Were there steps that these leaders or their successors could have taken to assure the realization of socialism, or at least to prevent the collapse of the Soviet Union? Does Putin's increasing interest in restoring Russia as a great power suggest that nationalism is of greater concern to the citizens of Russia than the creation of a socialist society? When I began to study Russian history in the early 1950s, most historians would not have considered these questions germane or interesting. The transformation of Russia in the hundred years since the Bolsheviks assumed power in Russia makes them unavoidable.

I would not have been able to write this book had I not had

the experience of teaching Russian history for more than forty years. Students in my courses have often raised difficult questions, and I am grateful to them for having stimulated me to broaden my knowledge of certain aspects of Russian history. The staff at Oneworld, Victoria Warner and Rebecca Clare, as well as the copy editor, Anthony Nanson, were most helpful at every stage of the writing of the first edition of the book. Shadi Doostdar, who supervised the preparation of the present edition, has been very supportive in my composing of the update of the 2009 edition. The anonymous reader of the manuscript made valuable comments that I took into account in revising the manuscript. David Inglesfield, the copy editor, made many suggestions that have improved this work. Finally, I would like to express my special thanks to my good friend Marc Raeff, who read the first edition of the book with his usual care and made many suggestions for its improvement. Of course, I am responsible for any errors and deficiencies that remain.

Abraham Ascher
New York, September 2017

MAPS

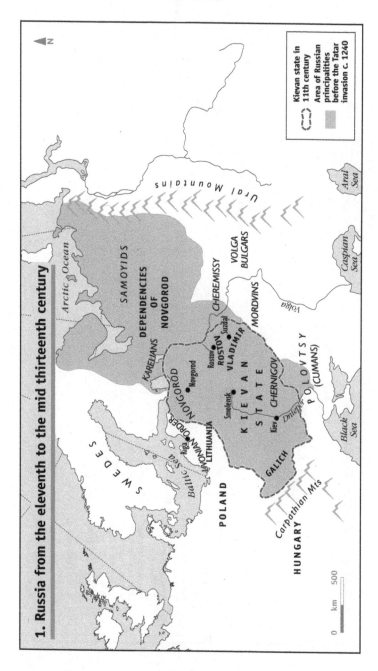

1. Russia from the eleventh to the mid thirteenth century

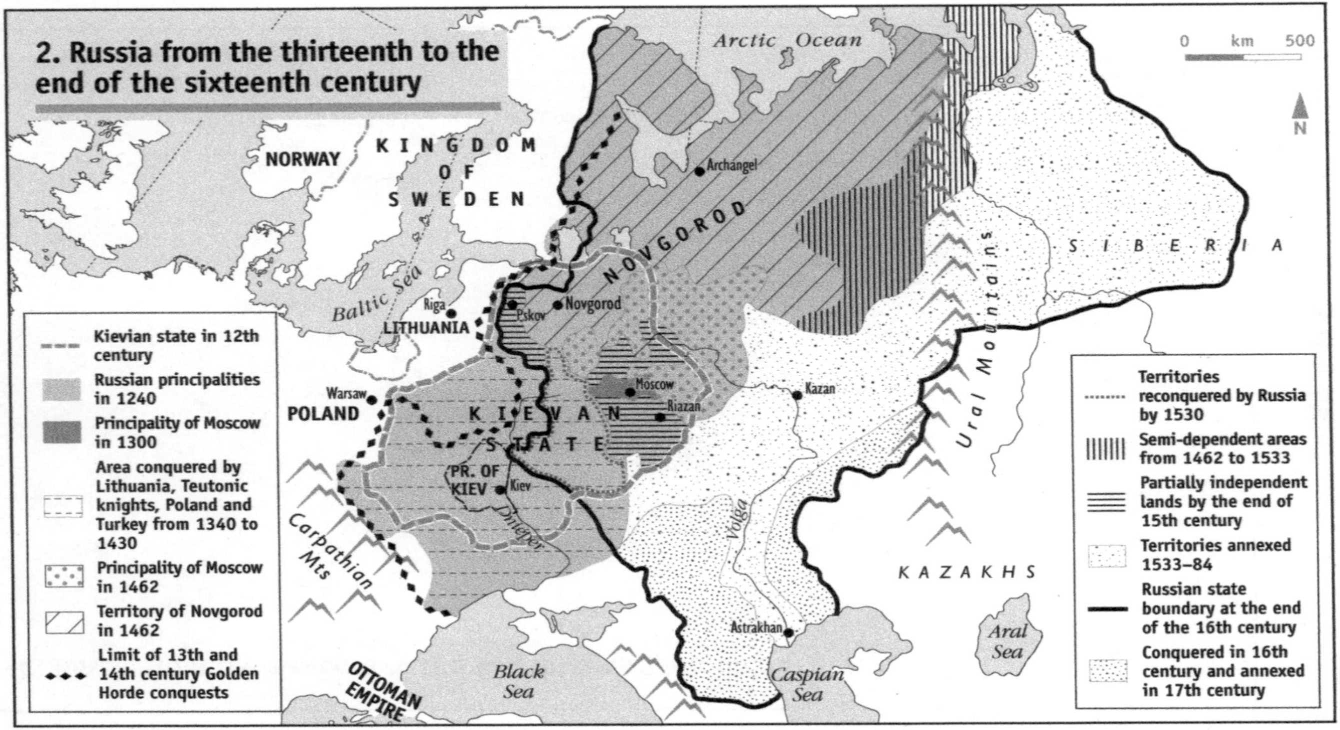
2. Russia from the thirteenth to the end of the sixteenth century
Arctic Ocean
0 km 500
N
NORWAY
KINGDOM OF SWEDEN
Baltic Sea
Riga
LITHUANIA
Archangel
NOVGOROD
Pskov
Novgorod
Moscow
Riazan
Kazan
Warsaw
POLAND
KIEVAN STATE
PR. OF KIEV
Kiev
Dnieper
Carpathian Mts
OTTOMAN EMPIRE
Black Sea
Volga
Astrakhan
Caspian Sea
Ural Mountains
SIBERIA
KAZAKHS
Aral Sea
Kievian state in 12th century
Russian principalities in 1240
Principality of Moscow in 1300
Area conquered by Lithuania, Teutonic knights, Poland and Turkey from 1340 to 1430
Principality of Moscow in 1462
Territory of Novgorod in 1462
Limit of 13th and 14th century Golden Horde conquests
Territories reconquered by Russia by 1530
Semi-dependent areas from 1462 to 1533
Partially independent lands by the end of 15th century
Territories annexed 1533–84
Russian state boundary at the end of the 16th century
Conquered in 16th century and annexed in 17th century

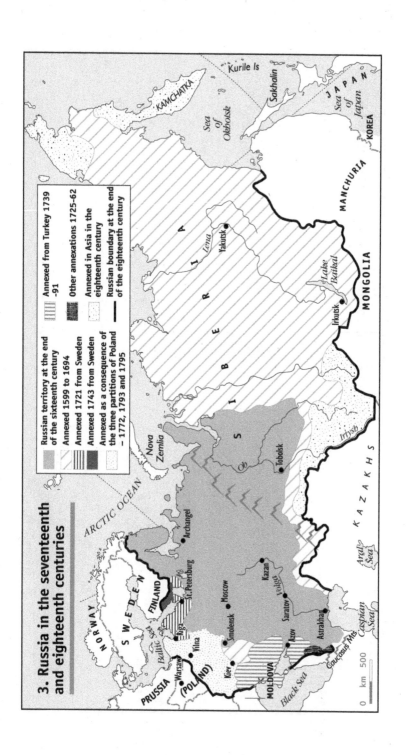

3. Russia in the seventeenth and eighteenth centuries

Russian territory at the end of the sixteenth century

Annexed 1599 to 1694

Annexed 1721 from Sweden

Annexed 1743 from Sweden

Annexed as a consequence of the three partitions of Poland – 1772, 1793 and 1795

Annexed from Turkey 1739 -91

Other annexations 1725-62

Annexed in Asia in the eighteenth century

Russian boundary at the end of the eighteenth century

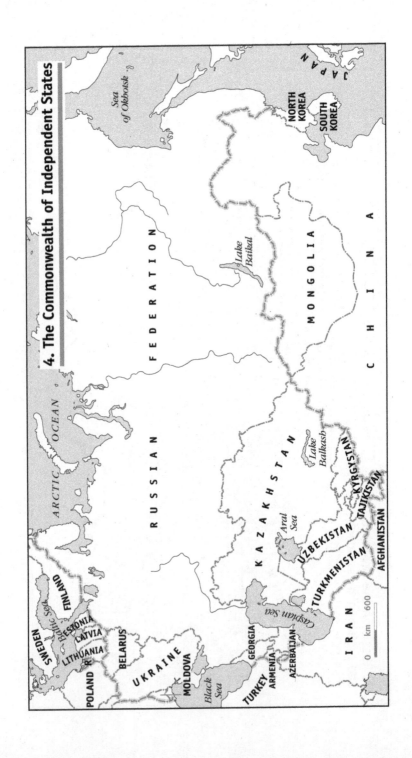

4. The Commonwealth of Independent States

1

THE BEGINNINGS

For over a century and a half, intellectuals and scholars interested in Russia have differed sharply over the essential characteristics of the country's economic, social, and political institutions, and its culture. Much of the time, the debate centered on the question of whether Russia was part of Western European civilization or of Asian civilization, or whether it had somehow amalgamated basic features of both. That this was not a debate taken lightly became clear as early as 1836, when the philosopher P. Ia. Chaadaev published the first of his 'Philosophical Letters', in which he bemoaned Russia's cultural isolation and its failure to make a signal contribution to world culture. Neither 'of the East nor of the West', Russia, according to Chaadaev, had no great traditions of its own; 'alone in the world, we have given nothing to the world, we have taught it nothing . . . we have not contributed to the progress of the human spirit and what we have borrowed of this progress we have distorted . . . we have produced nothing for the common benefit of mankind.' Chaadaev's sweeping and harsh pronouncements had the effect, in the words of the political thinker and activist Alexander Herzen, 'of a pistol shot in the dead of night'. Tsar Nicholas I declared Chaadaev insane and put him under house arrest. Among Russia's educated elite, Chaadaev's disparagement generated excitement of a different sort. Intellectuals took Chaadaev's views seriously and initiated a passionate debate that quickly divided them into two groups, the Slavophiles and the Westerners, and in one form or another their historical and philosophical discussions continue to this very day. An observer of contemporary conditions in Russia reported from Moscow in the *Times Literary Supplement* of 19 November 1999 that 'In Russian intellectual life, a conversation that was cut off and redirected after the Bolshevik Revolution has resumed its course. Its basic theme: East, West, whence, and whither Russia?'

The Slavophiles and Westerners of the early nineteenth century were not at odds with each other over all public issues. For example, both groups believed that such deeply rooted features of Russian society as serfdom and government censorship should be abolished. But beyond that they parted company. The Slavophiles were profoundly religious and revered Russian Orthodoxy, a faith they considered to be much more spiritual than Western Christendom, which they disdained as allegedly under the thrall of cold rationalism. They also disdained Western conceptions of law as destructive of the social bonds that hold society together. In Russia, the Slavophiles claimed, people settled conflicts not by litigation but by discussing their differences in a kindly manner and by unanimous agreement. Nor did the Slavophiles believe in the efficacy of constitutional government, then widely advocated in the West, though they did condemn the arbitrary bureaucracy that meddled in the lives of the Russian people. And the Slavophiles did not favor the institution of private property for peasants, preferring instead the tradition of communal ownership of land that had evolved in many parts of the Russian countryside. They insisted that the attempts of reformers ever since Tsar Peter the Great in the early eighteenth century to introduce Western institutions and values into Russia should be rejected, for they undermined the meritorious features of Russian civilization.

By contrast, the Westerners, a group with diverse views on how to improve conditions in Russia, tended to be secularists and were highly critical of the historical path their country had followed.

Although they were no less patriotic than the Slavophiles, they insisted that Russia was a backward country in need of fundamental change. Some Westerners were socialists, some were liberals, but they all respected the achievements of Europe in science and, more generally, in education, and they favored the replacement of tsarist autocracy with constitutional government.

There is good reason for this sharp divergence of opinion on Russia's past. The history of the country is highly complex, and on many critical developments the evidence is so scant that a consensus is hard to come by. Of course, the histories of nearly all countries are replete with uncertainties. But in the case of Russia an additional factor has stimulated controversy. Ever since the ninth century AD the country has been subjected to a wide range of different influences whose impact it is hard to gauge. Until the mid thirteenth century, the economic, social, and political institutions of Rus, as the country was then known, bore certain similarities to those in Central and Western Europe. But the Mongol invasions of 1237, which marked the beginning of two centuries of foreign domination, deepened the isolation of Rus from Western Europe that had begun in the late twelfth century, and influenced cultural trends in various ways. Cut off from the West, Russia remained largely unaffected by the Protestant Reformation in the sixteenth century, the scientific revolution of the seventeenth, and the Enlightenment of the eighteenth, all movements that promoted individualism and rationalism.

Russia also differed from most European countries in several other respects. The Industrial Revolution, which beginning in the mid eighteenth century produced vast economic and social changes in the West, did not take hold in Russia until late in the nineteenth century. Moreover, serfdom, an institution that had largely disappeared in Central and Western Europe by the sixteenth century, became firmly entrenched in Russia in 1649 when a new Code of Law reaffirmed the subservient condition of peasants. Serfdom was not abolished until 1861. Furthermore, the principle of autocracy, long challenged in the West and seriously undermined by the French Revolution of 1789, remained the guiding principle of government in Russia until 1917. Initially, the word 'autocrat' in the Russian lands referred to a ruler who was independent of any foreign power. But in the late fifteenth century, and even more so in the sixteenth, the term referred to a leader with unlimited power. Not all proponents of autocracy agreed fully on its precise meaning, but all tended to favor a definition akin to the one that appeared in 1832 as the first article of the *Fundamental Laws of the Russian Empire* (the first volume of the Digest that listed all laws still in effect): 'The Emperor of all the Russias is a sovereign with autocratic and unlimited powers. To obey the commands not merely from fear but according to the dictates of one's conscience is ordained by God himself.' In short, the emperor's powers were boundless and in theory the tsar could do as he wished because he alone was answerable to God. The tsar set policy, he established the laws of the land, and he was responsible for their enactment. By the early twentieth century, this view of governmental authority was the single most divisive issue in the political conflicts that preceded the collapse of tsarism.

In the meantime, the make-up of the Russian state, originally populated predominantly by Slavs, had changed dramatically. The steady expansion of Russia to the east, south, and west, which began in the sixteenth century and lasted until late in the nineteenth century, transformed the country into a multinational empire in which some fifty-five percent of the population was not ethnically Slavic. Among other things, this development hindered the emergence of a nation state, a political association with a relatively homogeneous population that shares a sense of nationality. The minorities, of which there were more than 150, spoke their own languages, retained their own cultural traditions, and often were heirs of a long and proud history. Although Christianity of the Orthodox persuasion was the state religion, with more adherents than any other faith, by the nineteenth century several other Christian denominations had sizable followings, as did Islam and Judaism.

GEOGRAPHY

By the early twentieth century Russia appeared to many within the elite to be a clumsy giant.[1] A vast empire comprising one-sixth of the earth's surface, stretching from the White Sea and Arctic Ocean to the Black and Caspian Seas, to Persia, Afghanistan, India, and China, and from the Baltic Sea to the Pacific Ocean, it was almost three times the size of the United States. The absence of natural boundaries within this huge territory had facilitated both internal migration and territorial expansion, but at the same time it deprived the country of natural defenses against invaders, a frequent threat over the centuries. Populated in the early twentieth century by some 130 million people, the country was blessed with abundant natural resources, though these were unevenly distributed throughout the land. In a rough triangle from Lake Lagoda to Kazan to south of the Pripet Marshes (near Kiev), mixed forests predominated. This is the region central to what came to be Muscovy; the climate is severe and most of the land is poor, inhospitable to agriculture. Rye was the staple crop of this zone, though barley, oats, and wheat were also grown. Near Novgorod some flax and hemp were cultivated. Because of climatic conditions the region regularly endured droughts and devastating famines.

Another zone, known as the taiga, consists largely of conifer forests and stretches north to the tundra and east for hundreds of miles all the way to the Pacific Ocean. The subsoil of the tundra, which extends along the Arctic coast and inland between the valleys and comprises about fifteen percent of Russia's land mass, is permanently frozen. Plants in this region grow for only about three months of the year. Its economy depended heavily on the fur trade and to a lesser extent on fishing and the extraction of tar, pitch, and potash and more recently on coal and minerals. The shore along the White Sea is also rich in salt. Siberia, a huge sector of this region, was known mainly for its furs and some gold.

A third zone, the steppes, south of the above-mentioned zones, comprises about twelve percent of the Russian land mass.

A treeless expanse from the western border to the Altay mountains in Central Asia, it included the so-called bread basket of the empire. It has a variety of rich black-earth soils, enjoys dry warm summers, and was in many ways ideal for grain cultivation. But even here the rainfall is low and tends to be erratic, another cause of the periodic famines in Russia.

The extensive and elaborate system of natural waterways, such as the Volga, Dnieper, and Don rivers, the Caspian, Black, and Baltic Seas, Lake Ladoga, and Lake Baikal, greatly facilitated commerce and internal migration. But one serious drawback has hampered commerce. Only Murmansk, founded in 1915 in the extreme north-west of the country (next to Finland), has access to an open, ice-free ocean and is therefore navigable throughout the year. On the other hand, Russia's natural resources are enormous. No other country can boast of so large a variety of minerals, and only the United States is richer in resources. The empire had about twenty percent of the world's coal supplies, located primarily in the Donets (Ukraine) and Kuznetsk (in mid Siberia) basins. Its huge oil and gas reserves may have exceeded half the world's total supply. And there were vast supplies of iron, manganese, copper (of relatively low quality), lead, zinc, aluminum, nickel, gold, platinum, asbestos, and potash. Well endowed by nature, Russia seemed destined for a long period of leadership on the world scene.

But because it failed to discard its archaic social and political system, Russia could not take advantage of the advances in modern science and technology that, beginning in the seventeenth century, steadily enriched and transformed Western societies. By the nineteenth century Russia lagged far behind much of Europe in economic development, national literacy, and the standard of living of its people. To understand this backwardness it is necessary to study history, but one should not assume that all students of history will agree on why Russia developed as it did. The question touches on the highly sensitive issue of national identity and is often discussed by even the most learned scholars in charged language that tends to foster disagreement rather than consensus on the nature of Russia's past and destiny.

THE RISE OF KIEV

The very first problem that the student of history encounters is the origin of the Russian state. According to the Normanist school of historians,[2] the beginnings of a Slavic commonwealth can be traced to AD 862, when the tribes known as 'Varangian Russes' sent an urgent message to Scandinavian princes for help: 'Our whole land is great and rich, but there is no order in it. Come to rule and reign over us!' The oldest of three Scandinavian princes, Riurik, settled in Novgorod, in the north, which allegedly became 'the land of Rus'. His younger brothers are said to have gone to 'Byeloozero' and 'Izborsk' to serve as rulers. Riurik, the Normanists claim, fundamentally shaped the culture and political institutions of Russia, which during its first two centuries assumed a distinctly Scandinavian character.

Although archeological evidence supports the presence of Scandinavians in Rus in the ninth century, the Normanist interpretation has been widely challenged and is no longer accepted in its original form. Historians[3] have demonstrated that long before Riurik appeared on the scene, Slavs in Kiev had assimilated the cultural achievements of numerous peoples who had lived in southern Russia since the sixth century, among them the Cimmerians, the Scythians, the Sarmations, the Goths, and the Khazars. In contacts with Hellenic, Byzantine, and Oriental civilizations, these peoples had developed their own material culture, art, and customs that were no less advanced than those of the Scandinavians. Although the Russian dynasty beginning in the ninth century was Norman, and Scandinavian influences on Russia were significant, the basic culture of Russia was essentially indigenous.

Whatever the differences over the origins of Russia, all historians now agree that the Kievan state or Kievan Rus, which emerged in the ninth century and existed for some four centuries, was the first large and powerful Slavic state and that it strongly influenced the course of Russian history. The Kievan era can be divided into three fairly distinct periods. During the first, from 878 to 972, the princes of Novgorod, successors of Riurik, expanded into the south and created a vast empire stretching from the Baltic to the Black Sea and from the Carpathian mountains to the Caspian Sea. The idea behind the expansion was essentially commercial, to gain control of a vast network of commercial highways in the Pontic and Caspian regions. Prince Oleg, who initiated the expansion in 878 or 879, constantly waged war and when he defeated the Magyars (who migrated to present-day Hungary) the Kievan principality seized control over the whole Dnieper from Kiev to the Black Sea. During his reign the Russians engaged in extensive trade with the Greeks, the profits from which became the basis of Kievan prosperity.

During the second period, from 972 to 1139, Kievan princes sought to stabilize the new state, and a principal means to that end was the adoption of Christianity. Apparently, Prince Vladimir (977?–1015) concluded that if Kiev was to become a major power it would have to abandon paganism and end Russia's religious isolation. Not much is known about the religious faith of the Russians up to this time, but there is substantial evidence that the Kievans worshiped clan ancestors, who were regarded as guardians and protectors. There is also evidence that Slavs revered rivers, nymphs, and other spirits as well as trees, woods, and water sprites. In addition, they worshiped gods of lightning, thunder, the great goddess Mother Earth, and Veles, believed to be the protector of commerce. Only the upper classes, it seems, prayed in temples in which priests officiated.

How and why Kiev came to adopt Christianity remains unclear. Legend has it that Prince Vladimir sent an emissary to the leaders of the main faiths to examine the beliefs of each. In the end, he allegedly rejected Islam because it forbade alcohol, which 'is the joy of the Russian', and Judaism, because it was the religion of a dispersed people without a state. More likely, political considerations prompted Vladimir to opt for Christianity. In 987–8 the Byzantine Emperor Basil sought military support from Vladimir to help him fend off attacks from foreign enemies. In return, Basil promised Vladimir the hand of his sister, Anna, an offer that broke with a long-standing Byzantine court tradition against marriage with foreigners. Deeply honored and pressured by dignitaries at his court who had already converted to Christianity, Vladimir accepted the offer, which was conditioned on his baptism. In February 988 Vladimir was baptized and adopted the Christian name of Basil. The Byzantine emperor, behaving in a most un-Christian manner, now refused to live up to his side of the bargain. In a rage, Basil attacked Byzantium and after several victories he achieved his goal, marriage to a Christian princess.

As is often true of converts, Vladimir became an ardent advocate of the new faith. Determined to root out paganism, Vladimir ordered the destruction of all statues of pagan deities, directed the entire population of Kiev, Novgorod, and other cities to be baptized in the local rivers, and took the initiative in having Christian churches built throughout the realm. He also created a church hierarchy and church schools to educate the children of the elite in the doctrines of Christianity. Kiev, where an elegant cathedral was built, soon emerged as the ecclesiastical center of Rus. The metropolitan, ordained by the patriarch of Constantinople, resided in the city, which now also served as the political center of Rus.

For the Russians and for many people in the rest of the world, the country's conversion to Christianity signified that it was now part of the civilized world, not only because the people had turned to monotheism but also because the conversion added momentum to making permanent the written language (Cyrillic), the early form of which had been invented in the mid ninth century by St Cyril and St Methodius. For centuries to come, Christianity shaped much of the nation's culture. It was of critical importance that Russian Christianity came not from Rome but from Byzantium, where the church was clearly subordinate to the secular ruler. In the West, the church asserted its independence and at times even claimed to be superior to the princely authorities, but in Russia the church tended to buttress the temporal ruler's claim to supreme power.

When Vladimir died in 1015 Kievan Rus's prestige had risen appreciably, but, plagued by intermittent outbursts of bloody clashes between political dignitaries, it was nevertheless a politically unstable principality. The underlying problem was the absence of a clearly defined rule for succession; on the death of a prince, his sons often waged war against each other, and only after some had died could a semblance of stability be restored. For example, Iaroslav (1015–54) succeeded Vladimir but did not become sole ruler until 1036, when his brother Mstislav died. Despite this instability, Kiev developed into a remarkably prosperous state with political institutions that were, in many respects, as sophisticated and efficient as those in Central and Western Europe.

KIEV'S ECONOMY

For its economic well-being, Kiev depended on both agriculture and trade, which explains the existence of some three hundred cities with a combined population in the twelfth century of about one million people out of a total of between seven and eight million. Some four hundred thousand of the urban dwellers lived in the three major cities, Kiev, Novgorod, and Smolensk. The land in the southern regions of the principality was very fertile; so rich, in fact, that after one ploughing it produced excellent harvests for a number of years without any further tilling. The ax was the main agricultural tool, but ploughs were also widely used for the production of spelt, wheat, buckwheat, oats, and barley. Apple and cherry orchards were widespread in what is today Ukraine. Kievans also engaged in horse and cattle breeding. Slaves, indentured laborers, and freemen performed most of the agricultural work on one of three types of larger estates belonging to princes, boyars (senior nobles), or to the church.

Kievans engaged in lively domestic as well as foreign commerce. The north depended on the south for grain, in return for which the south obtained iron and salt. At the same time, the cities imported agricultural goods and exported tools and other manufactured goods. Foreign trade proceeded largely along the Dnieper river and then across the Black Sea to Constantinople, which became the main southern outlet for Russian goods such as furs, honey, wax, and slaves (after the tenth century the Russians stopped the selling of Christian slaves). The Russian traders, in turn, brought back wines, silk fabrics, art objects (in particular, icons), jewelry, fruits, and glassware. Kiev also engaged in fairly extensive trade with the Orient, exporting furs, honey, wax, walrus tusks, woolen cloth, and linen, and importing spices, precious stones, silk and satin fabrics, and weapons of Damask steel as well as horses. The sacking of Constantinople in 1204 by the knights of the Fourth Crusade put an end to the Black Sea trade, but some of the slack was taken up by the overland trade between Kiev and Central Europe that had developed in the twelfth century. The Russians supplied Europe with furs, wax, honey, flax, hemp, tow, burlap, hops, tallow, sheepskin, and hides, and imported manufactured goods such as woolen cloth, linen, silk, needles, weapons, glassware, and metals such as iron, copper, tin, and lead.

By the standards of the Middle Ages, the gross product of Kiev was impressive. A small minority, most notably the princes of the major principalities, can be said to have been successful capitalists who enjoyed considerable wealth. On the other hand, laborers were not 'workers' in the modern sense of the word. Most of the people worked on the land as free peasants and most of the manufacturers were artisans who produced their wares in small establishments. Slaves, generally foreigners captured in wartime, were used to perform household services, but the total number was small.

It should be noted that feudalism, the dominant social and political order in Central and Western Europe by the eleventh century, did not take hold in Kievan Rus. A personal relationship between nobles under which a lord (the suzerain) granted a fief to a vassal in return for certain military and economic obligations, feudalism was the political and military system of medieval Europe in the region roughly west of Poland. Kievan Rus was organized differently. The upper classes, consisting of the prince's retinue and an aristocracy of wealthy people, merged into the social group known as the boyars, whose power and prestige derived from their possession of large landed estates. By the early thirteenth century, the number of princes, many with relatively small landed estates, had risen substantially, and they came to be regarded as the upper crust of boyardom. Though highly influential, the boyars did not constitute an exclusive social order. Through outstanding service in a prince's retinue a commoner could rise to the position of boyar, though this did not occur very often. Moreover, the boyars did not enjoy legal privileges as a class. For example, they were not the only people who could be landowners. By the same token, many boyars retained close ties to one or another city.

The middle class in Kievan Rus was quite large, in fact proportionately larger than in the cities of Western Europe at the time, and consisted of merchants as well as a stratum of independent farmers who were fairly well off. The lower classes were divided into several groups. The most numerous were the *smerdy*, peasants or hired laborers who were personally free, paid state taxes, and performed military service in wartime. But the *smerdy* did not enjoy full ownership of their property. For example, at a *smerd*'s death his sons inherited his belongings, but if he had no sons the property went to the prince, who was authorized to assign a share to unmarried daughters. But unlike the serfs in the West, the *smerdy* were not legally bound to the land and were not subject to the arbitrary will of the landowner.

The political system of Kievan Rus can best be described as an amalgam of three features, the monarchic, the aristocratic, and, for want of a better word, the 'democratic'. Although these were closely intertwined, for pedagogical reasons it is best to discuss each feature separately.

Designed originally to prevent discord, the political system had evolved by the eleventh century into an incredibly complicated structure that, ironically, tended to generate interminable conflict. Its underlying principle, known as the rota system, was that each member of the House of Riurik was entitled to a share in the common patrimony, the ten lands of the Kievan kingdom. The senior prince was to occupy the throne of Kiev and the other thrones would be distributed according to the place of each prince in an elaborate genealogical tree of the family. (The only exception was Novgorod, where the prince was elected from the princely family at large.) Thus, upon the death of the senior prince all other thrones would be redistributed. In theory, the scheme seemed ideal, but as the number of princes multiplied the system became hopelessly confusing. For example, according to the official rules, the elder son of the first brother in a princely generation was considered genealogically equal to his third uncle (that is, the fourth brother). Inevitably, disputes arose over claims to specific thrones and increasingly these were settled by the sword.

Initially, each member of the Riurik clan considered himself to be the social and political equal of every other member. But the Prince of Kiev, looked upon as the 'father' of the younger princes, enjoyed certain prerogatives that gave him special status. He assumed the title of 'suzerain prince' or 'grand duke', and in that capacity assigned the junior princes to their provinces, adjudicated disputes between them, and, most important, acted as the guardian of the entire realm of Rus. When major decisions had to be reached – for example, whenever Kiev faced attacks by foreign enemies – the Prince of Kiev would convoke a family council of all the princes. By the end of the twelfth century, the elaborate system no longer worked as designed. Increasingly, the grand duke treated the smaller princes as his vassals and the principle of genealogical seniority was often disregarded.

Although quite powerful, the princes could not act entirely on their own. In the administration of the realm, the implementation of legislative measures, the codification of laws, and the conclusion of international treaties, the princes needed the approval of the Boyar Council, which represented the aristocracy, the second branch of the political structure. On occasion, the Boyar

Council acted as a supreme court. The precise functions of the Council were generally determined by custom rather than law. Significantly, the boyars were not obliged to serve any one prince and could leave at any time to work for the ruler of another principality. Even if a boyar received land from a prince, that did not oblige him to serve his benefactor in perpetuity. The land became the private property of the boyar, who was not regarded as the vassal of any one prince.

The *veche* (popular assembly) represented the third, 'democratic', element in the political system of Kievan Rus. All city freemen could participate in its deliberations and its votes, and residents in nearby towns could also attend meetings of the assembly, although generally only the men in the capital showed up. Custom dictated that all decisions be unanimous, but on occasion differences were so sharp that the *veche* could not reach any decision. Princes, mayors, or groups of citizens could convoke meetings of the assembly, which tended to follow the lead of the princes and boyars in matters of legislation and administration. But after the mid twelfth century some assemblies grew more independent and even played a role in the selection of princes and sometimes went so far as to call for the abdication of a ruler.

The socio-economic and political order of Kievan Rus was thus quite unique, not to be confused with the feudal order dominant in the West. For about two centuries, that order functioned relatively efficiently, but during the years from 1139 to 1237 it began to falter. Rivalries between princes and between cities and principalities sharpened, leading to an ever looser federation of Russian states. The growth of regional commerce further weakened the bonds between the principalities. Kiev focused on trade with Byzantium and, as already noted, after 1204 with Central Europe; Smolensk and Novgorod turned their attention increasingly to commerce in the Baltic region; Riazan and Suzdal sought to expand their trade with the Orient. The boyars in the various principalities grew stronger and became less and less interested in maintaining close contact with their neighbors. Although the various Russian states did not exactly view their neighbors as 'foreigners', they did begin to look upon them as 'outsiders'. That the bonds of unity had been frayed became evident in 1237 when the Russians proved incapable of mounting a united stand against the advancing Mongols (also known as Tatars), who had reached Rus and soon threatened the entire realm. The Mongols had given ample warning of their intentions fourteen years earlier, in 1223, when they invaded the south-eastern region then inhabited by the Polovtsy (or Cumans). The Polovtsy appealed to the Russian princes for help but only a few agreed to join the fight. In a fierce battle on the river Kalka the Mongols scored a great victory, but for some reason they withdrew, only to return with a larger force in 1237.

THE EMERGENCE OF THE MONGOL EMPIRE

In several respects, the Mongol Empire, one of the greatest in world history, remains an enigma to historians. It is hard to explain how one million people succeeded in imposing their rule over one hundred million in a huge area stretching from the Pacific Ocean to the Adriatic coast, from China to Hungary. Although the Mongols dominated Russia for close to two and a half centuries, from 1240 to roughly 1480, there is still no consensus among scholars about the extent to which they influenced the course of Russian history. That this long tutelage of the Mongols profoundly affected Russia at the time can hardly be disputed. The critical question is whether the conquerors left a lasting imprint on Russian political, cultural, and social institutions.

In the twelfth century, the Mongols were only one of numerous tribes and clans that lived in the easternmost part of what is today Mongolia, and their emergence as the dominant force was essentially the work of one man, Chingis Khan (Great Emperor), whose original name was Temuchin. Born in the mid 1160s, Temuchin as a young man came to believe that it was his destiny

to achieve greatness. One source of his conviction apparently was
the legend that one of his forefathers had been born some time
after the death of the mother's husband. The woman claimed to
have had a vision of a divine being visiting her at night. It has
been suggested that this was an adaptation of the story about the
Virgin Mary, which is plausible because Nestorian Christianity
had a following among the Mongols. In any case, Temuchin, an
intelligent and wily young man, became an outstanding warrior
who ingratiated himself with Togrul, the ruler of the Keraits, one
of the more powerful Mongol tribes.

As Togrul's adviser, Temuchin succeeded in changing the
rules of steppe politics, which had hampered the development
of a stable order. Under the prevailing rules, the loyalty of vassals
to their suzerains lasted only so long as it seemed useful to both
sides. Each vassal, in other words, was free to abandon his suzerain to join the service of another one. Thus, no one tribal leader
could form a large and stable khanate. Temuchin concentrated
on securing a large personal following and soon challenged
Togrul himself, who was killed probably as a result of Temuchin's
cunning plans. Having seized power, Temuchin created a special
unit of 150 guards who were charged with protecting him night
and day against a surprise attack, a favored political stratagem
among the Mongols. Then Temuchin divided the entire army
into units of 1,110 men and enforced rigid discipline in each
unit. At the same time, he insisted that all political and military
leaders be directly and clearly subordinate to him and forbade
them from changing their loyalties.

Once he had established his authority over the tribes in his
region (by 1206), Temuchin adopted the title Chingis Khan and
then step by step vastly expanded his domain. He defeated the
Tanguts, a people of Tibetan origins, and in 1211 he launched a
four-year campaign against the Chin Empire; within four years
he subjugated northern China and Manchuria. He strengthened
his forces immensely by incorporating into his army Chinese
army engineers and by employing literate Chinese as civil
servants. Then, moving westward, he conquered Khorezm in

western Turkestan, an area of the utmost importance for international trade, since it lay at the crossroad between China and the Mediterranean world and between India and southern Russia. In the years 1221–3 the Mongols penetrated Russia, from which Temuchin mysteriously retreated after his great victory at the river Kalka.

Chingis Khan died in 1227 leaving a two-fold legacy that inspired his successors to continue his policy of military expansion. On the one hand, he had claimed to be driven by a religious obligation to establish universal peace and a universal state. If he conquered the world he would bring stability and order to humankind, which, in return, would have to pay the price of permanent service to the new state. Under the new dispensation, the poor would be protected from injustice and from exploitation by the rich. On the other hand, Chingis Khan glorified the military life as a high calling that was deeply satisfying. 'Man's highest joy', he declared, 'is in victory: to conquer one's enemies, to pursue them, to deprive them of their possessions, to make their beloved weep, to ride their horses, and to embrace their daughters and wives.'

Chingis Khan had turned his army into the best in the world. Consisting for the most part of superbly trained cavalry accompanied by a gifted engineering corps, it adopted highly sophisticated strategies and tactics to weaken the resolve of the enemy to resist. Long before attacking a stronghold, the Mongols sent secret agents to the region to wage psychological warfare. The agents would spread the word that the Mongols intended to grant religious toleration to dissenters, to help the poor resist exploitation by the rich, and to aid wealthy merchants by making the roads safe for commerce. But at the same time the agents warned that these commitments would be kept only if there was a peaceful surrender. In the event of resistance, the punishment would be devastating.

Once the Mongols had decided on a battle, they would proceed to surround and annihilate the enemy. Applying a strategy known as the ring, the Mongols would occupy a huge area around the enemy and then would gradually approach their quarry. Uncanny in their ability to coordinate their advances, the commanders applied steady military pressure on the enemy. If the enemy lines failed to crack, the Mongols would feign retreat. The enemy, assuming that the invading forces were in disorderly retreat, would rush forward only to be surprised by the Mongols' orderly resistance. The Mongol columns then surrounded the defenders, who found no way of escaping the ring. The Mongols persisted in fighting until the enemy had been utterly destroyed.

MONGOL DOMINATION

In 1235, Ugedey, Chingis Khan's son, decided to attack Europe. After defeating the Bulgars and other peoples in the eastern parts of Russia, 120,000 troops under the command of his nephew Batu reached north-eastern Russia and inflicted one defeat after another on the local armies. Batu caught the Russians by surprise by attacking in wintertime, a season considered inhospitable to the movement of large armies. The Mongols, used to severe winters, were warmly attired with furs and rode horses trained to gallop on snow, and their armies moved swiftly across the many frozen rivers and lakes. In addition the Mongols benefited from miscalculations by the Russians and Western Europeans. The Russians believed that the Volga Bulgars would put up strong resistance, but their forces crumbled quickly, enabling the Mongols to capture Riazan in 1237. Shortly thereafter the Mongols seized control of Moscow and in 1238 they entered the city of Vladimir, which they destroyed. The invaders then defeated the army of the Grand Duke Iuri II, turned south, and after capturing Kiev in 1240, began to move towards Hungary and Poland. The Western Europeans, disdainful of the Russians as heretics and schismatics, made no effort to help them fend off the Mongols, who in 1241 entered Silesia and almost took Vienna. Only the death of Great Khan Ugedey that year saved the rest of Europe from invasion. Eager to influence the selection by clan leaders of a new leader, Batu withdrew from the West and returned to southern Russia.

But the Mongol army did not retreat from Russia, over which they established a rather elaborate system of rule that reduced the Russians to a subordinate position without eliminating all autonomous political life of the local population. It is this duality of the Mongol domination that has led to much controversy about the impact of the long period of foreign rule on the history of Russia.

On the other hand, the Great Khan's authority was considered absolute. Once elected by clan leaders, no one could challenge the ruler, who relied upon the army as the backbone of the administrative structure of the Mongolian Empire. The Great Khan issued his orders to army commanders, who acted as civil governors of the districts in which their armies camped. At the same time, most Russian princes retained their posts, but they were clearly in a subordinate position. They were required to travel to Saray, which was the capital of the Golden Horde, the autonomous state the Mongols had set up west of the Ural mountains, to kowtow before the Khan, pledge their allegiance to him, and be confirmed in their offices. Any prince who resisted this humiliating ritual was quickly executed.

Yet the Mongols showed little interest in exercising direct control over the Russian lands. Their concern was to collect taxes and to secure recruits for their army, but beyond that they allowed Russian princes to administer their lands. There were only two exceptions to this mode of rule: in south-west Russia (Ukraine) the Mongols removed the existing administrative structures entirely and replaced them with their own, whereas in Novgorod Mongol agents left the Russian authorities firmly in control at all times. In the late thirteenth and early fourteenth centuries some Russian princes and grand dukes assumed the burden of collecting the tribute for the conquerors, which enhanced their local power and their standing among the Mongols. Eventually, some of these princes grew strong enough to challenge the authority of the conquerors.

Such challenges would probably have failed had the Mongol Empire not suffered from endless internal discord. In principle, the Great Khan in Mongolia was the absolute ruler, but the distances between the different regions of the realm were so vast and communications between them so slow that local khans often ignored their leader with impunity and at times even sought to take over the entire empire. In the 1360s and 1370s, the conflicts reached such intensity that the Golden Horde was virtually paralyzed, enabling Russian princes to play off one khan against another and in the process strengthen their own authority.

In the meantime, the impact of Mongol rule on Russia had been substantial. For one thing, the Mongols caused enormous physical damage. A number of cities were entirely destroyed and as a consequence Russian industry (enamels, jewelry, ceramics, glasswork, stone-cutting, building crafts) suffered a devastating blow from which it did not recover until the mid fourteenth century. It has been estimated that during the first three years of the invasion, from 1237 until 1240, some ten percent of the population was killed. Moreover, because of the decline of industry, internal trade declined markedly, though it should be noted that the Mongols' interest in international trade did stimulate foreign commerce.

A major consequence of Mongol rule was the continuing decline and eventual disappearance of the *veche*, the 'democratic' institution of Kievan Russia in which the lower classes had been able to express their discontents. Their major grievances were taxation and conscription, which placed a special burden on them. Princes and boyars, who frequently managed to come to terms with the foreign rulers, were inclined to support the khans' elimination of the *veche*, a potentially troublesome institution for local Russian authorities. By the mid fourteenth century, the *veche* had ceased to be a significant political institution in much of the country.

Another major political change during the era of Mongol rule was the replacement of the rota system, under which Russia had remained a unified state, by the appanage system, under which each province became a separate, divisible, permanent property of a particular prince. Princes no longer moved from one province to another on the death of a prince higher on the ladder of the House of Riurik. And each prince could dispose of his property at will to his wife, sons, daughters, or other relatives, however distant. Historians[4] differ over the reasons for the disintegration of the Russian state into ever smaller appanages, but there is agreement on certain general factors that made it possible. Although the Mongols did not initiate the establishment of the appanage system, they found it advantageous because it made much more difficult a unified stand of the Russians against them. But the geography of the country probably played a more important role. A striking feature of northern Russia was the complex network of rivers and streams, all flowing in different directions, and as people began to colonize new regions they naturally moved along the waterways. This diffusion of people led to the formation of small river provinces separated from each other by natural boundaries of virtually impassable wilderness. Princes, who often supervised the colonization almost on a day-to-day basis, tended to look upon the new settlements as their own creation and even as their own property. And there were no dignitaries such as boyars to offer resistance to their claims of supremacy. Many of the appanage princes were hardly rich even by the standards of the fifteenth century and often they were no more affluent than independent owners of private estates. In view of the political disintegration of Russia, it is remarkable that the Mongol yoke was ever discarded and that a new, unified state under the leadership of Muscovy emerged. How that happened will be the subject of the next chapter.

Before exploring that theme, however, a few more words should be said about the long-term legacy of the Mongol domination. Although the Mongols left much of the administration to Russian dignitaries, they did contribute significantly to the undermining of the relatively free society of Kievan Rus by introducing certain elements of what has been called a 'service-bound society', though the process of establishing such a society was not completed until the seventeenth century. The following are some of the Mongol practices that left their mark on Russia: the obligation placed on the nobility to serve the state; the right of the ruler to confiscate the estate of a nobleman pronounced guilty of treason; the imposition on townspeople as well as peasants of a *tiaglo* (literally 'burden' or taxes); the introduction of such harsh judicial practices as capital and corporal punishment. Torture became a regular feature of Russian criminal procedures only after the Mongol conquest. It would be misleading to attribute the changes in the institutions and traditions of Kievan Russia solely to the influence of the Mongols, but it would be equally misleading to discount that influence.

2

THE RISE OF
MUSCOVITE RUSSIA

Little is known about the origins of Moscow, a town that within two centuries enjoyed a spectacular rise from obscurity to prominence and that by the seventeenth century had developed into the center of a vast empire ruled by an autocrat whose powers were unmatched by any European monarch. According to the *Russian Chronicles*, a primary source for the early history of Russia, in 1147 Iurii Dolgoruki (George of the Long Arm), Prince of Suzdal, invited Prince Sviatoslav of Novgorod-Seversk to Moscow. The host entertained his guest with a 'mighty dinner', which suggests the existence of a structure of some consequence. Nine years later Iurii laid the foundation of Moscow by constructing a wooden wall around that building. This small fortress, situated at the western corner of Kremlin (Fortress) Hill, comprised one-third or at most one-half of the territory that the citadel occupies today.

Iurii's decision proved to be remarkably astute. Moscow's proximity to the headwaters of four major rivers – the Oka, Volga, Don, and Dnieper – facilitated commerce with various parts of Russia. Close also to several major overland routes, Moscow evolved into a natural depot for refugees fleeing the declining Kievan region, which was repeatedly attacked by Tatar hordes.

Moreover, the city's location deep within the Kievan federation endowed it with a measure of military security. The enemy would attack surrounding cities and then, either exhausted or content with their plunder, would fall back without proceeding to Moscow. Between 1238 and 1368 the city was sacked only once, in 1293; no other city in northern Russia escaped enemy attack for as long a time. It was during this period, in 1263, that Daniel, the youngest son of Alexander Nevsky, the highly effective ruler of Vladimir, became the ruler of Moscow, which was now the capital of a permanent principality. Daniel is considered the founder of the princely house of Moscow.

The princes of Moscow made the most of these material advantages. As junior princes they could not even aspire to the throne of a major principality and therefore devoted all their energies to expanding their patrimony, generally by the most expedient means. One of Russia's most accomplished historians, V. O. Kliuchevsky, has aptly referred to the earliest rulers of Moscow as 'robbers of the most unblushing type'. But in addition they were crafty opportunists. If they observed that a neighboring prince was momentarily weak, they attacked him without provocation. On other occasions they resorted to treaties or outright purchase in order to enlarge their territory. Although most of them were neither colorful nor exceptionally gifted, the Muscovite princes seemed to accommodate their policies instinctively to the often changing circumstances. They rarely undertook an action for which they were too weak, and they did not shrink from forming alliances with the heathen 'devourers of raw flesh', their Mongol oppressors. In short, steadiness, caution, flexibility, and moderation were the hallmarks of their policies. As one commentator noted somewhat ruefully, they did not even carry their 'tendency to get drunk after dinner' to excess.

No one exemplified these tendencies more strikingly than Ivan I, nicknamed Kalita or 'Moneybags', who ruled Moscow from 1328 to 1340. Some historians believe that he received this name because of his stinginess, but in many folktales Ivan is depicted as a generous prince who always carried a moneybag so that on his travels he could distribute alms to the poor. Whatever the real reason for his name, he was certainly shrewd in handling money. His lavish gifts to the Khan of the Golden Horde were designed to safeguard his principality against attack.

Ivan initially ingratiated himself with the Golden Horde in 1327, when he led an army against the Grand Duke of Tver, who had refused to pay the tribute demanded by the Mongols. As a reward for his victory over Tver, the Khan bestowed on Kalita the title 'Grand Prince of Vladimir', a position of great prestige that for a hundred years was retained without interruption by the Muscovite rulers. Kalita then assumed responsibility for collecting tribute throughout northern Russia. He performed this task efficiently and ruthlessly, always making sure that some of the funds remained in his coffers. These profits went towards purchasing additional land, which Ivan acquired from impecunious princes, private landlords, and ecclesiastical institutions. The Khan, grateful to be relieved of the burden of collecting the tribute himself, gave his blessing to Ivan's unremitting accumulation of territory.

One of the most significant aspects of Ivan's reign was the transformation of Moscow into the spiritual center of the nation. The repeated Mongol incursions into Kiev had induced Metropolitan Maxim to abandon that city in favor of Vladimir in 1299. The choice had proven unfortunate, however, for the secular authorities and the metropolitan had begun to quarrel, a situation that was soon exploited by Ivan's brother Iuri, then ruler of Moscow, who established cordial relations with Maxim's successor, Peter.

During a visit to Moscow in 1326 Peter died, an event that later metropolitans interpreted as evidence of divine selection of the city to be the seat of the Russian church. One legend that gained currency in the late fourteenth century maintained that Peter had actually died in Ivan's arms after uttering the following prophesy:

> My son, if thou shouldst hearken unto me, and shouldst build the Church of the Holy Mother, and shouldst lay me to rest in thy city, then of a surety wilt thou be

glorified above all other princes in the land, and thy sons and grandsons also, and this city will itself be glorified above other Russian towns, and the Saints will come and dwell in it, and its hands will prevail against its enemies. Thus will it ever be as long as my bones lie therein.

Many Russians came to believe in the authenticity of the incident because two years after Peter's death Metropolitan Theognost suddenly decided to settle in Moscow. From that time the spiritual and secular authorities worked in close harmony, a development crucial to Moscow's rise to preeminence in Russia.

CHALLENGES TO MONGOL RULE

Ivan Kalita's policy of enhancing Moscow's power and prestige was pursued with remarkable vigor by his grandson Dmitrii Donskoi, who assumed the title of grand prince in 1359. A talented and courageous ruler, Dmitrii determined to challenge the Mongol overlords. Buoyed by his success in fending off the combined military attacks of Lithuania and Tver in the 1360s and early 1370s, he began to defy the Mongols by refusing to pay the annual tribute. In 1378 he added insult to injury by defeating the Mongols in a minor battle near the Vozh river. This enraged the proud Khan Mamai, who realized that if he did not subdue the rebellious Dmitrii, Mongol authority would evaporate all over Russia. Mamai assembled a huge army and in 1380, after forming an alliance with Lithuania, crossed the Volga and advanced towards Moscow.

In an attempt to settle the issue without bloodshed, Mamai offered Dmitrii peace in return for the resumption of tribute in the amount customary before 1371. The grand prince responded by appealing to other Russian princes to join in a crusade against the Tatars. Several answered the call and by the summer of 1380 he had assembled an army of thirty thousand men, most from his own principality. Khan Mamai's army was roughly the same size, but he enjoyed the advantage of superior cavalry forces.

On 8 September, the two armies stood poised for battle at Kulikovo Pole (Snipes' Field), a plain between the upper Don and its tributary, the Neprivada. In accordance with the traditions of steppe warfare, before the fighting began one of the Tatars challenged the Russians to a duel. A monk accompanying Dmitrii's army accepted the challenge and galloped full speed towards his opponent. They collided with such tremendous force that both died on the spot. Minutes later, the two huge armies lunged at each other along a seven-mile front.

For four hours, Mamai's troops relentlessly assailed the Muscovite army, which was on the verge of total collapse. But Dmitrii had cleverly held a large detachment of his best troops in ambush in a nearby forest, and just when all seemed lost, he called on his reserves. The sudden appearance of fresh troops not only breathed new life into the Muscovite army but demoralized the Tatars. The tide of battle turned completely; Mamai abruptly fled, his army disintegrated, and Grand Prince Dmitrii captured the Mongol camp along with large quantities of booty. The Russian force had lost about one-half of its men, including the commander in chief and several other high-ranking officers. Nonetheless, it was a superb victory – and the first time that a large Mongol army had been routed by Russians in a major test of strength. In the nineteenth century one historian interpreted it as nothing less than 'a sign of the triumph of Europe over Asia'.

In the wake of the battle, Grand Prince Dmitrii's stature rose immeasurably in Russia, not only by virtue of his victory but also because of his personal bravery. 'He was the first in battle', notes a contemporary account of the conflict, 'and killed many Tatars.' At one point he singlehandedly took on four Mongol attackers and was knocked unconscious. At the end of the battle his officers found him under a pile of dead bodies. His armor was slashed to pieces, but he was only slightly wounded and capable of resuming command.

Dmitrii's joy at defeating the Mongols was short-lived. In 1382, only two years after the battle at Kulikovo, Khan Tokhtamysh appeared in north-eastern Russia with a large army determined to seek revenge and to reassert Tatar authority. Caught off guard, Dmitrii, demonstrating none of the acumen or courage he had displayed two years earlier, fled to the north to organize a new army. He apparently had persuaded himself that the powerful stone walls of the Kremlin would withstand any Tatar siege. But as soon as he left Moscow, pandemonium broke loose in the city. Wealthy citizens sought to save their lives by quitting the city, but the commoners demanded that everyone remain to help strengthen the defenses against the impending attack. When the well-to-do Muscovites persisted with their escape plans, civil disorder erupted. Many of the people who had packed their bags were killed, and their property was looted as commoners seized control of the city. Distrusting the local nobility, the rebellious peasants chose a Lithuanian visitor, Prince Ostei, to command the garrison. The Muscovites fought bravely, held off Tokhtamysh's army for three days, and might have won a great victory had the Mongol commander not resorted to a cruel deception. On the fourth day of the siege, the Khan sent a message to the beleaguered defenders abjuring any intention of causing harm and requesting merely some 'small gifts' and an opportunity to visit the city. Naively, the Muscovites opened the gates to the Kremlin and dispatched a religious procession, led by Prince Ostei, to greet Tokhtamysh and offer him presents. As soon as the last members of the group had cleared the Kremlin gates, the Khan's henchmen pounced on the stunned and defenseless Muscovites, killing the prince and many of his companions. Other Mongols rushed through the open gates or climbed over the walls on ladders that had been held in readiness for the attack. The next few hours were ghastly, as Mongol soldiers indiscriminately cut down local residents, killing, by one estimate, no less than ten thousand people.

Tokhtamysh, it appeared, had restored the supremacy of the Golden Horde over Moscow and perhaps over all of Russia. But it soon became evident that because of endless internecine struggles between rival khans the Mongols could not exploit their victory of 1382. The Tatars could still cause considerable devastation, as they did when they looted the countryside around Moscow in 1408–9, but a sustained military campaign against the Russians was now beyond their means. In fact, the Mongol Empire was slowly disintegrating.

Had Muscovy itself not been weakened by fierce dynastic feuds the Russians might have shortened the foreign domination by fifty years. The conflicts can be traced to a decision of Grand Prince Vasili I, who died in 1425, not to bequeath his throne to his brother Iurii, who followed him in seniority, but to his son Vasilii II, who was then only ten years old. Iurii, claiming to be the rightful heir, declared war against Moscow and thus initiated the only military conflict between descendants of Ivan Kalita. It was a long conflict lasting some twenty-five years and it was marked by ghastly brutalities. In one clash Vasilii II captured his cousin Vasilii the Squint-Eyed and proceeded to blind him. The custom of blinding pretenders to the throne was widely practiced in Byzantium, but in Russia this form of punishment had been used only once before (in the twelfth century), and consequently it shocked many Russians. No doubt, Vasilii came to regret his brutal behavior, for when he was captured in 1446 by Dmitrii Shemiaka, the brother of Vasilii the Squint-Eyed, he was similarly blinded. Now known as 'Vasilii the Dark', he resumed the struggle as soon as he was released from captivity. Despite his infirmity, he led a new revolt and crushed his enemies once and for all. He also succeeded in expanding the boundaries of Muscovy, and when he died in 1462 the principality comprised some fifteen thousand square miles. It was now twenty-five times as large as it had been at the time of Ivan Kalita, some 120 years earlier. Formally, Vasilii recognized the Golden Horde as the supreme authority in Russia, but he delivered only a small portion of the customary tribute. The Tatars were no longer able to enforce their will and Muscovy had, since its founding three hundred years earlier, evolved into a major state that enjoyed virtual independence.

Moscow did not owe its preeminence in Russia solely to its accretion of material power. By the fifteenth century it had also greatly enhanced its spiritual importance by replacing Constantinople as the religious center of the Greek Orthodox Church. This shift resulted from a decision by the patriarch in Byzantium in 1439. That year, he proclaimed religious unity between Orthodoxy and Roman Catholicism in order to gain Western help against the advancing Turks. To the Muscovites, the union was nothing less than heretical and they unceremoniously confined their own metropolitan, Isidor, to the Chudov monastery in the Kremlin for having dared to invoke the pope's name while celebrating a solemn mass in the Cathedral of the Assumption. A few years later the Russian bishops, strongly encouraged by Vasilii II, elected Bishop Iona of Riazan as the metropolitan of the Russian church. They did this without even consulting the patriarch in Constantinople.

Moscow's spiritual independence became final in 1453, when Constantinople fell into the hands of the infidel Turks, an event that Russians came to regard as just punishment for Byzantium's heretical dealings with Rome. Within a few decades a Russian monk named Filofei contended that both Rome and Constantinople had lost their standing in the spiritual world by abandoning the true faith. 'Two Romes have fallen,' he asserted, 'and the third stands, and a fourth shall not be.' Moscow, of course, was the 'Third Rome', entitled to moral supremacy in Christendom and destined for eternal life because only there had heresy been shunned. Filofei's doctrine, as Robert O. Crummey pointed out, 'quickly entered the mainstream of Russia's ecclesiastical thinking', bolstering the prestige of the Muscovite principality.

MOSCOW'S EXPANSION

In 1462, when Vasilii II died and was succeeded by his son Ivan III, the Grand Duchy of Moscow was only one of several Russian lands. The grand duchies of Tver and Riazan as well as the city states of Novgorod, Pskov, Viatka, Yaroslavl, and Rostov were still independent. To the west of Moscow, the land of Smolensk (present-day Belarus) and much of Ukraine were under the authority of Lithuania. Eastern Galicia was part of Poland and Carpatho-Ukraine belonged to Hungary. Most people in these territories considered themselves to be Russian, and Ivan III, a man at one and the same time ambitious, ruthless, and pragmatic, adopted as his mission the unification under his rule of as much of these Russian lands as possible. His methods were diverse. Some lands (most notably Novgorod and Tver) he simply appropriated by force, some he purchased, and others he acquired through inheritance. At the time of Ivan's death in 1505, only Pskov and one-half of the principality of Riazan remained separate states within Great Russia, and neither of these was strong enough to pose any military or political threat to Muscovy.

Ivan, who acquired the title of 'Gatherer of Russian Lands', had taken several other steps to centralize the state and magnify his authority. In 1472 he married the Byzantine princess Zoe Palaeologa, a move that to many in the West seemed to portend far-reaching political changes on the international scene. But to Ivan himself the marriage symbolized increased status as a ruler within Russia itself. In diplomatic documents Ivan frequently referred to himself as 'Tsar of all Rus' and 'autocrat', by which he meant to suggest not so much that he exercised unlimited authority within his realm as that he was independent of all foreigners. He established a royal army and thus freed himself from having to rely on the goodwill of other princes in time of military emergency, and he introduced a measure of legal uniformity by issuing a code of law. Also, court etiquette and ceremonials became ever more elaborate, and beginning in the 1490s the Byzantine crest of the double eagle was affixed to all state documents. In this way Ivan gave currency to the notion that his marriage to Zoe had conferred upon him the position of logical successor to the Byzantine emperors. The double eagle remained the official crest of tsarist Russia until the revolution of 1917.

Ivan's son Vasilii III (1505–33) proved to be a worthy successor to the throne. He, too, devoted himself to the two-pronged policy of external expansion and the accretion of power by the ruler in domestic affairs. Convinced that the country's insecure borders, especially in the south and south-west, posed a threat to the state, Vasilii insisted that the centralization of the administrative machinery must be tightened and opponents to his policies must be dealt with harshly. Although he did not execute many people who stood in his way, he did imprison and exile a large number of them. He was similarly ruthless in his treatment of the upper social stratum of the territories he conquered. After he forcefully annexed Pskov in 1510 he ordered the arrest of leading members of society and had them sent to Moscow. He then sent entire families from Moscow to Pskov to replace those he had expelled. Vasilii continued this process of population transfer until the leading stratum of Pskov society was replaced. The rest of the population, now leaderless, was an amorphous mass incapable of offering resistance to his authority. In 1522 Vasilii annexed the remaining half of Riazan and once again consolidated his power by sending the local elite to Moscow and replacing it with his own agents.

The steady enlargement of the Muscovite state and growth in the ruler's power were inevitably accompanied by fundamental administrative changes. Until the mid fifteenth century, during the appanage period mentioned in the preceding chapter, the core of the military consisted of the grand ducal *dvorianstvo* (nobility) and the sons of the boyars (the highest service aristocracy). Under the command of the grand duke himself, these warriors were nevertheless free to serve or not to serve in the military without risk to their rights of ownership of their estates. There was thus no connection between military service and landownership, as there was in much of the West at the time. Those who served in the army were rewarded with administrative or judicial posts that carried financial incomes. During periods of warfare, the grand duke could also order service princes and the Moscow boyars to participate, with their retinues, in military campaigns. Still, in the appanage period both the princes and the boyars were free to move from one principality to another. The grand princes of Moscow also utilized the services of Tatar troops, who were assigned various towns to 'feed on' (*kormlenie* system), that is, the commanders could impose taxes on the towns, of which they could keep a share. All these three groups were cavalrymen. The infantry were drawn from merchants and the Cossacks (literally 'free warriors'), a stratum first mentioned in written records in the mid fifteenth century and who gained fame as horsemen.

From about the 1470s, when Ivan III embarked on his program of expansion, the need for troops increased dramatically. It has been estimated that in the period from 1492 until 1595 Moscow was as often at war as it was at peace. The country fought three Swedish wars and seven wars with Poland-Lithuania and Livonia, and waged an almost continuous struggle against the Tatars, who had not yet been fully crushed. To finance the huge military expenditure, Ivan introduced the *pomestie* system, under which men received an allotment of land (a *pomestie*) in return for military service and the supply of a certain number of cavalrymen. In principle, the possession of a *pomestie*, like the obligation of military service itself, was to be temporary, but generally the piece of land was granted for the lifetime of the recipient. But the possession of a *pomestie* was conditional, dependent on the discharge of military obligations, and thus clearly different from an *otchina*, a piece of land that passed from parent to offspring.

To implement the *pomestie* system, Ivan needed vast stretches of fertile land, a commodity in short supply. The boyars, who owned much of that land, could not be easily deprived of their holdings, for they were the leading force in society. Ivan therefore turned to Novgorod, where he forced the church to hand over to him more than half its holdings. He also transferred many Novgorod nobles to other regions of the realm after depriving them of their land. By 1500 Ivan had accumulated about 2.7 million acres of land in Novgorod alone. Within a few decades, the *pomestie* system had been firmly established and it significantly changed the character of military service, and in some important respects the character of the Muscovite state. Not only could the *pomeshchik* (the holder of a *pomestie*) not move freely from one principality to another and transfer his allegiance from one prince to another, but gradually, in the course of the sixteenth century, service to the state became a corporate, hereditary obligation of every member of the upper classes. Only the tsar could exempt a nobleman from service. Moreover, the obligation to serve the state devolved from father to son, which helps to explain the evolution of Russia into what came to be known as a 'service state'. Boys were educated for service at an early age and at fifteen they entered one or another branch of the state services. And in the course of the sixteenth century the distinction between *pomestie* and *otchina* was gradually erased. As a consequence, every nobleman who had a landed estate was obliged to serve the state.

Another major effect of the *pomestie* system was to weaken the urban centers and urban industries, for large numbers of state servitors moved to their lands in the countryside and thus deprived the towns of many of their best customers. Towns also suffered from the fact that many landlords built up their own handicraft industries on their estates. The slow development of towns in Russia in the sixteenth and seventeenth centuries can thus in good measure be attributed to the *pomestie* system. Finally, it should be noted that the gentry who were granted their landed property by the ruler were politically more reliable and pliant than the boyars. This was obviously an important factor in the centralization of political authority by Muscovite rulers.

To appreciate the significance of the grand prince's accretion of power, one needs to keep in mind that during the appanage period in the fourteenth century the state was hardly distinguishable from a manorial property and the administration was primarily designed to exploit the assets of the manor. The population living in an appanage did not constitute a community or a union of subjects whose purpose was to achieve the specific goals of public welfare and social order. The tasks of the population were to keep the economy functioning and to supply men for the army. The state machinery was located in the prince's palace and the ruler looked upon the principality as his private patrimony, a political system that has been described as 'patrimonialism'.

To be sure, certain key issues, such as war and peace, the framing of a prince's will, and the arrangement of matrimonial alliances for the ruler's family, were considered by a 'prince's council' operating under the chairmanship of the prince. But this council was not a permanent body and did not have clearly defined jurisdiction or even established procedures. It was an informal institution enabling the prince to obtain advice. Still, it was important as a precedent for the later *boyarskaia duma*, an institution that will be discussed below.

Although the prince had amassed great personal power he still needed local officials to implement his directives, to maintain order, and to dispense justice. Known as *namestiniki* in the larger districts and *volostele* in the smaller ones, the officials were all also referred to as *kormlenshchiki*, a word that derives from *kormlenie*, which means 'feeding'. Local officials quite literally fed themselves by imposing taxes and fees on the population under their jurisdiction, a portion of which they could keep. Often, individuals were appointed to administrative posts for a year or two for the specific purpose of enabling them to acquire an income after a period of service in the army or the capital. It was a system of local government that was neither rational, uniform, nor free from widespread abuse.

In the late fifteenth and the sixteenth century, princes in Moscow established departments (*prikazy*) in the capital city for the purpose of centralizing the administration of the entire country. Then, also in the sixteenth century, the *boyarskaia duma* was turned into a permanent institution charged with supervising the work of the departments as well as drafting laws for approval or rejection by the ruler. All its members were appointed by the tsar and thus were beholden to him. The ruler picked a few members from the lower nobility, but he chose most of them from the leading boyar families according to a highly elaborate system known as *mestnichestvo* (code of preference). The system was based on a genealogical table or 'ladder' that determined the standing of each noble on the basis of the government offices held by his ancestors. Special offices kept careful records of each family's service and the assumption was that the selection of officials on the basis of these records would eliminate conflicts between nobles over their rights to government positions. In practice the system had precisely the opposite effect, for it was often impossible to determine the precise positions of dignitaries on the hierarchical ladder, and nobles threatened with a loss of status almost invariably would put up a spirited defense of their privileges. For the rulers, such conflicts were not entirely unwelcome. 'Instead of uniting to oppose the encroachment of absolutism on their ancient privileges,' the historian Kliuchevsky has written, 'the Moscow nobles, in order to uphold family honor, fought one another, sometimes in bodily conflict and to the considerable detriment of their venerable beards.'

IVAN THE TERRIBLE

This was the unwieldy and inefficient state inherited by Ivan IV, the Terrible (1547–84), one of the more mercurial, colorful, articulate, and unscrupulous rulers of Russia. He was also one of the more enigmatic rulers, a man who has been the subject of diverse evaluations by historians. Some have depicted him as a demented sadist and lecher whose main goal in life was to satisfy his basest instincts and whose policies ultimately led to the collapse of the state. Others have praised him – without necessarily condoning all his crimes – as a gifted leader who subjugated the selfish nobles and established a personal autocracy that not only unified the state but also extended its power. The Soviet historian Robert Wipper, one of the more respected representatives of this school, contended that 'the enhanced attention to Ivan's . . . cruelties, the stern and withering moral verdicts on his personality, the proneness to regard him as a man of unbalanced mind, all belong to the age of sentimental enlightenment and high society liberalism.' Yet another group of historians has claimed that despite Ivan's personal aberrations he was beloved by the people, who looked upon him as pious and well intentioned. It seems certain that in his own time he acquired the epithet *Grozny* – which is generally translated as 'terrible' but can also mean 'awe-inspiring' – not because of his immoral conduct but because the common folk considered him their champion against the enemies of Muscovy.

The few surviving records of Ivan's reign do not give a clear picture of the man. His most enduring trait appears to have been his moral instability. In his personal life and in affairs of state he regularly alternated between 'lofty mental flights and shameful moral degradations'. Thus, he meticulously adhered to religious ritual, often rising at 4:00 A.M. to pray for two or three hours. Yet when it suited his purposes he defied the church and disregarded its teachings. In 1568, for example, he publicly humiliated a popular metropolitan who had dared to criticize his conduct; a year later the ecclesiastic was dead, either strangled or burned alive by one of the ruler's closest servants. Similarly, Ivan was genuinely devoted to his first wife, but within eleven days of her death he chose her successor. He also cherished his eldest son but in a fit of anger bludgeoned him so severely that the young man died.

The contradictory impulses that inhabited Ivan's soul were nowhere more apparent than in the political arena. On the positive side, he introduced imaginative reforms in several branches of government, cowed the unruly boyars, and scored a succession of stunning victories over the troublesome Tatars. Yet he governed with such recklessness and barbaric cruelty that when he departed the throne his politically unstable country was on the verge of economic collapse. On the mere suspicion that Novgorod was planning to betray him Ivan had the city sacked and sixty thousand men, women, and children massacred – but he took pains to send lists of victims to various monasteries so that requiem masses could be performed in their honor. He even made generous personal contributions to help defray the cost of these rituals.

Although a professed believer in the divine origin of autocratic power, Ivan in practice made a mockery of this principle of government. In 1575, for example, he whimsically conferred his crown upon an obscure Tatar prince, Simeon Bekbulatovich, and retired to Moscow to live as a humble boyar. Bekbulatovich made a pretense of governing, although he does not seem to have exercised any real power. In 1576, Ivan ended the grotesque joke and reascended the throne, to rule for another eight years. There was surely a touch of madness in all this, but if we assess the total impact of Ivan's politics, we are tempted to agree with the historian who described his system of rule as 'the madness of a genius'.

The tsar's lack of equilibrium can be accounted for quite easily. Given his childhood experiences, it would have been remarkable if he had grown up to be a well-balanced adult. The death of his father when Ivan was only three had plunged the Kremlin into a ferocious duel for power between rival factions. For the next fourteen years the country was on the brink of civil war as two boyar families, the Shuiskys and the Belskys, jostled ruthlessly for dominance. Power seesawed between them, and whichever family held sway plundered the state treasury and massacred members of the opposition, often in full view of the young Ivan. Nominally, Muscovy was ruled by an oligarchy, but disorder verging on anarchy spread throughout the realm.

These experiences engendered in Ivan a profound hostility towards the boyars and, more significantly, a lasting distrust of people in general. Not surprisingly, the violence and bestiality he observed also rendered him callous and even cruel. By the time Ivan was ten years old, a biographer reports, his 'great amusement was to throw dogs down from the top of the castle terraces and enjoy their anguish'. And when he was thirteen he 'began to go about the streets . . . thrashing the men he met, violating the women, . . . always applauded by those about him'.

But Ivan was not simply a playboy and sadist. Intelligent, well read, and fiercely ambitious, he felt destined for a place in history through his role as the nation's leader. In 1547, he took the unprecedented step of having himself formally crowned in the Uspenskii Sobor, the Cathedral of the Assumption in the Kremlin, as 'Tsar and Autocrat of All Russias'. During the ceremony the claim was put forth that the cross and regalia on Ivan's head and shoulders had been sent to the Grand Prince of Kiev in the twelfth century by the Byzantine Emperor Constantin Monomachus. On another occasion, Ivan contended that his authority had an even more distinguished pedigree. 'The beginnings of our autocracy', he declared, 'is of St Vladimir [956–1015]. We were born and nurtured in the office of Tsar, and do possess it, and have not ravished what is not our own. From the first the Russian autocrats have been lords of their own dominion, and not the boyar aristocrats.'

As tsar, Ivan immediately faced a series of crises, and in his handling of them we can observe how he gradually changed from a cynical despot into a shrewd politician. In June 1547, several citizens of Pskov visited the tsar in the village of Ostrovka to complain about the arbitrary actions of their governor. Ivan responded to their petition by having boiling brandy poured on them and having their hair and beards singed by candles. The unfortunate delegation had just undressed and lain down on the floor, ready for execution, when an excited messenger interrupted the proceedings with dreadful news. A new fire – one of a series that had erupted in Moscow in recent months – was raging in the capital, and the whole city was threatened with destruction. The tsar abruptly halted the torture and turned his attention to the catastrophe.

The devastation in the capital proved to be staggering. Twenty-five thousand houses were destroyed and at least seventeen thousand Muscovites were burned to death. Over eighty thousand people were left homeless, including many nobles who lived inside the Kremlin walls. The tsar's own palace, the metropolitan's palace, the treasury building, the Arsenal, two monasteries, and several churches – all within the citadel – had been reduced to ashes. For a time Ivan was obliged to forsake the Kremlin for the nearby village of Vorobievo.

The dazed survivors could not believe that a disaster of such magnitude was accidental, and they began to look for scapegoats. Before long the story gained currency that sorcerers had torn human hearts out of corpses, dipped them into pails of water, and then spread the fire by sprinkling the streets with this brew. When some boyars attested to having observed this very practice, suspects were promptly arrested, tortured to yield confessions, and executed.

But the aroused Muscovites were not satisfied. Many interpreted the fire as divine punishment for Ivan's sins, and they openly advocated rebellion. At the same time, a group of boyars circulated the rumor that the Glinskys, a powerful family at court, had caused the conflagration. These boyars summoned the populace to a general meeting in front of the Uspenskii Sobor, where one of them demanded to know who had burned the city. 'Princess Anna Glinskaia [Ivan's maternal grandmother] through sorcery', roared the crowd – whereupon the boyars urged the people to seek revenge on the Glinsky family.

Not finding Iurii's mother in Moscow, the mob assumed that she had sought the tsar's protection and they marched on to Vorobievo. The commoners refused to believe Ivan when he disavowed knowledge of Anna Glinskaia's whereabouts, and they actually threatened to kill him if he did not cooperate. After some heated exchanges he managed to persuade them that he was speaking the truth, and many began to have second thoughts about their conduct. Shrewdly taking advantage of the crowd's vacillation, Ivan quickly ordered the seizure and execution of the ringleaders. This resolute action enabled the tsar to weather the storm, but the events took their toll: Ivan came close to having a nervous breakdown.

When Ivan regained his equilibrium, he seemed more mature, responsible, and wise than ever before. He recruited thoughtful counselors and introduced policies that augured well for Muscovy. He publicized these policies, as well as the principles that would guide him as sovereign, at mass meetings in Red (or Beautiful) Square, a large oblong plaza just outside the

Kremlin walls. At one of the meetings, in 1549, Ivan treated the assembled crowd to an altogether unusual spectacle, a public confession by the ruler himself. After denouncing the boyars for exploiting his subjects, he acknowledged his past failures to protect the subjects from 'oppression and extortion'. Then, identifying himself fully with the common folk, he called for a new era of Christian love. 'Henceforth,' he vowed, 'I will be your judge and defender.' This speech, both brilliant and demagogic, did much to raise his popularity among the people.

During the next few years, Ivan's constructive domestic program and military successes contributed to a steady increase in his prestige. He strove to eliminate corruption among government officials, introduced a measure of local self-government, modernized the army, improved judicial procedures, and attempted to root out abuses in the church. Without doubt, the major reason for Ivan's popularity at mid century was his decisive blow against the Tatars, whose murderous raids into Muscovite territory had not ceased altogether. In addition to plundering Russian cities, the Tatars made a practice of capturing Russians and selling them as slaves. It has been estimated that in 1551 some 100,000 Muscovites languished in Kazan, the Tatar khanate closest to Moscow. That year, Ivan personally led an army of 150,000 men against Kazan, and in 1552, after a series of bloody clashes, he succeeded in capturing the city. Overjoyed, the commoners proclaimed him 'Conqueror of the Barbarians – Defender of the Christians'. Four years later Ivan neutralized another Tatar stronghold by capturing Astrakhan. Muscovy then controlled the entire basin of the Volga, and thereafter Russians could colonize lands in the south, south-west, and east. The path to Siberia had been opened.

REIGN OF TERROR

Despite his domestic and military achievements, Ivan remained too suspicious of his boyars to enjoy peace of mind. By the mid

1550s his position on the throne was secure, but he could never free himself from the fear that at the first sign of weakness the nobles would betray him. Although the fears were probably exaggerated, the boyars' behavior during one crisis certainly gave him fresh cause to doubt that they had learned much since the chaotic days of the 1530s and the early 1540s.

In 1553, Ivan suddenly developed a high fever. His doctors could find no cure and gave up hope of saving his life. On his deathbed Ivan proclaimed his son Dmitrii, an infant, as his successor, and called upon the boyars to swear an oath of allegiance to his heir. Several dignitaries demurred on the grounds that they feared another period of anarchy if the infant ascended the throne. The real reason for their recalcitrance was less noble: they simply did not wish to take orders from the lowly Zakharini, the relatives of Ivan's wife, who would have ruled during Dmitrii's minority. More important, the boyars themselves wanted to seize power. While Ivan lay on his bed in agonizing pain, he could hear the boyars quarreling about the succession in an adjoining room. The tsar could not help suspecting that as soon as he died the contentious boyars would slaughter his entire family. He ultimately prevailed upon most of them to sign the oath of allegiance, but he put little trust in their word.

Miraculously, Ivan recovered from the illness – only to suffer an overwhelming personal loss. In order to offer thanks to the Lord for restoring his health, he undertook a long and arduous pilgrimage to the Kirillo-Belozersky monastery with his wife and infant son, and while the royal party was changing boats on the Shesna river a nurse accidentally dropped the baby into the water. The child drowned, and the tsar returned to the Kremlin an embittered man.

For several years Ivan kept his rage under control. Then several events occurred to completely unsettle him. First, his beloved wife, Anastasia, died in 1560, a loss whose importance it is hard to exaggerate. She had exercised a soothing influence on the tsar that curbed his most violent instincts. Shortly after her death he dismissed two of his most sensible advisers,

Sylvester and Adashev. Both had for some reason been hostile towards Anastasia, and Ivan had convinced himself that the two had caused her death by deliberately failing to obtain the necessary medical supplies. Four years later Prince Andrei Kurbsky, one of Ivan's most distinguished generals, defected to Lithuania, apparently out of fear that the tsar would also turn against him. News of the defection infuriated Ivan and reinforced his lack of trust in the boyars. After brooding over these events for several months, he inaugurated a series of polices that are among the most outlandish in both Russian and world history.

One day late in 1564, Ivan and his family quietly departed from the Kremlin. The destination was the village of Alexandrovsk, to which the tsar's personal effects as well as his sacred images, crosses, and treasure chests had already been sent. In the meantime, two royal proclamations were issued in Moscow. The first reminded the subjects of the brutal conduct of the boyars during Ivan's childhood, disparaged their loyalty to tsar and church, and announced the sovereign's sorrowful decision to abdicate. The second, addressed to the commoners of the realm, suggested that Ivan did not really expect his abdication to be taken seriously. Its assurances of concern for the people's welfare were clearly designed to provoke so strong an outcry over the tsar's departure that he would be able to return to power with greater authority than ever.

Ivan had judged the people's mood with uncanny shrewdness. As one historian noted, 'Everyone stood petrified at the proceedings. Shops were closed, offices deserted, and voices hushed. Then, in a panic of terror, the city broke forth into lamentations, and besought the metropolitan, the bishops, and certain of the boyars to go to Alexandrovsk, and to beg the tsar not to abandon his realm.'

When the emissaries from Moscow arrived in Alexandrovsk, Ivan had a prepared statement in readiness. He agreed to reassume the burdens of office, but only if the populace would accept certain conditions that he intended to elaborate at a later date. The emissaries felt they could not reject this novel arrangement and retired to Moscow to await the tsar's pleasure. When Ivan returned to the Kremlin in February 1565, his appearance had been transformed. Whether from genuine torment over the advisability of resuming power or from anxiety that his stratagem might boomerang, the thirty-five-year-old tsar had become an old man in the short period of eight weeks: 'His small, gray, piercing eyes had grown dull, his hitherto animated, kindly face had fallen in and now bore a misanthropic expression, and only a few stray remnants remained of his once abundant hair and beard.' The change, it soon turned out, was more than physical. Ivan had decided on an entirely new regime, under which all traitors would be summarily executed and all boyars he deemed disloyal would be banished from court. In effect, the new order amounted to nothing less than a monstrous police dictatorship.

To root out sedition, he established the so-called *oprichnina*, a separate state with its own administration directly under his authority. (The other half, the *zemshchina*, retained its previous structure.) In the new state, thousands of people were evicted from their homes and replaced with loyal supporters, a process of expropriation that continued until the *oprichnina* encompassed almost half of the state. In addition, Ivan created a special police force, the 'Blackness of Hell', whose members dressed in black clothes, rode black horses, and carried a dog's head and a broom. Their duty was to sweep treason from the land and eliminate the tsar's enemies.

Ivan unleashed a reign of terror. Many innocent people were slaughtered on the slightest pretext, and often on no pretext at all. In a contemporary account, Heinrich von Staden, a German adventurer who served in the *oprichnina*, described how Ivan impulsively murdered one of Muscovy's leading boyars, Ivan Petrovich Cheliadin, and threw the corpse into a filthy pit. 'The grand prince', von Staden continued, 'then went with his *oprichniki* and burned all the [landed estates] . . . in the country belonging to this Ivan Petrovich. The villages were burned with their churches and everything that was in them, icons and church ornaments. Women and girls were stripped naked and forced in that state to catch chickens in the field.' Most of the time the *oprichniki* did not content themselves with subjugating women to such indignities; a favorite sport was rape, and Tsar Ivan not only approved of but also participated in it.

After a few years Ivan turned against the leading *oprichniki*, probably because he believed that they, too, had committed treason. He justified the action by spuriously claiming that they had disregarded his orders in committing atrocities. The slaughter of the *oprichniki* was accomplished in the style to which they were accustomed. Thus, according to von Staden, one prince was 'chopped to death by the harquebusiers with axes or halberds. Prince Andrei Ovtsyn was hanged in the Arbatskaya Street of the *oprichnina*. A living sheep was hung next to him. Marshal Bulat . . . was killed and his sister raped by five hundred harquebusiers. The captain of the harquebusiers, Kuraka Unkovskii, was killed and stuck under the ice.' Ivan even ordered that the handsome young Fedor Basmanov, with whom the tsar had indulged in homosexual relations, be brutally put to death. Before being executed, these dignitaries were publicly whipped in the marketplace and forced to sign over all their money and land to the crown.

It is not known exactly how many people perished during the *oprichnina*'s existence, but the number surely ran into the thousands. Insofar as the terror was designed to weaken the powerful aristocrats and eradicate separatist sentiments, it no doubt succeeded, and in so doing laid the basis for the subsequent development of untrammeled autocracy in Russia. Ivan himself emerged from the carnage as a ruler whose authority no one dared challenge.

On the other hand, the *oprichnina*'s reign of terror so weakened the country militarily that in 1571 Ivan could not fend off a Tatar army that plundered a large portion of the capital. He was also too weak to realize one of his most cherished dreams, the annexation of Livonia, which would have given Muscovy control over the Baltic. Time and again he attempted to conquer the territory, but in the end he had to acknowledge failure.

Ivan spent his last three years in mental agony, in large measure because of his inability to control his temper. In November 1581, he unintentionally killed his son and heir, leaving him in a state of near hysteria. According to the most plausible account, the tragic incident was triggered by an earlier encounter between the tsar and his daughter-in-law, who was then pregnant. Ivan came upon her clad only in a nightgown and was shocked by her immodesty. Losing his self-control, he slapped the woman so hard that within a day she miscarried. When the tsarevich complained to his father, Ivan again lost his temper and violently struck his son with the iron-tipped staff that he always carried with him. Unhappily, the blow fell on the tsarevich's temple and knocked him to the ground, where he bled profusely. Despite the heroic efforts of the court doctors and the sovereign's fervent prayers, the twenty-seven-year-old heir to the throne died four days later.

In deep despair, Ivan became convinced that his son's death was God's punishment for his sins. He now called his boyars together and, pronouncing himself unworthy to rule, asked them to choose a successor. Suspecting a trap designed to test their loyalty, the boyars pleaded with him to stay in power. The grief-stricken tsar obliged, although he was by this time a broken man, much of the time incapable of exercising effective leadership. He died in the spring of 1584 after a serious illness, leaving behind a larger realm but one that had been greatly weakened by the turmoil the ruler himself had inflicted upon the country.

3

TIMES OF TROUBLES AND GRANDEUR, 1584–1725

With the death of Ivan IV, Russia entered a period of unprecedented turbulence. For a few years it seemed as though the country, rife with discontent, would disintegrate and split into numerous independent regions governed by usurpers or adventurers. In the words of Giles Fletcher, an English visitor to Russia in 1588, the tsar's 'wicked policy and tyrannous practice (though now it be ceased) hath so troubled the country and filled it so full of grudge and mortal hatred ever since, that it will not be quenched (as it seemeth now) till it burn again into a civil flame'. Fedor, Ivan's son, who assumed the throne in 1584, was utterly incapable of exercising leadership, let alone coping with a state in disarray. In his childhood Fedor had been an 'undersized white-faced stripling who was disposed to dropsy and possessed an unsteady, quasi-senile gait'. He grew up to be a feeble-minded adult far more interested in spiritual matters than in affairs of state. When he received foreign dignitaries, he could not refrain from 'smiling, nor from gazing first upon his scepter, and then upon his orb'. Nothing gave him greater pleasure than to run from one church to another ringing the bells and having mass celebrated. As Ivan himself sadly noted, Fedor behaved more like a sexton than the son of a tsar.

Immediately after his father's death the boyar dignitaries began a struggle for influence over the imbecile tsar that lasted four years and was at times accompanied by bloody rioting in the streets. Finally, in 1588, the thirty-four-year-old Boris Godunov, a boyar allegedly of Tatar origin and the subject of Moussorgsky's famous Russian opera, emerged as the tsar's principal counselor. Although barely literate, Godunov was an intelligent and uncommonly sensible man who administered the country virtually unopposed for some ten years. English visitors to Moscow considered Boris so powerful that they referred to him as 'lieutenant of the empire' and 'lord protector of Russia'. His astute and moderate policies succeeded in producing a measure of calm throughout the realm. He eschewed risky foreign adventures, made serious efforts to help the destitute, and tried to lighten the burden borne by the peasants. Through a series of shrewd, if not altogether honorable, maneuvers he succeeded in elevating the Moscow metropolitanate to a patriarchate. This change added measurably to the prestige of the Muscovite church and also to that of the tsar and Godunov himself. Above all, the years from 1588 to 1598 were a period of internal calm, a welcome change after the tumult of Ivan's reign.

The calm ended in 1598, when Fedor died without leaving a single relative who could advance a legitimate claim to the throne. The metropolitan took it upon himself to summon a *zemskii sobor*, or national assembly, to elect a new tsar. Boris was naturally the leading candidate, but to everyone's surprise he stubbornly turned down every suggestion that he campaign for the position. The crafty boyar actually longed to be tsar of Muscovy, but he did not want to be beholden to the *zemskii sobor* for his election, nor did he want the election to serve as a precedent. If he was to be tsar, he intended to found a new dynasty, thus permitting his children to succeed him. Unable to agree on another candidate, the assembly turned to Godunov anyway and acceded to all of his stipulations. But as ruler in his own right, Boris did not fare as well as he had previously. To be sure, he continued many of his enlightened policies, which in some respects anticipated the innovative work of Peter the Great later in the seventeenth century. He recognized the need for Russians to master Western technology and technical skills, for example, and therefore attempted to found a university in Moscow. But the clergy, who feared the introduction of heretical ideas from non-Orthodox countries, blocked the plan. Instead, Godunov sent eighteen young men to the West to study, a bold move that had no impact on Russia, for not one of the students returned.

Godunov's reform program, however, was dealt a more serious blow by nature. In the fall of 1601, large areas of Russia were blanketed by a very early frost that destroyed much of the crop. Many people went hungry, and in order to provide work for the needy, Godunov introduced the equivalent of a public works program: the building of a conduit for water from the Moscow river to the Kremlin. This well-intentioned measure, however, only worsened the situation in the capital, for as soon as people heard of the relief project they streamed into the city. The weather did not improve during the following two years, and food shortages became even more acute. Between 1601 and 1603, 100,000 people are believed to have died of starvation in Moscow; several hundred thousand more perished in other parts of the country.

The people held Godunov responsible for their suffering and readily believed the horrendous stories that his boyar opponents hastened to circulate. They charged him with ruthless ambition, corruption, and such misdeeds as having Moscow raided by a foreign power in order to divert attention from domestic difficulties. He was even accused of poisoning Tsar Fedor. But the most startling charge of all was that he had engineered the murder of Ivan the Terrible's last child, the nine-year-old Dmitrii, in order to pave the way for his own accession. The events surrounding the death of Dmitrii in 1591 are actually so bizarre and the accounts of them so contradictory that they may justly be considered one of Russia's most intriguing detective stories.

Dmitrii was born in 1582 to Ivan's fourth wife, Maria Nagaia, but, since the church normally permitted a man no more than three marriages (an exception had been made to allow Ivan to take a fourth wife), the youngster was canonically ineligible for the crown. Fiercely ambitious, Dmitrii's mother would not relinquish her son's claim to what she considered his patrimony. In order that Maria be prevented from plotting against Tsar Fedor, she and her entire family were exiled to Uglich, a town that Ivan had bequeathed to Dmitrii as an appanage. There Maria and her relatives plied the boy with hatred for Fedor and Godunov, so much so that Dmitrii used to direct his playmates to make snow statues of the despised leaders, whose heads, arms, and legs he would then chop off. Godunov no doubt heard of these games through his informers, just as he heard of the frequent visits Maria paid to soothsayers to find out how long Tsar Fedor and the tsaritsa would live. Godunov probably also learned that by 1590 Maria's clan had organized an elaborate conspiracy designed to wrest power for her son.

A few months later, in 1591, Dmitrii suddenly died from mysterious knife wounds. The boy's family lost no time in charging that government agents had murdered the boy, and once this story spread, the people of Uglich staged a violent rebellion against the tsar's officials. At the same time, fires set by arsonists in the employ of the Nagois broke out in Moscow. The plan was to discredit the government and foment a national uprising, but Tsar Fedor's troops quelled the disorder within a few days. Maria was forced to take the veil, and many members of her family were exiled to remote provincial towns.

Godunov then appointed a commission to investigate the death of Dmitrii, which it eventually determined to have been accidental. But when the charge of murder was revived twelve years after the accident, many people chose to believe that Godunov had in fact arranged to have the child killed. In the face of these slanders and intrigues, Boris lost his composure and instituted a terroristic regime bound to horrify everyone who recalled the barbarities of Ivan the Terrible. Inevitably, Godunov's opponents attracted growing support, but they still could not dislodge him. The intriguers, who apparently included members of the Romanov family, therefore dreamed up another scheme. In a sudden reversal, they claimed that the assassination attempt had failed and that Dmitrii, the 'legitimate claimant' to the throne, was alive and eager to assume his rightful position. In 1604, a pretender known as the False Dmitrii appeared in Poland and was received in semi-private audience by King Sigismund, who recognized the potential usefulness of the impostor in subduing Muscovy. The pope and the Jesuits also supported the pretender, who had converted to Catholicism, in the hope that he would deliver the Muscovites over to the Roman Catholic Church.

In October 1604, the pretender led a motley army of three thousand Poles, Ukrainians, and Don Cossacks into Muscovy. The army met with little success until April 1605, when Boris died suddenly, perhaps as a result of poisoning. His son Fedor succeeded to the throne, only to be deposed a few weeks later. Both boyars and commoners went over to the False Dmitrii in large numbers, and in June 1605 the impostor triumphantly entered the Kremlin and butchered the Godunovs. The invaders spared Ksenia, Boris's daughter, but only because the pretender wanted her as his mistress. A few boyars then summoned Maria Nagaia, the real Dmitrii's mother, from her convent to the Kremlin, and in an incredible scene she pronounced the impostor her long-lost son. She later admitted that she had lied because she feared for her life.

The next eight years, from 1605 to 1613, are known as the Time of Troubles, a period when the country was literally plunged into anarchy. The pretender quickly alienated his new subjects by inviting numerous Poles to Moscow and barring Russian peasants from the Kremlin grounds. The boyars, ever inventive when their interests were at stake, claimed that the new tsar was not the real tsar after all and organized a Russian army, led by Prince Vasilii Shuisky, to rout the Poles in the citadel. The False Dmitrii tried to escape by jumping out of the palace window, but he injured himself as he landed, was apprehended by Shuisky's men, and was immediately killed. In May 1606, a crowd of nobles and commoners gathered in Red Square to proclaim Shuisky the Tsar of Russia.

By this time, conditions in the country had deteriorated to such an extent that the new ruler found it impossible to maintain order. Violent class warfare raged in several regions of the state, brigandage was rampant, and both the Poles and the Swedes intervened in Russian affairs. During the next two years a score of new pretenders appeared, all of whom rallied some support among disaffected Muscovites of various social classes.

In 1607, the cause of the second pretender, the most successful of the lot, presented the Polish Catholic clergy with an amusing moral dilemma. The clergy sought to bolster his claim to the Muscovite throne by arranging for Marina Mniszech, wife of the False Dmitrii, to acknowledge him as her husband, but this second impostor was so physically unappealing that when Marina saw him she purportedly shuddered. Nevertheless, she was eventually persuaded to overcome her revulsion, a change of heart occasioned in part by her ambition to be tsaritsa and in part by her father's desire to be close to the seat of power. Although the priests and her father seemed not the slightest bit disturbed by her lying about the pretender's identity, they could not suffer Marina to commit the sin of cohabiting with a man they knew was not her husband. A public marriage would have exposed the entire scheme as a fraud, and the dilemma could only be resolved by means of a secret marriage ceremony.

Recognized by his 'wife', the new pretender marched into Muscovy in June 1608 and encamped in Tushino, nine miles from the capital. There the 'Brigand of Tushino', as he was nicknamed, set up a government and laid siege to Moscow. Two tsars now vied for supremacy, and many nobles who nurtured a grievance against Shuisky moved to the 'second capital' to support the Brigand. At this time there emerged a sizable group of boyars, known as the *perelety*, who regularly shuttled back and forth between the two centers; the allegiance of the *perelety* at any particular moment depended on the attractiveness of the promises and privileges and land grants made by the 'rulers'. But the

Brigand did not remain in Tushino for long. His relentless plundering of the countryside turned the people against him, and in December 1609 they drove him from the town. A few months later, a Tatar officer killed him in revenge for his alleged murder of the ruler of Kasimov.

To add to the confusion, a rebellious force deposed Shuisky in 1610 and offered the crown to Wladyslaw, son of King Sigismund of Poland, on the understanding that he would convert to Orthodoxy. According to the *Russian Chronicles*, Wladyslaw 'was to be reborn to a new life, like a blind man who has recovered his eyesight'. The only difficulty was that Sigismund wanted the crown for himself. He dispatched an army against Muscovy, captured Smolensk, and then entrenched himself in the Kremlin after burning much of Moscow. At the same time, the Swedes occupied Novgorod and offered one of their princes as a candidate for the throne. As one historian put it, by 1611 the Muscovite state was in 'universal and complete disruption'.[1]

Salvation came from an unexpected source. In Nizhni Novgorod, a well-to-do butcher and merchant named Kuzma Minin took it upon himself to form a national movement to oust the enemy. An efficient organizer and public-spirited citizen, he convinced the city commune to impose new taxes for the creation of an army of liberation. Other cities joined in the effort, and many lesser nobles who had suffered from the chaos rushed to his support. Minin also had the good sense to call on the able Prince Dmitrii Pozharsky to lead the army.

After four months of preparation, Minin and Pozharsky joined with a Cossack force headed by Prince Trubetskoi and advanced on the capital. Their army of ten thousand men faced Polish forces numbering fifteen thousand, but the Russians cleverly invested the city for three months before launching an attack in October 1612. That assault gave them control of every part of the city except the Kremlin, where the Poles continued to hold out. Cut off from supplies, the defenders could not hope to resist for long, and when the food shortage among the Poles became acute they reportedly resorted to cannibalism. After five days they surrendered, and the critical stage of the struggle for liberation was over. The heroic efforts of Minin and Pozharsky are memorialized by a statue of the two men that stands at the edge of Red Square.

SOCIAL CONDITIONS

To reestablish authority in the country a man had to be found whom the people would accept as sovereign. Early in 1613 a *zemskii sobor* was convened, and after much wrangling the delegates settled on sixteen-year-old Michael Romanov, who was distantly related to the old dynasty. The family tie endowed Michael with the mantle of legitimacy, but the boyars who supported the election were also motivated by another consideration. Fedor Sheremetev, member of an old and distinguished family, revealed it in a private letter written at the time: 'Let us elect Misha [Michael] Romanov, he is young and still not wise, he'll be agreeable to us.' Even though the assembly unanimously elected him tsar, Michael initially refused the honor because his mother felt he was too young to cope with the turbulent conditions in the country. Only after a delegation from the *zemskii sobor* assured her that the nation stood ready to obey Michael and to end the civil strife did he agree to serve. On 11 July 1613, Michael was formally crowned in the Uspenskii Sobor, thus initiating a dynasty that was to rule Russia for three hundred years.

Although none of the three Romanovs who reigned through most of the seventeenth century – Michael (1613–45), Alexis (1645–76), and Fedor (1676–82) – was an inspired leader, the country, exhausted from the chaos of the Time of Troubles, regained its unity and a measure of stability. This is not to say that Russia remained free of fundamental changes and profound conflicts. Without doubt, the most significant change occurred in the legal status of peasants, who comprised at least eighty percent of the population. At roughly the time when serfdom in Western Europe was in decline, that institution became firmly entrenched in Russia. This development not only epitomized the differences between Russia and the West but deeply affected the course of Russian history for the next three centuries.

In the course of the sixteenth century, the Muscovite peasants' right of free movement and the freedom from obligatory service to the landlords were gradually undermined, though precisely how that happened is still unclear. We do know that with the growth of national expenditure on the numerous wars the government increased the tax burden on peasants and sought to prevent them from moving freely to distant regions where they could escape detection by tax collectors. We also know that peasants tended to obtain a loan (*ssuda*) from landlords to enable them to cultivate their lands, and, since they had to pay off their debts (usually over many years), they were not free to move to other parts of the country. At the same time, nobles with *pomestie* became more dependent on a reliable workforce, since constant wars imposed a growing burden of military service upon the nobles, causing their absence from their estates. The less affluent noble land-owners faced the additional problem of having their agricultural laborers attracted to the estates of richer landowners. The labor shortage became so severe in the sixteenth and early seventeenth century that it was not uncommon for landlords to engage in 'peasant abductions'. A landlord would pay off a peasant's debt to another landlord and then triumphantly secure the services of that peasant. These 'abductions' provoked considerable contro-versy between landlords, and to prevent them communal authori-ties and small landowners would go to such extreme measures as placing the peasants in chains, imposing excessive quit-rents on them, or using force to prevent their departure. Not infrequently, riots broke out over the issue of transferring peasants from one landlord to another.

These were the general circumstances in the countryside at the time that serfdom took hold, but unfortunately we have virtually no documents on how the institution evolved. One school of histo-rians[2] contends that the critical event was the issuance by Tsar Fedor (1584–98) of a *ukase* prohibiting peasants from leaving the land they occupied. Other historians[3] reject this theory because it places too much weight on one decree, which has never been located, in explaining a development that took many decades. It seems most likely that serfdom evolved gradually in response to economic pressures on state authorities and nobles, who were intent upon maintaining a steady supply of agrarian labor in the countryside. What we do know is that in 1649, when the General Law Code (*Ulozhenie*) was published, the institution of serfdom was firmly established and the legal conditions under which a majority of Russians lived were spelled out in some detail. Before describing those conditions, it is worth noting that about twenty percent of the peasants belonged to the category of 'state peasants', who were also tied to the land but were economically and in other respects better off than the serfs. Their number increased steadily and by the mid nineteenth century there were more state peasants than landlords' peasants in Russia.

Russian serfdom is not easy to define, because it both resembled its Western counterpart and yet contained features characteristic of slavery, under which some human beings were the property, pure and simple, of their masters. Russian peasants were serfs in that they could not move from one location to another without formal permission. In return for a plot of land, serfs in Russia had to pay either a quit-rent (*obrok*) or work for the landlord for a specified number of days – normally two or three – each week (*barshchina*, comparable to the *corvée*). Unlike a slave, however, the Russian serf retained a measure of civic individuality. He was a taxpayer, he was entitled to a plot of land, he could not be arbitrarily converted into a household worker, and he could not be deprived of his personal belongings 'by violence'. Under certain circumstances, the serf was legally entitled to lodge a complaint with the authorities about levies or labor that landlords sought to impose on him.

But the Code of 1649 contained some provisions that gave the landlord the right to treat his serfs as property. For example, if a nobleman or any of his relatives or servants killed a peasant of another noble, the master of the guilty party had to hand over as compensation the 'best peasant' under his authority together with the peasant's wife, children, and property. More important, landlords eventually secured the right to sell their serfs to another landlord with or without land and without keeping intact the serf's family. The landlord also decided on whether or not his serfs might marry and served as a judge in his domain with the power to order serfs to be flogged, imprisoned, or exiled to Siberia. Serfdom in Russia was a harsh institution and came close to slavery.

The economic and social life of many peasants was dominated by the commune (*mir*), an institution unique to Russia and obscure in its origins. Apparently founded in the fourteenth century by groups of peasants who believed that cooperative farming would be most efficient, the commune in time came to regulate the local affairs of the villages. Its officials, elected by peasant householders, maintained order, regulated the use of arable land, and assumed responsibility for the collection of taxes imposed by the state. About eighty percent of the communes periodically redivided the land among villagers to maintain an equality of allotments assigned to peasant families, whose size would naturally vary over the years.[4] Thus, there was no tradition of private landownership among the bulk of the country's population, and as long as the peasants did not own the land they worked, they lacked the incentive to improve efficiency. This factor as well as the vagaries of Russia's climate help explain the low level of productivity and low standard of living of the vast majority of the population.

Not surprisingly, peasant unrest was a frequent occurrence. One of the more dramatic eruptions of violence took place in 1670 in the south-eastern regions of the Volga, when Stenka Razin, who hailed from an old, established Cossack family, succeeded in rousing a large number of poor peasants to follow him in a campaign against the boyars and rich landlords in general. A charismatic leader, Razin raised an army of some six thousand men that inflicted several defeats on government troops and within a year captured the city of Astrakhan, where the rebels looted at will and slaughtered many landlords. Razin's army then marched along the Volga, where several towns (Saratov, Samara), having heard of the atrocities the rebels had committed in Astrakhan, surrendered without putting up any resistance. By the summer of 1670 it seemed as though Razin would march all the way to Moscow. Only now did the government take the uprising seriously. It dispatched a large army, well equipped with artillery, to the war zone, and after some initial setbacks the government's forces defeated Razin in a major battle near Simbirsk. Razin managed to escape and continued the struggle in what had now turned into a virtual civil war, but in the spring of 1671 he was captured. Government troops brought him to Moscow, apparently with his neck chained to a scaffold mounted on the rear of a wagon. The tsar himself questioned him and then ordered officials to torture him. According to the historian Paul Avrich, Razin was 'beaten with the knout, his limbs were pulled out of joint, a hot iron was passed over his body, and the crown of his head was shaved and cold water poured on it drop by drop, "which they say causeth very great pain"'. The government also dealt harshly with the rebels, killing, according to one contemporary estimate, about 100,000 of them. The official brutality was meant to teach the peasants a lesson, but it did not prevent future peasant uprisings, some of them as vast and bloody as Razin's.

The peasants were not the only social group whose rights were legally defined and constricted by the *Ulozhenie* of 1649. The premise of the Code, a thoroughly conservative document, was to subordinate all subjects to the state. Concerned, above all, to ensure the army had a steady supply of recruits and the treasury an adequate supply of funds, the government divided the population into hereditary groups, each of which was assigned a specific status and obligations. The burghers were legally bound to remain in the towns where they lived and were granted a monopoly over commerce and industry. The nobility (*dvorianstvo*) were the only social group granted the right to own estates worked by servile labor, a prized privilege that had the effect of limiting the number of people who could obtain a *pomestie*. The purpose of this regulation was to reduce the competition for land, which was in short supply. At the same time, the nobles, many of whom were far from affluent, were prohibited from selling themselves into servitude. The purpose of this measure was to ensure an adequate supply of soldiers and state servants. In effect, Muscovy was now a state in which, as the reformer Michael Speransky noted early in the nineteenth century, there were only two estates: 'slaves of the sovereign, and slaves of the landlords. The former are called free only in regard to the latter.'

RELIGIOUS CONFLICT

It was also a state stubbornly resistant to the very idea of reform. In 1653, when Patriarch Nikon, then a favorite of Tsar Alexis, sought to introduce minor changes in religious ritual and texts, a social convulsion erupted that led to permanent discord within Russian Orthodoxy. Nikon's purpose was as much political as spiritual: he hoped to bring the Russian liturgy and customs into conformity with those of Constantinople in order to facilitate the planned rapprochement between Muscovy and the Ukraine, where the church had remained faithful to Greek practices. Thus, for example, he proposed that the spelling of 'Jesus', incorrectly inscribed in Muscovite texts, be amended; that in making the cross, three rather than two fingers be used; that the 'Alleluia' be chanted thrice instead of twice during services; and that religious processions move in the direction of the sun rather than counter to it.

Because of the low educational level of the Russian people and clergy, religious ritual mattered far more to them than dogma. In their eyes the slightest deviation from established practices, such as the reforms advanced by Nikon, amounted to heresy. The archpriest Avvakum, who led the opposition to the changes, recalled his initial reaction to them: 'We [the zealots of the church] gathered together to think it over. We saw that winter was about to overcome us. Our hearts became cold, and our legs trembled.'

The opposition mounted a campaign against the reforms, to which the patriarch and the government responded with a ruthless campaign of their own. Some of the zealots, including Avvakum, were exiled to Siberia, while others were anathematized, and a feverish hunt was launched for icons that in any way differed from the Byzantine model. Homes were searched for the offending images, which were then publicly destroyed, sometimes by the patriarch himself. By the 1660s the *Raskol*, or Great Schism, had torn the church asunder and left in its wake a group of dissenters who came to be known as *Raskolniki*, or Old Believers.

In the meantime, personal differences terminated the relationship between Patriarch Nikon and Tsar Alexis. The arrogant and impetuous manner of the patriarch, and his belief that ecclesiastical supersedes temporal power, thoroughly alienated the tsar. At a church council that Alexis held in his Kremlin palace in 1666–7, he denounced Nikon for innumerable transgressions of Muscovite law and for offenses against the sovereign and the boyars. In a move that officially affirmed the supremacy of the secular ruler over the church, the council deposed Nikon and banished him from Moscow. Yet the campaign for reform continued and was even intensified. The council formally cursed and anathematized all dissenters, and the tsar ordered that the tongues of two recalcitrants be cut out, a punishment then considered fitting for blasphemy. Such interference by the state in essentially ecclesiastical matters accelerated the process of subjugating the Russian Orthodox Church to temporal authorities.

The Old Believers felt that the state hampered the road to eternal salvation, a conviction that bred fanaticism in their ranks. Many dissenters sank into such despair over the state of affairs that they became convinced that the end of the world was imminent. They proclaimed that the apocalypse would occur in 1666 or in 1669, and when both years passed without catastrophe they forecast that the end would come in 1698. They even claimed to know precisely how the ultimate calamity would take place: 'The sun would be eclipsed, the stars fall from the sky, the earth would be burned up, and on the Day of Judgement the last trumpet blown by the Archangel would summon together the righteous and the unrighteous.' Confident about the accuracy of their prophesy, many thought it senseless to remain on earth and risk being contaminated by heresy. Above all, they would not recant despite intense government pressure to do so. As a result, between 1672 and 1691 there were thirty-seven horrifying mass immolations in which more than twenty thousand dissenters voluntarily burned themselves to death. In addition, the government burned many Old Believers at the stake, among them the archpriest Avvakum.

Far from unifying Russian Orthodoxy, Nikon's reforms generated irreconcilable conflicts among the people. It has been estimated that in 1889 there were some thirteen million dissenters, among them Orthodoxy's most devout followers, out of a total population of about ninety million. Moreover, the religious schism of the 1660s reinforced the practice of governmental persecution of religious minorities, a practice that remained more or less a permanent feature of Russian state policy until the late twentieth century.

PETER THE GREAT

The seventeenth century, which had witnessed an array of unprecedented disasters, ended with the reign of a person who was in many ways the most impressive and innovative tsar in Russian history. Peter the Great, as he came to be known, contended that if Russia was to develop into a powerful and enlightened nation, many ancient customs and traditions would have to be abandoned and extensive reforms of the country's institutions on the Western European model would have to be implemented. It was a worthy and even noble vision of modernization and Westernization, but unfortunately for Russia, Peter had little understanding of human nature, and it never occurred to him that he might be able to persuade his people, many of them, to be sure, ignorant and superstitious, of the desirability of rapid change by means other than raw compulsion. In the end, his attempt to 'civilize Russia with the Knout' failed and he did not succeed in 'binding together a nation lacking in cohesion'. Nonetheless, it must be said that hardly an institution of national significance remained unaffected by his initiatives. He laid the foundations of modern Russia.

Peter was physically and otherwise a gargantuan figure. Almost seven feet tall, he had great physical strength and remarkable manual dexterity, and his interests were astonishingly broad. He claimed to have mastered fourteen trades as well as surgery and dentistry. When courtiers and servants took sick they tried to conceal it from Peter, for if he thought that medical attention was needed he would gather his instruments and offer his services. Among his personal belongings Peter left a sackful of teeth, testimony to his thriving dental practice. Peter was also a man with a strong sadistic streak. He delighted, for example, in forcing all his guests, including the ladies, to drink vodka straight – the way he liked it – and in large quantities. Johann Korb, the secretary of the Austrian embassy in Moscow from 1698 to 1699, described a particularly gruesome incident at one of these festive occasions: 'Boyar Golowin has, from his cradle, a natural horror of salad and vinegar; so the Czar directing Colonel Chambers to hold him tight, forced salad and vinegar into his mouth and nostrils, until the blood flowing from his nose succeeded his violent coughing.'

Peter's personality, like that of Ivan the Terrible (whom he greatly admired), was molded largely by traumatic childhood experiences. His mother, Natalia Naryshkin, was the second wife of Tsar Alexis, the second Romanov ruler. From the moment she moved into the Kremlin early in 1671, Natalia had been obliged to contend with the animosity of the Miloslavskys, relatives of Alexis's first wife, who had died in 1669. As a result, Peter, who was born in 1672, spent his first four years in a tense atmosphere. The situation was compounded in 1676 when Alexis died; Fedor, Peter's half-brother, succeeded to the throne and the Miloslavskys took control of the Kremlin.

The new ruler, however, was sickly and his death in 1682 stirred a serious crisis over the succession. Peter's other half-brother, Ivan, was entitled to the throne, but everyone knew that he could not possibly govern. Aside from being mentally deficient, he was virtually blind and suffered from a speech defect and epilepsy. The nobles therefore ignored his claim and proclaimed the ten-year-old Peter tsar on the understanding that his mother would act as regent during his minority. But the Miloslavskys refused to be shunted aside and appealed to the *streltsy* (specially trained musketeers), who staged a three-day riot in their support. Some of the most dramatic scenes took place on the Porch of Honor in the Kremlin, the striking entrance to the royal palace that was covered with scarlet carpets on festive occasions. In the hope of calming the *streltsy*, Natalia courageously appeared at the top of the stairs together with Peter and Ivan. But the soldiers refused to end their rebellion; they demanded that the tsaritsa hand over to them her foster father, the aged Artamon Matveiev. When she complied, they hurled him into the square, where he was cut to pieces in full view of Peter, who watched the gory proceedings without betraying a trace of emotion. The *streltsy* continued their rampage, brutally murdering more than a dozen people. The ghastly disorders came to an end only when it was agreed to make Sofia Miloslavsky, Peter's half-sister, regent and both Peter and Ivan co-tsars, a novel arrangement that Sofia claimed was divinely inspired. After this triumph by the Miloslavskys, Natalia and Peter moved to the village of Preobrazhensk, some three miles from the center of Moscow. The horrors of 1682 remained indelibly inscribed in Peter's mind and seem to have bred within him a moral callousness that became ever more pronounced as he matured.

At Preobrazhensk, Peter received a formal education of only the most rudimentary kind, but he was highly intelligent, had a fine memory and remarkable curiosity, especially in regard to things mechanical, and therefore educated himself in those fields that appealed to him. Gifted with his hands, he quickly acquired a certain proficiency in carpentry, masonry, and metalwork. Sailing and boatbuilding also intrigued him, but his greatest passion was to 'play' with live soldiers. At the age of eleven he procured guns, lead, powder, and shot for his soldiers and within a few years built his own six-hundred-man army, the nucleus of the future imperial guards.

One night during the summer of 1689 Peter received the alarming news that Sofia planned to have herself crowned tsaritsa and that she had dispatched several companies of *streltsy* to arrest him. Without bothering to get dressed, Peter leaped on a horse and raced off to the monastery-fortress of Holy Trinity, forty miles from Preobrazhensk. Sofia, who had in fact lost popularity among the musketeers, found herself unable to mobilize them in support of her seizure of power. Consequently, Peter and a group of loyal soldiers managed to crush the plot without firing a shot. He sent Sofia to a convent, exiled some of her advisers, and had one of them hanged, but for about seven years he allowed his mother to run the government and only in 1696 did Peter assume the burdens of power.

In the interim he was a regular visitor to the so-called 'German suburb' that lay between Preobrazhensk and the Kremlin. Between 1689 and 1694 he spent much of his time there with Dutch and English merchants, whom he pumped for information about the latest mechanical devices and political developments in Europe. It was there that his interest in the West was first seriously aroused.

THE WESTERNIZER

As a sovereign, Peter's most distinctive trait was his activism; in foreign as well as domestic affairs he continually initiated new policies. Although not a profound thinker, he had the capacity to grasp difficult problems and devise solutions. His prodigious energy and drive are perhaps best exemplified by the fact that he rarely stayed in any one place more than three months; he insisted on being at the center of the action, whether it was the battlefield, the negotiating table, the torture chamber, or a shipyard. He made heavy demands on himself and his people, but not primarily for reasons of personal glorification. Unlike his predecessors, he did not identify himself with the state but considered himself its first servant, and he justified his exacting policies on the grounds that they promoted the interests of Russia. In view of these extraordinary exertions, as well his frequent debaucheries, it is not surprising that he developed a nervous twitch on the left side of his face that sometimes distorted into a grimace.

Peter was also highly eccentric, a trait he demonstrated most dramatically in 1697 when he visited the West, an unprecedented undertaking for a Muscovite monarch. One of his purposes was to seek allies among European kings for a military crusade against Turkey, but his major reason was to study Western industrial techniques, especially shipbuilding, and to engage skilled craftsmen and naval officers to send back to Russia. Because the tsar wanted to feel free to work in the industrial establishments he visited, he traveled under the name of Peter Mikhailov, an alias that deceived almost no one.

Peter's five months in Holland were filled with diverse activities: he inspected factories, workshops, hospitals, schools, military installations, and an observatory. In each place he asked detailed questions, and whenever possible he took part in the work, at least for a short while. He even attended lectures by famous anatomists and insisted on watching them dissect cadavers.

Early in 1698 he moved on to England, where, after a cordial welcome by King William III, he again made the rounds, including a visit to the House of Lords. On hearing the interpreter's report on the debates, he declared, 'When subjects thus do speak the truth unto the Sovereign, it is goodly hearing. Let us learn in this of the English.' This was mere talk, of course, but Peter was serious about studying English methods of shipbuilding, and for this purpose he settled for a few weeks in Deptford, which was close to a government dockyard. In the spring Peter returned to the Continent, arriving in Vienna in May 1698. He intended to proceed to Venice, but news of another conspiracy fomented by his half-sister and a new rebellion led by four *streltsy* regiments caused him to change his plans. By this time he had been abroad for fifteen months, and he rightly feared that if he prolonged his absence he might lose power. In any case, he had every reason to be satisfied with his accomplishments, for in addition to improving substantially his technical knowledge, he had recruited 750 specialists in naval affairs, engineering, and medicine and had purchased an impressive array of military supplies.

Within a day of his return Peter shocked his Muscovite subjects by personally cutting off the beards of leading nobles as well as the long sleeves of their surcoats. Somewhat later he issued decrees requiring everyone except peasants and clergymen to appear clean-shaven and wear Hungarian or German dress on pain of having to pay an annual tax. Another measure that disturbed the people was the Westernization of the Russian calendar: the New Year was to be celebrated on 1 January instead of 1 September, and beginning with the new century the years would be counted not from the presumed date of the world's creation but from that of Christ's birth. Thus, the year 7208 became 1700. Peter reasoned that only by means of these seemingly trivial innovations could the Russian people rid themselves of their backward 'Asiatic' customs and become energetic, enterprising citizens.

The people, especially the lower classes, did not take kindly to Peter's reforms. The beard in particular contributed significantly to preserving the 'image of God' in which they believed man to be made. They thought that by shaving it off they would be reduced to the level of cats and dogs and would court eternal damnation. The depth of feeling on the subject is amusingly illustrated by the following incident. In 1705, two young men approached the Metropolitan of Rostov for advice, complaining that they would sooner lose their heads than their beards. The prelate countered with a rhetorical question: 'Which of the twain, I pray you, would grow again the more easily?'

A further cause for dismay among Peter's subjects was his brutal treatment of the rebellious *streltsy*. Peter lost no time in initiating extensive investigations, but no one seemed able or willing to answer all the questions to his satisfaction. Consequently, he began to doubt everyone's loyalty and decided to massacre subjects indiscriminately in Red Square. According to some accounts, the tsar himself participated in the executions. On one occasion, he is said to have cut off eighty-four rebel heads with a sword. In all, over twelve hundred *streltsy* were exterminated, and many of their heads were left in the streets of Moscow over winter in order to terrorize the population. Peter was unquestionably a tyrant, who early in his reign resolved to make it clear that he would insist on absolute obedience to his word. Local rebellions, some quite massive, from time to time raised doubts about the loyalty of some of his subjects, but after 1698 his authority was sufficiently secure to allow him to concentrate on military affairs and domestic reform, his chief interests.

Russia waged war, usually at Peter's instigation, during most of his thirty-six-year reign. In the period from 1689 to 1725, the country enjoyed only one full year and thirteen isolated months of peace. Determined to bring about the political unification of all the Russian people and to rectify his nation's exposed frontiers in the south and west, Peter became entangled in military conflicts with Sweden, Turkey, and finally Persia. Occasionally, he suffered painful defeats, but on balance Russia emerged from the encounters a far stronger nation.

His most costly and most rewarding war, the one with Sweden, lasted from 1700 to 1721 and is known as the Great Northern War. Sweden was then one of the leading European powers, and until 1718 her armies were commanded by the brilliant and daring strategist King Charles XII. When Peter defeated the Swedes in 1709 in the famous Battle of Poltava, he not only saved Russia from conquest but propelled the country into the forefront of European diplomacy. At the war's end, twelve years later, when the Treaty of Nystad was signed, Sweden was thoroughly humbled. Russia gained control of the Baltic coast from Riga to Vyborg, having confirmed possession of the provinces of Livonia, Estonia, Ingria, and a part of Karelia. Thus consolidated,

Russia's position as a major European power has survived to the present day.

Peter fêted the victory in grand style. For seven days and nights, he compelled the leading nobles to remain in the senate building to celebrate. He himself, 'half-demented with joy at having brought the struggle to a successful issue, and forgetful alike of years and gout . . . danced upon the tables [and] sang songs'. Then, allegedly in response to the urgent pleas of the senate, he agreed to accept the titles of emperor and 'Father of the Country'. This marked the official birth of the Russian empire.

These festivities took place not in the Kremlin, but in Peter's new capital, St. Petersburg, which he called his 'paradise' and 'darling'. Three considerations prompted him to build a city in the swamps at the head of the Gulf of Finland near the mouth of the Neva river: his love for the sea, a desire to perpetuate his memory, and hatred for the Kremlin. For twenty years beginning in 1703 the royal coffers were ransacked to create this 'great window for Russia to look out at Europe' or, as some have called it, Russia's 'window to the West'. The conquests ratified by the Treaty of Nystad gave Peter the territorial security for his capital that he had so persistently sought.

Because of the cold, damp climate around St. Petersburg, Peter had to rely heavily on forced labor to complete the grueling task of erecting the new capital. There was much grumbling among the workers, who suffered from various illnesses, especially dysentery, but Peter would not be deterred. The historian Kliuchevsky did not exaggerate when he wrote: 'It would be difficult to find in the annals of military history any battle that claimed more lives than the number of workers who died in [the building of] St. Petersburg.' And the financial cost ran into millions of rubles. Peter engaged the distinguished French architect Jean-Baptiste Leblond and other Western experts to design the city and its palaces, and paid them all extraordinarily large sums of money. Leblond's chief work was the tsar's country residence at Peterhof. With its formal gardens, terraces, fountains, and cascades it resembles the palace gardens at Versailles.

St. Petersburg became the official capital of Russia in 1718 and remains to this day one of the world's most beautiful cities.

Peter took rather novel measures to bolster the country's military strength. He built a sizable navy, a significant innovation, since Russia had never before aspired to being a naval power. The eight-hundred-ship fleet contributed substantially to Sweden's defeat, though it should be noted that the navy did not long survive Peter as an effective force. More lasting was his creation of a standing army that by 1725 consisted of roughly 200,000 troops. Its effectiveness was enhanced by Peter's insistence on rigorous, up-to-date training, the use of the most modern weapons, and the hiring of foreign officers.

None of Peter's ambitious projects could be implemented without money, which was always in short supply. From 1705 to 1707, for example, the government's expenditure exceeded its income by twenty percent. To cope with this problem, Peter repeatedly overhauled the system of taxation, constantly increasing the burden on the common people, and in 1724 he imposed a soul tax on all males of the non-privileged classes. This tax, which in effect extended serfdom by abolishing the legal distinctions between serfs and other groups of bondsmen, was a fiscal triumph: direct taxes now brought in 4.5 million rubles instead of 1.8 million. By granting various exemptions and privileges Peter also stimulated the development of industry during the first decades of the eighteenth century, but despite initial gains, many of these enterprises went out of business by mid century owing to the inferior grade of their products.

One of Peter's most enduring reforms was the establishment in 1722 of the Table of Ranks, a key feature of Peter's determination to promote the idea that service to the state was a subject's highest calling and paramount obligation and to encourage efficiency. According to the Table of Ranks, there were to be fourteen ranks in three areas of service – the military, the civil, and the court – and theoretically at least, and often in practice, the criteria for advancement were to be merit and length of service. All who entered state service were to start their careers at the bottom, at rank 14, and commoners who reached rank 8 would be accorded the honor of hereditary nobility, which meant that their children would be nobles. In stipulating a gradual rise in status and regular salary for state servants, Peter sought to encourage lifelong service for all officials. The same concern prompted Peter to prohibit nobles who took public posts from returning periodically to their estates to manage them.

Finally, Peter reorganized the administrative structure of the state. He granted urban communities a degree of self-government, replaced the sluggish central departments with Swedish-style 'colleges', and established a senate that served as the highest judicial and administrative organ and was to govern when the tsar was away from the capital. To promote greater efficiency, he also divided the country into provinces, which in turn were divided into districts. In 1721 he completed the process of subjugating the church to the state by substituting for the patriarchate the 'Most Holy Governing Synod', a body of ten clergymen appointed by the tsar. The chief procurator, a layman whose job it was to supervise the work of the synod, was also appointed by the monarch. It is noteworthy that in formulating many of these reforms Peter relied on the advice of Gottfried Wilhelm von Leibniz, the German mathematician and philosopher who supplied the tsar with numerous concrete suggestions in return for a handsome annual retainer.

Although they were by no means fully successful, and although many left their mark primarily on the privileged class, the Petrine reforms are generally considered to have raised the quality of government in Russia. Their very durability – some lasted as long as two centuries – supports this conclusion. In addition, it was Peter who placed the idea of Westernization on the agenda of Russian historical development. Henceforth the merit of this idea, as much as any other, would be debated by those Russians who speculated about their country's future.

Much as he prided himself on his accomplishments, Peter was constantly anguished by one question that he was never able to answer to his own satisfaction: would he be succeeded by a man capable of carrying on his work? His rightful heir, Alexis, born to his first wife, Eudoxia, in 1690, turned out to be lazy and totally indifferent to affairs of state. In any case, the relationship between Peter and Alexis deteriorated into open and bitter antagonism. In 1718, Peter charged his son with having conspired to overthrow him in a *coup d'état*. The evidence in support of the charge was far from conclusive, but that did not prevent Peter from investigating and torturing numerous suspects. Alexis himself was found guilty of treason and sentenced to death by a special council of 127 officials summoned by the tsar. But before the sentence could be carried out Alexis died in the fortress of Saints Peter and Paul in St. Petersburg, apparently from wounds inflicted by his torturers. The government announced that he had succumbed to apoplexy, but it was widely believed he had been murdered.

Alexis's demise only compounded the problem of succession. In May 1719, Peter's surviving son died at the age of three, and the tsar was again left to ponder the future of his realm. In 1722, Peter abolished the existing rules of succession and decreed that henceforth the incumbent could appoint his heir. For some reason Peter himself failed to do so, and the upshot was that after his death early in 1725 the succession became a subject of precisely the sort of passionate controversy that he had hoped to forestall.

4

DECLINE AND REVIVAL IN THE EIGHTEENTH CENTURY

For nearly forty years after Peter the Great's death in 1725, during the 'Era of Palace Revolutions', Russia was ruled by thoroughly undistinguished sovereigns. Most rulers succeeded to the throne by means of palace upheavals executed by the Corps of Guards, a privileged stratum of the regular army. Intrigue, plots, and corruption prevailed at court while favorites, often foreigners, administered the country. It has been said that during the reigns of Empress Anne (1730–40) and her successor, Elizabeth (1741–62), 'lovers ruled Russia'.

Moreover, the major concern of most rulers during that era was their private amusement, which often assumed bizarre forms. According to the historian Michael Florinsky, during the reign of Anne, 'the imperial residences were filled not only with animals and birds, especially those trained in the performance of tricks, but also with giants and dwarfs, hunchbacks and cripples, beggars and fools, while a large retinue of women, especially selected for their ability to chatter, spent hours spinning stories for the empress's entertainment.' In 1740, she amused herself by organizing an elaborate wedding ceremony in which Prince A. M. Golitsyn, scion of one of Russia's most illustrious families, was married to a 'Kalmyk woman of outstanding ugliness' in a 'mansion built of ice'.

Empress Elizabeth was a slight improvement. The daughter of Peter the Great, she suffered a terrible disappointment in 1727 when her fiancé, the Bishop of Lubeck, died shortly before they were to be wed. Elizabeth's grief was apparently genuine, but even so it is hard to think of her as the devoted wife of a clergy-man, for with a single-mindedness reminiscent of her father's, she lived life to the fullest. In fact, she conducted herself so scandal-ously that the Spanish ambassador in St. Petersburg was moved to remark that the empress 'shamelessly indulged in practices which would have made blush even the least modest person'. Her preoccupation with amorous adventures left Elizabeth little time for other activities, and Russian statesmen and foreign diplomats were forever seeking an opportune moment to persuade her to sign important documents.

She did, however, take seriously the question of the succes-sion. Since she had no children, she invited the son of her sister Anne to come to Russia to prepare himself for the crown. The boy, whose name was Peter, had been born in 1728 to Anne and her husband, the Duke of Holstein. Anne died when Peter was only a few weeks old, and as a result his upbring-ing had devolved completely upon his father. When the duke himself died thirteen years later, Peter made the long journey to St. Petersburg. He arrived knowing only the German language and German customs, but within a year of his arrival he converted to Orthodoxy and was forced to accept Russia as his home.

Having handpicked her immediate successor, Empress Elizabeth next sought to provide for her family's permanent retention of the crown. To that end, she began to consider a bride for the future Peter III; in 1744, she settled on Sophia Augusta Frederica of Anhalt-Zerbst, whose father, a petty German prince serving as governor of Stettin, was delighted by the prospect of so brilliant a match. Mother and daughter eagerly undertook the arduous trip to Russia, and after the fifteen-year-old girl had been converted to Orthodoxy and rebaptized Catherine, she was married to Peter in 1745 in a glittering ceremony in the Church of Our Lady of Kazan in St. Petersburg.

It was destined to be a disastrous union. The two were completely ill-suited to each other. Catherine was serious, intelligent, somewhat intellectually inclined, strong-willed, energetic, and, above all, ambitious. By contrast, Peter was sickly, dull, stubborn, and 'phenomenally ignorant'. He never matured, Kliuchevsky has noted: 'Grave matters he viewed jejunely; jejune matters he treated with the gravity of an adult.' He knew no greater pleasure than to play with his dolls and toy soldiers, amusements that continued to preoccupy him even after his marriage. His one cultural accomplishment, playing the fiddle, could not be appreciated by Catherine, who was tone deaf; but those in a position to judge her husband's performances could testify to her good fortune in this instance. Physically, Peter was unprepossessing. At the age of fourteen he had the physique of a ten-year-old. Moreover, as an adolescent he contracted smallpox, which left his face disfigured. It is believed that the marriage between Catherine and Peter was never consummated. In the early 1750s she had her first of a long series of love affairs that became the talk of St. Petersburg. By this time she had become estranged both from Peter and from Empress Elizabeth and it seemed that she would not be able to realize her ambition to play a major role in affairs of state.

Not until late 1762, when Empress Elizabeth suddenly died, did the wheel of fortune finally turn in Catherine's favor. Peter III succeeded to the throne, but his conduct and policies offended so many people that few Russians in positions of influence expected him to remain in power for long.

Some of Peter's actions were favorably received, especially by the privileged classes. Because Russia after Peter the Great enjoyed fairly long periods of peace – there was no war during the years from 1725 to 1733 and from 1743 to 1757 – the services to the state of the nobles were no longer as essential as they had been. During that period the nobles received one concession after another that lightened their burden but at the same time increased their power over the serfs. Thus, in 1760, landlords obtained the right to deport to Siberia serfs judged to be delinquent. Moreover, the deported serfs were credited towards the landlords' quota of recruits they had to supply to the army. The capstone of these measures was the so-called emancipation of the gentry in 1762. Henceforth, nobles no longer owed any service to the state and, except during wartime, they could resign from the army and the civil administration. They now also enjoyed the privilege of traveling abroad freely and could enter the service of foreign powers. But it would be wrong to conclude that nobles were now 'citizens' in the Western sense of the word. The authorities could still inflict corporal punishment on them and could with impunity confiscate their hereditary estates. Tsar Peter did, however, issue several other decrees that liberalized the autocratic regime. He abolished the security police, discouraged the arrest of political dissidents, and ordered more lenient treatment of Old Believers, many of whom were allowed to return from the foreign countries to which they had fled to escape Empress Elizabeth's persecutions.

But Peter also adopted many policies and practices that alienated important groups within the nobility. For one thing, he substantially reduced the authority of the senate, whose members had exercised a considerable amount of power ever since the time of Peter the Great. More important, Peter's obsession with things German shocked the members of his court. Because he revered Frederick the Great of Prussia, he abruptly extricated his country from the war it had been waging against the German state on terms clearly disadvantageous to Russia. To everyone's amazement, he frequently appeared in public dressed in a Prussian uniform, and once, during a state banquet, he interrupted the proceedings by rising from his seat and 'prostrating himself headlong' before the bust of Frederick. As if this were not enough, Peter forced rigid Prussian drill exercises upon his nobles and gave precedence to 'Holstein Guards', soldiers imported from Germany, over the Russian guards. Time and again he referred to Russia as 'an accursed land'.

His private behavior did not create a better impression. Hardly a day went by that he remained sober until bedtime. Claiming to be an accomplished actor, he would entertain guests at his palace by contorting his face in various ways. On seeing one of the tsar's performances, a lady at court exclaimed that 'whatever else he looked like as he was making . . . [the facial expressions], he did not look like a tsar.' Andrei Bolotov, a memoirist of the period, accurately summed up the feelings of the people: 'The Russians were gnashing their teeth with rage.' Thoroughly inept politically, Peter not only antagonized one social group after another; he also publicly humiliated Catherine and thus presented the growing opposition with a natural leader around whom it could rally. Catherine took advantage of the tsar's political isolation and on 9 July 1762, while Peter was away from St. Petersburg drilling his Holstein Guards, she led thousands of soldiers and nobles into the Church of Our Lady of Kazan to be formally proclaimed Empress of Russia by the Archbishop of Novgorod. Three days later she went to Peterhof, the imperial palace, and seized it without resistance. Peter sensed the hopelessness of his situation and quietly abdicated. He ended his erratic and perverse reign of six months incarcerated in a chateau in Ropsha, a few miles from St. Petersburg. From prison he pleaded with Catherine to be magnanimous, but on 16 July he died, apparently murdered by soldiers. Whether or not Catherine played any role in the deed is an open question, but many contemporaries were convinced that she had a hand in the tsar's death. Horace Walpole, son of Britain's famous prime minister, referred to her as 'Catherine Slay-Czar'. Most knowledgeable people in Europe, aware that she had no legal right to the throne, doubted that she would be able to retain power. But Catherine proved to be far more formidable than anyone suspected; she quickly crushed several conspiracies, and in so doing demonstrated her determination to rule with an iron hand.

THE REIGN OF CATHERINE II

In the public mind outside of Russia, Catherine's long reign, from 1762 to 1796, has gained notoriety because of her phenomenal love life. Her amorous adventures were unquestionably remarkable, but it would be a mistake to dismiss her as a sovereign whose only interest was private pleasure. Nor would it be accurate to regard her as a self-centered woman who merely used men to satisfy her carnal needs. To be sure, from 1752 until her death she had no fewer than twenty-one lovers, generally men in the prime of life with impressive physiques. It is also true that the older she grew, the younger were the men she chose. When she was in her early sixties, for example, she took a twenty-two-year-old lover. She was passionately devoted to each of her amours at the time of their liaison and she retained a certain affection for them all afterward. 'God is my judge', she stated in 1774, 'that I did not take them out of looseness, to which I have no inclination. If fate had given me in youth a husband whom I could have loved, I should have remained always true to him. The trouble is that my heart would not willingly remain one hour without love.'

Two of Catherine's lovers exercised substantial political influence – she even helped Stanisław Poniatowski acquire the Polish throne long after their affair ended – and all were handsomely rewarded by the empress. One, Gregory Potemkin, who became a valuable helpmate, allegedly received the stupendous sum of fifty million rubles, out of the total of ninety-two million that she lavished on lovers.

Yet despite her time-consuming preoccupations with sensual pleasure, Catherine was a dedicated and hardworking sovereign. Not since Peter the Great had Russia been governed by a ruler as energetic, devoted, and successful as she. She wielded decisive power in formulating and executing state policies in both domestic and foreign affairs.

Indeed, she had great ambitions for Russia, but their implementation often proved to be beyond reach. For instance, in the late 1760s the empress proclaimed that 'Peace is essential to this vast empire; what we need is a larger population, not devastation . . . Peace will bring us a greater esteem than the always ruinous uncertainties of war.' But the exigencies of events and her longing for glory prompted her to undertake several aggressive moves. In 1763, for example, she ordered her troops to seize the Duchy of Courland, which was subsequently incorporated into the empire. Thrice she was instrumental in promoting the partition of Poland, and each time she annexed a portion of that unhappy country. Her most significant gains were made at the expense of Turkey, against which she waged a vigorous war in disregard of her generals, who feared that she was overextending the country's military. But the Russian army prevailed over the Turks, who in the Treaty of Kuchuk-Kainardzhi (1774) made vast concessions. Russia acquired Azov, as well as stretches of land along the shores of the Black Sea, and the right of free navigation in that sea for its merchant fleet. Moreover, Turkey gave up the Crimea, which Russia annexed nine years later. In subsequent wars with Turkey (1787–92), Russia took possession of Ochakov and the shores of the Black Sea all the way to the Dniester river. Russia now controlled what were widely regarded as her natural borders in the south.

Catherine did not succeed in destroying the Ottoman Empire as she had hoped, but she certainly weakened it substantially and greatly enhanced the power of Russia. Under her auspices, the size of Russia increased by 200,000 square miles and the population rose from nineteen to thirty-six million. These successes in foreign policy, more than any other accomplishments, earned Catherine the title of 'Great'. But it should also be noted that in the long run Russia's territorial expansion proved to be a mixed blessing – for it increased the number of disgruntled subjects within the Russian Empire. For example, the empire incorporated a sizable Polish population (probably more than two million), most of whom yearned to be part of an independent Polish state. In the nineteenth century the 'Polish question' was a perennial problem for Russian leaders and twice (in 1831 and in 1863) the Poles staged bloody revolts that were put down at great cost. Also, the annexation of Poland for the first time placed within the Russian Empire a large number of Jews (about 500,000), who by the early twentieth century numbered about five million. Unwilling to be assimilated, distrusted by many Russians as an alien people with strange religious doctrines, the Jews were subjected to numerous economic, social, and political restrictions, which, in turn, prompted many of them to become hostile to the prevailing order.

There was also a discrepancy between the empress's avowed goals and her actions in the domestic realm. She claimed to favor an enlightened form of government based on 'European principles', and sought to demonstrate her devotion to progressive reform by corresponding regularly with Voltaire and other spokesmen of the French Enlightenment. She genuinely admired their writings and honestly believed herself to be their disciple, but she also knew that contact with the *philosophes* would fashion her reputation as a benevolent and thoughtful ruler. When she heard that Denis Diderot, editor of the learned *Encyclopédie*, was having financial difficulties, she paid him fifteen thousand francs for his library (which remained in Paris during his lifetime) and appointed him its librarian at an annual salary of one thousand francs. Moreover, when the French government prohibited the publication of the *Encyclopédie* because of the liberal views found in many of its articles, the empress offered to have it printed in Riga.

In her eagerness to impress the *philosophes*, Catherine on occasion lapsed into unrealistic descriptions of conditions in Russia. She told Voltaire that because she imposed such low taxes on her people 'there was not a single peasant in Russia who could not eat chicken whenever he pleased, although he had recently preferred turkey to chicken.' She also assured him that 'There are no shortages of any kind; people spend their time in singing thanksgiving masses, dancing, and rejoicing.'

Not all of Catherine's writings were devoted to self-glorification. In a serious vein she wrote extensively on social, pedagogical, and historical subjects, composed tragedies inspired by Shakespeare's, and wrote librettos for musical comedies. Her *Notes on Russian History*, dealing with the period from the ninth to the thirteenth century, is a massive, six-volume work in which she tried to show that Russia's development compared favorably with that of Western countries and that monarchical absolutism had made positive contributions to it. Despite weaknesses in spelling and grammar, and despite her lack of originality, Catherine's discourses impressed the *philosophes* as the product of a thinking person and therefore a kindred soul.

They were flattered beyond words by the attentions showered upon them by the gifted and powerful monarch. Even though Diderot visited Russia in 1773, and thus had an opportunity to check on some of the empress's claims about conditions in her country, neither he nor most of his colleagues ever publicly challenged her. On the contrary, Diderot heaped praise on her as a ruler committed to establishing freedom of conscience and described her as combining 'the soul of Brutus with the charms of Cleopatra'. Voltaire exclaimed, 'Long live the adorable Catherine,' and once, in a burst of enthusiasm, compared her to Saint Catherine, a title she had the modesty and good sense to reject.

Even a cursory examination of Catherine's domestic policies raises questions about the depth of her commitment to reform. With much fanfare she convoked a legislative commission in 1767 for the purpose of drawing up a new code of laws based on the most advanced legal doctrines. To guide the commission, she drafted a voluminous *Instruction*, composed of 653 sections, in which she expressed her views on every conceivable subject. Although she leaned heavily on the writings of Montesquieu, Beccaria, and Baron J. F. Bielefeldt, three well-known writers with enlightened views on legal questions, her social program turned out to be rather conservative. She was not prepared to reduce the privileges of the nobility and although she suggested an improvement in the lot of the peasants, she did not advocate abolition of serfdom, Russia's most glaring evil. In any case, the legislative commission was so large and its procedures so cumbersome that it accomplished very little. It failed to compile a new code, but it did provide the government with information leading to the administrative reforms enacted after the defeat of Pugachev.

In 1775, Catherine enacted a reform of provincial government that remained in force until 1864. It divided the prevailing
provinces into new entities of 300,000 to 400,000 inhabitants and
established a subcategory of counties (*uezdy*) of twenty to thirty
thousand inhabitants. The central government was empowered
to appoint the provincial governors, who functioned as executives with authority over their region's administrative and judicial
affairs. Governors could communicate directly with the sovereign, so had an especially powerful voice in administering the
provinces.

Two other notable reforms were the Charter of the Nobility
and the Charter to the Towns, both issued in 1785. The first
stipulated that no noble was to be deprived of his honor, life,
property, or title without a trial by his peers. If a nobleman was
found guilty of a serious crime, his hereditary estate would not
be confiscated, as had been the practice, but would go to his
heirs. Henceforth, nobles were exempt from corporal punishment, the poll tax, and the obligation to billet troops in their
homes. Finally, the nobles of each province could now form
a corporation headed by a general assembly and provincial
marshal of the nobility. The assemblies, to meet every three
years, were entitled to petition the crown, the senate, and various officials for redress of grievances and for specific administrative measures, but petitions had to be limited to matters of
concern to the local nobility. The authorities in St. Petersburg
pointedly did not make any provision for a national organization of nobles, which potentially could challenge the central
government.

The second reform created a corporate framework for
the towns. It provided for urban organs of government, to be
controlled by rich merchants, but their authority was so limited
that their accomplishments are generally regarded as negligible.

That Catherine merely paid lip service to principles of
enlightenment emerges with special force from her reaction to
Pugachev's rebellion, one of the bloodiest peasant uprisings in
Russian history. Emelian Pugachev, an unruly Don Cossack who

spent several years in the imperial army and fought in a number of campaigns in Poland and Turkey, had been imprisoned for his refusal to remain in the army after having contracted a serious illness. He escaped, settled in the territory of the Iaik Cossacks, an area east of the Volga river, where the local population had for some time been waging a struggle to maintain their autonomy. Pugachev gained support from these Cossacks and then enlisted support from other disaffected elements, notably peasants and Old Believers. In 1773, he proclaimed himself to be Tsar Peter III, Catherine's husband. He then proceeded to assemble a following of some thirty thousand men, whom he organized into a fierce though ragged army. His announced aims were simple: the elimination of rule by landlords and government officials, an end to serfdom, and the abolition of taxes and military service. In the name of these goals, Pugachev and his irregular troops ravaged the countryside, instituting a veritable reign of terror. Anyone who opposed him risked being killed by his merciless followers.

When Catherine first learned of the uprising, she was shaken, but she refused to act against the insurgents. She suppressed all news of the disorders because she feared that accounts of civil unrest would sully her reputation as an enlightened ruler who governed a happy nation. What would Voltaire and Diderot think if they heard about Pugachev? But in July 1774 the pretender stormed the important city of Kazan, and although he did not capture it he did burn much of the town to the ground. At this point, Pugachev held a large swath of territory in eastern Russia and it seemed likely that he might attack Moscow itself. Catherine could no longer ignore him. She amassed a large army, against which the rebel's ill-disciplined marauders were no match, and in the fall of 1774 the army crushed the insurgents. Pugachev, betrayed by his comrades, was taken prisoner and hauled to Moscow in a cage. The empress's ministers urged her to make an example of the power-hungry Cossack by subjecting him to various tortures, but she was too conscious of her professed principles for that. Instead, she ordered that he be tried in the Palace of the Kremlin. He was found guilty and executed on 11 January 1775. He was then strung on a pole, and sections of his dismembered body were put on public exhibition before being burned.

Only a few other rebel leaders were executed. The government preferred to have most of them branded, and their nostrils slit, and then sentence them to hard labor. The reprisals carried out against the rebellious peasants were the cruelest aspect of Catherine's policy. The army treated them so savagely that its program of pacification proved as costly in human lives as the uprising itself. All told, the insurrection claimed the lives of twenty thousand insurgents and three thousand officials and nobles. 'The Pugachev rebellion', the historian Nicholas Riasanovsky has noted, 'served to point out again, forcefully and tragically, the chasm between French philosophy and Russian reality.' The Pugachev rebellion has become enshrined in Russian history and folklore, revered by many peasants and radicals and deplored by the rest of society.

From this time on, Catherine grew ever more wary of liberalism, although she tried to conceal her true feelings under a barrage of lofty pronouncements. But when she learned of the progress of the French Revolution, which had been inspired by some of the ideas she had formerly embraced, she could no longer remain silent. 'One never knows', she wrote in January 1791, 'if you are living in the midst of murders, carnage, and uproar of the den of thieves who have seized upon the government of France, and will soon turn it into Gaul as it was in the time of Caesar. But Caesar put them down! When will this Caesar come! Oh, come he will, you need not doubt.' The execution of Louis XVI two years later drove her into a paroxysm of fury and fear: 'The very name of France should be exterminated! Equality is a monster. It would fain be king!'

In Russia itself, Catherine refused to tolerate ideas that displeased her. In 1790, for example, Alexander Radishchev, a sensitive and courageous man, created a sensation by publishing his *Journey from Petersburg to Moscow*, an exposé of the horrors of serfdom, despotism, and administrative corruption. The empress acknowledged that Radishchev was a man of 'imagination' and 'learning', but she could not forgive him for revealing that evils existed in Russia. 'The purpose of this book', she declared, 'is clear on every page: its author, infected by and full of the French madness, is trying in every possible way to break down respect for authority . . . to stir up in the people indignation against their superiors and against the government.' Radishchev was arrested, tried for fomenting sedition, and sentenced to death. The barbaric sentence was commuted, probably on Catherine's recommendation, to ten years' exile in Siberia.

By the empress's lights, her reign surely amounted to a success. Her most intense ambitions – to be popular in literate circles and to gain a reputation for having enhanced the glory and power of Russia – were realized. Yet in the closing years of her life she was tormented by the thought that the throne would pass to her unstable son, Paul, with whom she had never gotten along. Even though Paul's paternity was never definitively established, he assumed that Peter III had been his father and therefore believed himself entitled to rule instead of his mother. In part because she was aware that many Russians believed his claim to be legitimate, Catherine had always kept Paul at bay and even allowed several of her favorites to humiliate him. Moreover, her announced intention to disinherit him could only contribute to his hostility towards her and his anger over the weakness of his position. For some unknown reason, Catherine failed to designate her beloved grandson Alexander as her successor, and as a result, when she died in 1796 the royal court once again became the center of countless intrigues.

PAUL I

The forty-two-year-old Paul who ascended the throne was neither unintelligent nor uneducated, but he lacked the temperament to serve as a ruler. Filled with hatred for his mother, he often pursued policies simply because they differed from hers. But in addition his personality made him unsuitable for leadership. He was impetuous, highly irascible, vindictive, and utterly inconsistent. To be sure, he subscribed to some lofty ideals and did, in fact, introduce some significant reforms, but at the same time he believed firmly in absolutism. The ruler, in Paul's view, should govern the country paternalistically, improving the conditions of the people by promoting social welfare and education. But he also revered the conduct and traditions of Peter the Great and emphasized the exalted position of the ruler. He is said to have remarked that in his empire 'no one is great except the one to whom I speak and only while I am speaking to him.'

Paul began his reign, as have so many tsars, in a fairly liberal spirit. He did not seek revenge on his father's murderers, he freed Radishchev and several other political prisoners from exile, and retained most of his mother's advisers. One of his more important and lasting measures was to rescind (in 1797) Peter the Great's decree authorizing the sovereign to designate his successor. A cause of much of the political instability in the eighteenth century, Peter's decree was seen to be ill-conceived. Paul decreed that the succession was to be hereditary in accordance with the principle of primogeniture. Only males would be eligible to ascend the throne. The decree produced a measure of stability at the apex of the political structure during the last century of the Romanov dynasty.

In foreign policy, Paul initially abandoned his mother's belligerent approach, which had involved Russia in numerous wars and had drained the treasury. He pulled Russia out of the alliance ranged against France, but before long he became enraged at some of Napoleon's actions and resumed hostilities. Paul's policies towards the peasants, the vast majority of the people, were also contradictory. He claimed to favor easing the conditions of the serfs and restored their right to petition the crown; in April 1797, he issued a decree forbidding landlords from forcing serfs to work on Sundays. At the same time, however, he extended to merchants the right to buy serfs for work in industrial establishments, he increased the obligations imposed on certain categories of peasants, and he converted some 500,000 state peasants into serfs by turning them over to private landlords. And peasant uprisings were suppressed with the usual severity.

Paul's undoing was not so much his inconsistency as his unfriendly stance towards the nobility. He did not repeal the Charter of the Nobility, but in practice he curtailed the privileges of the nobles, who were now required to pay a tax imposed on their estates as well as certain other taxes. Moreover, he put strong pressure on nobles to serve the state, and nobles convicted of serious crimes could again be flogged. In the army, Paul insisted on more rigid discipline, greater efficiency, and the elimination of corruption. After about three years on the throne, Paul became more repressive. He banned foreign books, journals, and even foreign music, and he reimposed the restrictions on travel abroad. Censorship of the printed word grew more strict and was applied even to private correspondence. Unhappy with the performance of his officials, Peter dismissed one after another, often without good reason.

Senior dignitaries at court and a sizable corps of nobles conspired to overthrow Paul and install his son, Grand Duke Alexander, as tsar. It is certain that Alexander assented to the *coup d'état*, though it is not known whether he approved the murder of his father. It may be that the group of conspirators (army officers) did not actually plan to kill Paul when they entered his room at the Mikhailovsky Palace to demand his abdication in favor of his son. According to the most plausible account of the meeting, in the course of the encounter with the tsar the plotters heard footsteps and feared that men were coming to Paul's rescue. To prevent the failure of their plot, the intruders strangled Paul with an iron collar. It was Russia's last palace revolution.

5

RUSSIA AS A GREAT POWER, 1801–55

During the first half of the nineteenth century, the status of the Russian Empire in the international arena changed dramatically. After 1812 it reached the pinnacle of prestige and influence, but in the mid 1850s Russia endured a military defeat that exposed the internal weaknesses of the country, throwing into doubt its viability as a great power. Tsars Alexander I (1801–25) and Nicholas I (1825–55) reveled in Russia's enhanced status, but both seemed to sense that political and social changes would be necessary to retain that status. From time to time, they actually contemplated a wide range of reforms, and they even implemented a few, but none that fundamentally altered the structure of society. In the end, Russia in 1855 was, politically and socially, not appreciably different from the Russia of 1801.

It is tempting to attribute the tsars' failures to introduce far-reaching reforms to a lack of wisdom and to weaknesses of character. Perhaps more far-sighted and stronger rulers could have achieved more than Alexander and Nicholas in transforming Russia into a modern state, but it must be kept in mind that the tsars faced intractable problems. As indicated in previous chapters, economically, socially, and politically, Russia retained institutions – the autocracy, serfdom, a rigid social structure – that made change exceedingly difficult. The tsars and many of their advisers trembled at the thought that any fundamental change in their country's institutions would produce upheavals comparable to those of the seventeenth and eighteenth centuries. Fear that the whole structure of authority would then collapse paralyzed the tsars in their attempts to cope with some of the most critical problems facing the nation. The result was stagnation and a slow but steady growth in popular disaffection with the status quo.

Tsar Alexander I vacillated so frequently in pursuing his domestic and foreign goals that contemporaries often referred to him as the 'enigmatic tsar', the 'sphinx', and the 'crowned Hamlet'. Educated at the court of Catherine the Great by the Swiss republican Frédéric-César de La Harpe, Alexander received a good grounding in the ideas of the Enlightenment, to which he remained emotionally attached for much of his life. As a young man, he spoke often of the need to liberalize Russia, and even as sovereign he frequently supported the cause of reform. He went so far as to suggest that he favored a monarchy based on law rather than on personal whim and that he wished to improve markedly the condition of the peasants. At the same time, Alexander was ardently attached to the values of the military, to discipline and regimentation. In 1812, at the age of thirty-five, he came increasingly under the influence of religious mysticism, which affected his political views. He now advocated a restructuring of the world according to the doctrines of Christian morality, a hazy notion that underlay his advocacy after 1815 of the Holy Alliance. By this time, Alexander's liberalism was much less in evidence than his mysticism and his penchant for authoritarian rule. But Alexander was also a clever man, adept at dissimulation, and therefore succeeded in persuading many contemporaries that his liberalism was sincere even as he pursued policies that were conservative and at times reactionary.

In foreign affairs, he claimed to cherish peace and yet he waged aggressive wars against Persia, Turkey, and Sweden that enabled him to expand along the Black and Caspian Seas, to annex Bessarabia, and to incorporate Finland into the Russian Empire as a separate grand duchy. But his most notable success was his triumph over the outstanding military genius of the age, Napoleon Bonaparte, who had become Emperor of the French in 1804 and was determined to dominate Europe. No one would have predicted such a triumph. Indeed, initially, Alexander proclaimed Russia's neutrality in the European wars of the time, but by 1805 the tsar was worried by Napoleon's territorial ambitions and by his high-handed treatment of his opponents. Alexander now joined forces with Austria and Prussia to halt the French leader's advances, but within a two-year period (1805–7) Russia suffered three crushing blows, in the battles of Austerlitz, Jena, and Friedland. When Napoleon offered peace, the tsar readily agreed to negotiate. In July 1807, the two emperors met on a gaily decorated raft in the middle of the Nieman river, near the town of Tilsit, and reached an agreement that in effect permitted France to dominate Western Europe and Russia Eastern Europe. The arrangement suited Napoleon, at least temporarily, because it allowed him to concentrate on the struggle with Great Britain, the one major country he had been unable to subdue.

Over the next few years, Alexander fawned on Napoleon, but the Franco-Russian alliance was doomed to be short-lived. For one thing, the Russian nobles urged the tsar to break relations with France, fearing that 'the child of the revolution', as the French emperor was known, would export dangerous, liberal ideas that might ultimately infect Russia. More important, the interests of the two nations collided in one area after another. For one thing, Napoleon's plan for an independent Poland would deprive Russia of lands she had acquired during the recent partitions of that country. Another important source of friction was Russia's unwillingness to honor the Continental System, the economic blockade that Napoleon had mounted against Great Britain and that he expected other European states to honor. The system was so detrimental to Russian exporters and landlords that they persistently disregarded it, but Napoleon was not the kind of man to stand idly by and witness the subversion of his plans. There are also indications that the French emperor was affected by fits of megalomania during this period. He spoke confidently of conquering Moscow and then marching on to India. Flushed by his many military victories, in 1807 he told his brother, 'I can do everything now.'

NAPOLEON'S INVASION OF RUSSIA

On 24 June 1812, without bothering to declare war, Napoleon led his Grand Army across the Nieman river into Russian territory, thus initiating the most momentous struggle of his career. In a desperate effort to avoid hostilities, Tsar Alexander pleaded with his adversary to withdraw, but the invader would not be deterred. The French emperor had mustered an enormous force of some 600,000 men for the campaign, and although he seems to have lacked a precise plan, he pressed forward. If Napoleon ascribed the tsar's plea to personal weakness, he was soon to be disillusioned, for it turned out that in the face of severe provocation Alexander could summon up a tenacity and courage that startled his subjects as well as his foes. As one of his ministers aptly remarked, 'Alexander is too weak to rule and too strong to be ruled.'

For more than a century and a half it was generally believed that the Russian generals followed a 'Scythian strategy' in response to the invasion, that is, they deliberately lured the enemy into a devastated country, knowing that its subjects would refuse to give the invaders much-needed provisions. This interpretation is based, among other things, on a statement by Tsar Alexander to Armand de Caulaincourt, French ambassador at St. Petersburg and one of Napoleon's intimates: 'Your Frenchman is brave; but long privations and a bad climate wear him down and discourage him. Our climate, our winter, will fight on our side. With you, marvels take place where the emperor is in personal attendance; and he cannot be everywhere, he cannot be absent from Paris year after year.' These comments notwithstanding, no strategy of retreat was ever devised by the Russian high command.

In truth, the Russian army retreated because the generals correctly judged their forces to be too weak to stop the French. At most, the defenders could deploy 150,000 men, which meant that they were outnumbered four to one. An additional weakness of the Russian army, according to one authority on the subject, was the 'ignorance and military incompetence of many officers, even generals'. Furthermore, demoralization had set in because of widespread corruption among the officers and the barbaric discipline imposed on common soldiers. 'Much use was made of the bastinado [cudgel]. The principle was: beat two to death, train the third.' Rank-and-file soldiers found their brutal treatment so unbearable that they often committed suicide to escape it.

In view of these handicaps, General Barclay de Tolly, who made most of the major decisions for the Russian army during the first part of the campaign, had little choice but to pull back. In so doing he prevented Napoleon from achieving his prime objective in every previous war, the early destruction of the opposing force. With each successive day the French emperor occupied more territory, but he could not claim victory. Nor could he relax for a single moment: the enemy might suddenly decide to fight.

About six weeks after the campaign was launched, several of Napoleon's marshals warned him that he was falling into a trap. They pointed out that his military forces were already beginning to feel the strain of the long march: in the advance from Vilna to Vitebsk, for example, eight thousand of one army's twenty-two thousand horses had died. In addition, the retreating Russians had devastated much of the countryside. As a result, Napoleon's forces could not live off the conquered lands, as was their custom, and transporting supplies all the way from Poland presented tremendous logistical problems. But the most ominous sign for the French was that despite his territorial losses Alexander refused to sue for peace. Nonetheless, Napoleon continued the chase. 'If necessary,' he told one of his advisers, 'I shall go as far as Moscow, the holy city of Moscow, in quest of battle.' At that point Alexander would be forced to capitulate, 'for a capital to be occupied by an enemy is equivalent to a girl losing her honor'.

In the meantime, the Russian public unleashed a barrage of criticism at the generals for their failure to fight. Late in August the tsar yielded to the pressure of his counselors and appointed the sixty-seven-year-old Prince Michael Kutuzov commander-in-chief even though the sovereign passionately disliked him. Kutuzov was a highly respected officer, and in hopes of restoring national unity and bolstering morale in the army, Alexander set aside his personal feelings. One of the few who looked upon retreat as the most viable strategy, Kutuzov promptly announced that he intended to give up the ancient citadel, the Kremlin, and former capital without a struggle. But according to General Karl von Clausewitz, the noted German strategist who accompanied the Russian army, 'the court, the army, and the whole of Russia' clamored for battle. Kutuzov therefore decided, for essentially political reasons, to make a stand in defense of Moscow.

On 7 September a Russian force of 112,000 met a French army of 130,000 near Borodino, about seventy-five miles southwest of Moscow. Although the fighting lasted only one day, the bloodletting was savage. The Russians lost fifty-eight thousand men and the French fifty thousand, including forty-seven generals. The outcome can only be described as uncertain, for though the Russians withdrew again, their morale was high and their retreat orderly. Although the claim of many Russians that they scored a decisive military victory is overblown, there is no doubt that the Battle of Borodino was a great moral triumph for Russia. The French scoff at this claim, but after Napoleon had been deposed, he himself acknowledged Borodino's significance: 'The most terrible of all my battles was the one before Moscow. The French showed themselves worthy of victory, and the Russians worthy of being invincible.'

Several generals urged Kutuzov to engage the French again before Moscow, but the commander insisted on withdrawal. 'You fear a retreat through Moscow,' he told a conference of his highest officers, 'but I regard it as far-sighted, because it will save the army. Napoleon is like a stormy torrent which we are as yet unable to stop. Moscow will be the sponge that will suck him in.'

It was not a decision that Kutuzov took lightly. He understood that the fall of Moscow would be humiliating and depressing for his countrymen. When he entered his private quarters, he broke into uncontrollable weeping, but he would not change his mind.

Triumphantly, Napoleon marched towards Moscow, and on the morning of 14 September 1812 he reached the Sparrow Hills overlooking the city. He ordered Joachim Napoleon, King of Naples, to bring a deputation of city authorities to meet him at Moscow's principal gate. They were supposed to surrender the keys, as had been the custom in every other major town Napolean had occupied. To the emperor's astonishment, Joachim returned a short time later to report that he 'had not discovered so much as a single prominent inhabitant'. It soon became apparent that out of a population of 250,000 only about 12,000 remained. 'Moscow is empty!' the emperor cried out in disbelief. 'Incredible! We must enter. Go and bring some of the boyars.' Stubbornly, he continued to wait for a few hours. 'Finally, an officer, either anxious to please or convinced that everything desired by the emperor must take place, penetrated the city, caught five or six vagrants, and, pushing them forward with his horse, brought them into the presence of the emperor, imagining that he had brought a deputation.'[1] This action only compounded the injury to the ruler's pride, for 'from the very answers of these unfortunates, Napoleon saw that he had before him but a few pitiful day-laborers.'

Towards evening Napoleon finally entered the city, not in the mood of exhilaration he had anticipated but in one of gloom. Early the next morning he rode to the Kremlin, and the sight of the fortress raised his spirits. 'The city is as big as Paris,' he wrote to his wife. 'There are 1,600 church towers here, and over a thousand beautiful palaces; the city is provided with everything.' He occupied the royal palace and settled in for a much-needed rest. But before he could obtain even one night's sleep, the emperor was forced to flee for his life.

At eight o'clock in the evening of 15 September, a fire, presumably touched off by the careless French soldiers who were looting the city, erupted in one of the suburbs. Orders were given to extinguish it and the imperial party retired for the night. Two and a half hours later Caulaincourt was awakened by his valet, who told him that flames were spreading over a large part of the city. 'I had only to open my eyes', Caulaincourt recalled, 'to realize that this was so, for the fire was giving off so much light it was bright enough to read in the middle of the night.' A strong wind from the north drove the flames towards the center; the wooden houses burned like tinderboxes.

Additional fires broke out in other districts, and by four o'clock in the morning the conflagration had enveloped so much of the city that the emperor had to be roused from his sleep. Within a few hours the Kremlin itself was threatened. 'The air was so hot, and the pine-wood sparks were so numerous that the beams supporting the iron plates which formed the roof of the Arsenal all caught fire,' Caulaincourt remembered. It soon became too dangerous for Napoleon to remain in the Kremlin, and accompanied by his closest advisers and personal guards he managed to escape. He set up headquarters in a country mansion just outside Moscow. The metropolis continued to burn for another two days, and when the flames at last subsided about ninety percent of the city had been destroyed. Most of the structures in the Kremlin remained intact, however, and, fortunately for the French, the grain and fodder warehouses along the wharves also escaped, leaving the army with provisions for six months.

The burning of Moscow stunned and disheartened Napoleon, who now referred to the Russians as 'Scythians' and 'barbarians'. He could not control his anger: 'This exceeds all imagination. This is a war of extermination. Such terrible tactics have no precedent in the history of civilization . . . To burn one's own cities! . . . A demon inspires these people! What a people! What a people!' As soon as the fire had burned itself out, the French authorities conducted an investigation. They concluded that Count Fedor Rostopchin, governor-general of Moscow, had planned the burning and evacuation of the city. The investigators alleged that all the fire engines had either been removed or damaged and that fuses had been found in numerous buildings, including the imperial bedroom in the Kremlin. Finally, the French claimed to have discovered four hundred arsonists, whom they summarily tried and executed.

The evidence in support of this explanation is far from conclusive, and historians are still debating the question of responsibility. Rostopchin himself did not help to clarify the issue: initially, when he thought the burning of Moscow would be popular, he took credit for it; later, when he realized that the people deplored the action, he denied any connection with it. Of course, it served the interests of the French to place the blame on the Russians, if only to forestall being blamed for it themselves. For if the Russians came to believe that Napoleon had intentionally devastated their holy city, they would detest the invader with even greater intensity than before. Despite the emperor's elaborate investigations, this is precisely what happened. In truth, it is quite likely that no one deliberately set the fires, and that, as Leo Tolstoy argued in *War and Peace*, they broke out accidentally. Because the city was empty, no one extinguished them, and then the winds took over.

After Moscow was razed, Napoleon's occupation of the city could no longer pressure Alexander into suing for peace. Quite the contrary, the tsar held the French responsible for the disaster, and he became more adamant than ever in his refusal to deal with them. 'It is Napoleon or I, either he or I – we can no longer reign at the same time! I have found him out and he will not deceive me again.' Melodramatically, Alexander vowed that he would 'eat potatoes with the lowliest of my peasants in the depths of Siberia' rather than negotiate with the 'monster who is the misfortune of the entire world'.

Never before had Napoleon's plans misfired so completely. Never before had he so thoroughly misjudged the character of an adversary. Napoleon had captured the former capital, but he had not defeated Russia. Moreover, he soon saw that he could not stay in Moscow for long. Once winter set in he would find it difficult, if not impossible, to maintain contact with the rest of his empire and to secure adequate military supplies. His prolonged absence from Western Europe might well stimulate open resistance in conquered lands. Finally, discipline in the Grand Army, only one third of which was French, began to decline; numerous soldiers deserted and many others showed greater interest in looting than in maintaining French control over Russian territory.

For the first time in his career Napoleon was indecisive. He considered a four-hundred-mile march on St. Petersburg, but gave up that idea when his marshals convinced him that it was too risky, especially since inclement weather might soon hamper the movement of a large army. Out of sheer desperation he made three separate peace overtures to Alexander, but the tsar did not even bother to reply. On 18 October, Kutuzov inflicted substantial casualties on the French in a minor skirmish, and a day later – after five weeks in Moscow – Napoleon ordered his army to begin the march back to the West.

So great was Napoleon's anger at Alexander that he spitefully decided to annihilate the Kremlin. For three days Russians were forced to lay mines in palaces, churches, and other structures. As soon as the army had left, the explosions erupted, causing extensive damage to the Arsenal and to portions of the Kremlin wall and several of its towers. A fortuitous rainfall prevented most of the fuses from igniting, but if nature had not intervened Napoleon's barbaric action would probably have led to the destruction of most of the Kremlin.

Nature also contributed to the destruction of the retreating Grand Army. Short of supplies, military as well as food, ill-equipped to cope with the Russian winter, harassed by Kutuzov's troops and roving guerrillas, the vast military machine rapidly disintegrated. The horses collapsed in droves, mainly because they were improperly shod and could not keep their footing on the ice. 'For dozens of miles,' we are told, 'the roads were littered with corpses. Soldiers built shelters with the corpses of their comrades, piling them like logs.'[2] It has been estimated that no more than thirty thousand men survived the Russian campaign, that is, one out of twenty. The crushing defeat marked the beginning of the end of Napoleon's grand scheme to subjugate the entire European continent. For Alexander, it marked the beginning of the most glorious phase in his career; during the next few years he was not only one of the most influential but also one of the most popular monarchs in Europe.

DOMESTIC REFORM

In the meantime, however, Alexander's plans for domestic reform had faltered and his reputation as a liberal had suffered some blemishes. To demonstrate his repudiation of Tsar Paul's retrograde policies, Alexander in the first few years of his reign issued a series of progressive decrees. He removed restrictions on foreign travel, allowed the import of foreign publications, liberalized trade, outlawed some of the harsher features of the penal procedures, and abolished the secret police. The tsar also indicated his distaste for arbitrariness and promised to establish a governmental system that would be based on the foundation of law. To that end, he appointed a 'non-official committee' of liberal nobles to examine Russia's domestic and foreign policies and to devise proposals for reform. The committee deliberated in a rather unsystematic fashion for two years (from 1801 till 1803) and in the end did not accomplish anything of significance. But the committee's creation was a sign of the tsar's attempt to reach out to elements in society that wished to modernize Russia.

An even more striking sign was Alexander's appointment in 1808 of the gifted Michael Speransky to a high position in the Ministry of Justice. The son of a village priest, Speransky had been educated at a theological seminary, entered the civil service, and by dint of hard work and a sharp intelligence rose quickly through the ranks. Alexander was much taken with him and for several years relied heavily on his advice in political matters. In 1808 he asked Speransky to formulate a plan for constitutional reform, a project that the assistant minister of justice completed in October 1809. Scholars are still debating how radical Speransky's political views were; some contend that he was essentially an open-minded conservative whereas others argue that he envisioned a fundamental reordering of Russia's state institutions. The point is that Speransky's proposals for change were far-reaching without calling for an immediate overturn of the political structure or of social institutions. Thus, although the monarchy was to remain, it was to govern in accordance with the law. Speransky recommended the separation of powers between the executive, legislative, and judicial branches. A legislature was to be elected on the basis of a franchise defined by property qualifications, but its powers were to be limited. It would not, for example, have the authority to initiate legislation; it would, however, have the right to veto measures introduced by the tsar, and this would have amounted to a serious limitation on the ruler's prerogatives. On the question of serfdom, Speransky adopted a cautious approach. He favored abolition but because of the opposition of powerful social groups he urged that this be done gradually. In the meantime, the serfs would not be given any role in governing the country.

Tsar Alexander studied Speransky's recommendations for a constitution with great care and seemed to approve of them, but for reasons that he never articulated he did not try to implement them. He did, however, accept two of Speransky's other suggestions, both of which remained in effect until the revolution of 1917. The tsar reorganized the executive departments, spelled out in some detail the functions of each one, and prohibited them from a direct role in legislative and judicial matters. Secondly, Alexander redefined the functions of the State Council, a body appointed by him, by charging it with drafting legislative projects and with offering advice to the ruler on all matters. Although the tsar was not obliged to accept the Council's advice, now at least there existed an institution other than the autocrat's court or personal advisers that concerned itself with legislative proposals.

All in all, Speransky's efforts yielded modest results, and by 1812 the opposition to him from the elite became so intense that Alexander turned against him and exiled him, first to Nizhni-

Novgorod and then to Perm. Many nobles were envious of him for having risen from poverty to a position of paramount influence, but a more serious reason for their hostility to him was their fear that his reforms would undermine their social and political privileges. They also suspected Speransky of being an admirer of Napoleon and therefore of being a traitor to his country. With Speransky's departure, Alexander's interest in reform began to wane. True, in 1818, he commissioned Nikolai Novosiltsev, a senior official and close friend, to draw up a new plan for a constitution. Novosiltsev's constitution was more conservative than Speransky's, in part because it made no mention of ending serfdom, but it, too, remained a dead letter.

Alexander's most notable and certainly most controversial innovation in the domestic sphere, the creation of military colonies, has been both denounced as reactionary and praised as progressive. First set up in 1810, the colonies appeared to many people to be a crude attempt to militarize Russian society. But the motive behind their creation seems to have been idealistic and in keeping with the tsar's frequent expressions of support for liberal values. Alexander conceived of the colonies after a visit to the estate of General A. A. Arakcheev in the village of Gruzino, some seventy-five miles east of St. Petersburg. Arakcheev had turned his estate into a highly efficient enterprise, based on rational planning, a remarkable achievement in a country notorious for incompetence and slovenliness. The roads were well paved, the houses of the peasants, all identical in shape, were clean, and a bank set up by Arakcheev lent money without interest to peasants to enable them to buy agricultural tools and other items they might need to improve productivity. It occurred to Alexander that Russia's countryside could benefit greatly from the creation of colonies of soldiers based on Arakcheev's principles. During peacetime the men in uniform performed no useful function and the costs of their upkeep were a severe drain on the national treasury.

The idea was to transform the soldiers into peasant-soldiers who during peacetime would live with their families and would support themselves by devoting much of their time to agricultural work and to industry. Except during harvest time, most male colonists would spend two or three days a week on military drill and exercises. By 1825, some 750,000 men, women, and children lived in the colonies, which could field 126 battalions of infantry and 240 squadrons of cavalry. The ultimate goal was to place between one-quarter and one-third of Russia's male population in the new settlements, and to eliminate the draft altogether; in wartime all the soldiers needed by the armed forces would come from the colonies.

The colonies were a highly unusual experiment in social engineering. In every militarized village, each peasant received an identical amount of land as well as the agricultural tools, cattle, and furniture that he needed. The authorities established primary schools that all children between the ages of seven and twelve as well as adult illiterates were required to attend. Each colony had its own hospital and medical staff. Old people no longer capable of working were placed in 'invalid houses' and were cared for at government expense.

Economically, the colonies were in many ways successful: peasants in them were generally better off than their counterparts elsewhere in the countryside and poverty was altogether eliminated. Yet in the end the colonies proved to be a failure. Arakcheev's officers, who administered the settlements, were not very competent and often they were corrupt and tactless in their dealings with the colonists. Senior army officers despised Arakcheev, a crude and brutal man, and feared that he would exploit his powerful position to secure control over the army. The senior officers also believed that men who devoted much of their time to agricultural work would not be effective soldiers. And many nobles were concerned that once the draft was eliminated the government would no longer be as dependent on the landowners, thus weakening their position in society. At the same time, intellectuals turned against the colonies when they realized that the new institution would not lead, as they had initially hoped, to the elimination of serfdom.

But probably the most important reason for the colonies' ultimate failure as a social experiment was that the peasants themselves came to resent the extreme regimentation to which they were subjected. They wanted to be left alone, to have the freedom to do as they wished. This became dramatically clear in 1831 (six years after Alexander's reign had ended), when colonists reacted violently to a cholera epidemic. Blaming medical and hygienic measures for the epidemic, they randomly killed military officers and doctors and burned down hospitals and entire villages. They also went on drinking sprees and held wild parties in the fields. The authorities, realizing that the military colonies could become a dangerous threat to public order, began to dissolve them. A few survived until 1857, when the last of them were shut down.

POLITICAL FERMENT

The military colonies were only one cause of political ferment in Alexander's Russia. The tsar's professions of liberalism coupled with the grim conditions under which most Russians lived prompted people from the educated elite to question the status quo. But, ironically, Alexander's military successes in 1812 also had the effect of stoking discontent. A large number of Russian soldiers were stationed in the West, many of them in France, and their experience of conditions there, albeit in the limited constitutional regimes in Europe, made them painfully aware of their own country's backwardness and motivated them to take up the cause of reform. In 1816, a group of army officers, some of them attached to the general staff, founded the Union of Salvation in St. Petersburg. Its goals were never clearly articulated, but in general it subscribed to the replacement of the autocracy with a representative form of government and the adoption of a constitution. Although a small group, probably never more than twenty people, the Union included such dignitaries as Prince Sergei Trubetskoi, Sergei and Mathew Muraviev-Apostol, and Colonel Paul Pestel. In 1818 another society, the Union of Public Good, was founded to press for the advancement of education, social justice, economic welfare, and the abolition of serfdom. Its membership was larger, some two hundred people, but because of splits between radical and moderate elements, it was dissolved in 1821. However, Pestel, a republican and an advocate of regicide and thus one of the more radical activists, refused to give up and formed the so-called Southern Society in Tulchin in the Ukraine, where he was stationed. In the meantime, a more moderate Northern Society was formed in St. Petersburg and met regularly to discuss issues of public concern. Both societies favored a *coup d'état*, which they planned for the spring of 1826.

Before their plans could be implemented, Tsar Alexander died (on 19 November 1825), opening the way for what has sometimes been called Russia's 'first revolution'. It would be more accurate to say that the country experienced some political turbulence that could probably have been avoided had Alexander been less careless in making arrangements for the succession to the throne. Alexander was childless and consequently his brother Grand Duke Constantine was the heir apparent, but in 1820 Constantine had renounced title to the throne to enable him to divorce his wife and to marry morganatically a Polish Catholic woman. It was then agreed that Alexander's other brother, Nicholas, would be next in line to assume the throne. In 1823, Alexander directed Archbishop Philaret of Moscow to compose a manifesto declaring Nicholas the successor, but for some unfathomable reason the manifesto was not made public. It thus came as a shock to Russians to learn that Nicholas, widely disliked as a ruthless disciplinarian, would be the next tsar. Constantine was no less of a martinet, but, since he had been away from the capital for more than ten years, people had persuaded themselves that he was a liberal who favored the abolition of serfdom. Fearful that the guards would refuse to accept him as tsar unless Constantine publicly renounced his claim to the throne, Nicholas took an oath of allegiance to Constantine, in effect making him tsar. But that did not end the crisis, which was rapidly taking on all the aspects of an *opéra bouffe*. Constantine really did not want to be tsar, but, piqued by what he considered to be Nicholas's mishandling of the crisis, he refused to renounce the throne. Thus, Russia was without a ruler.

The crisis reached a climax when Nicholas learned that officers of the southern army were about to stage a *coup d'état*. He then ordered his staff to prepare a manifesto announcing his accession to the throne. Most men in the St. Petersburg garrison took an oath of loyalty to Nicholas, but about two regiments refused and, instead, marched to the Senate Square in St. Petersburg and loudly clamored for a constitution. All in all, some 2,300 soldiers joined the insurgents. A small crowd of civilians also came to protest in Senate Square, and it is said that when they called for 'Constantine and a constitution' they believed that 'constitution' was the grand duke's wife. The authorities sent four artillery pieces to the square and after a few volleys and the death of seventy rebels the Decembrist Uprising came to an ignominious end.

Alexander left behind a Russia much more powerful than it had been in 1801. The accretions to the empire were significant (Finland, the Grand Duchy of Poland, Bessarabia, regions in the Caucasus), and in the deliberations of European statesmen Alexander's opinions were given more than due weight. At the Congress of Vienna (1814–15), convoked to produce a settlement after the Napoleonic Wars, European statesmen humored the tsar by accepting his plan for a Holy Alliance, even though the British Foreign Minister Castlereagh was convinced 'that the Emperor's mind is not completely sound'. From now on, relations between nations as well as domestic affairs were to be based not on traditional principles of politics but, as Alexander would have it, on the 'sublime truths taught by the eternal religion of God our Saviour'. Political leaders would regard themselves as servants of providence and, 'thinking of themselves in their relation to their subjects and armies as fathers of families, they will lead them, in the spirit with which they are animated, to protect Religion, Peace and Justice.' Precisely what these words would mean when translated into policy was far from clear, but they did suggest a conservative thrust and were thus consistent with Alexander's drift to the right during the last years of his reign.

In internal affairs, Alexander's legacy was not impressive. After a flurry of reform during his first years on the throne, he either neglected domestic issues or adopted distinctly repressive policies. As early as 1804 the government reinstituted press censorship, and in 1807 it revived the security police as a permanent institution, which then played an increasing role in restricting the publication of books and journals. In 1818, the government declared that 'all questions pertaining to government policies may be discussed only in accordance with the wishes of the authorities, who know better what information should be given to the public; private persons must not write on political topics, either for or against.' Although this directive was meant to restrict the discussion of political subjects such as constitutional reform and the emancipation of the serfs, the government also placed severe restrictions on purely literary works.

Still, the government of Alexander I had made headway in promoting education. It established six universities, three lyceums, fifty-seven gymnasia (high schools), and 511 district schools. Nobles, who after 1809 were required to complete some formal educational training, could by the 1830s fulfill the requirement in Russia itself, whereas previously many had to attend universities abroad. But autocracy and serfdom, the two institutions that, more than any other, marked Russia off from the West, remained intact.

TSAR NICHOLAS I

By temperament and conviction Nicholas was not likely to undertake bold initiatives. Although a well-educated man who spoke several foreign languages (French, German, and English), he was not especially gifted intellectually and had little understanding or sympathy for anyone with convictions different from his. He was a deeply religious man, convinced that the hand of God guided his every action as an autocrat. He was also passionately devoted to military values. At the age of seven, John Keep has noted, 'he was learning how to make bombs out of wax and how to besiege a mock fortress.' Also, as a young student, he categorically refused to write an essay on the subject 'Military service is not the only kind for a nobleman.' When he became tsar he insisted that obedience, discipline, order, and regimentation must be the guiding principles of the Russian state. He deplored any questioning of his views and insisted on personally formulating state policies and making the decisions to implement them. At times his arbitrariness bordered on the ludicrous. On confirming the annulment of a marriage he wrote in the margin, 'The young person shall be considered a virgin.' Nicholas's thirty-year reign is justifiably considered the apotheosis of Russian absolutism.

The Decembrist Uprising left a profound imprint on his thinking and colored many of his actions as tsar. He himself supervised the investigation of 579 persons suspected of plotting the *coup d'état* and personally questioned many of them. Determined to crush the oppositional movement once and for all, he approved of severe punishments for many of the 289 found guilty. Five men were executed, thirty-one were given life sentences of exile in Siberia, and another eighty-five were sent there for shorter periods. Even many conservatives, noting that during the twenty-five years of Alexander's rule not a single person had been executed for political opposition, were shocked by the severity of the punishments.

And yet, during the first six years of his reign Nicholas showed some interest in reform. His first and perhaps most dramatic action was to dismiss the despised Arakcheev as minister of war. Then, in 1826, he established a committee charged with formulating reform proposals, but, since it contained no real progressives, it accomplished very little. In this early period Nicholas also tolerated some expression of liberal views and acted as a constitutional monarch in the Kingdom of Poland, albeit reluctantly. And he formed a committee under the guidance of the rehabilitated Michael Speransky to codify the laws of the Russian Empire, which had not been systematically assembled since 1649. The committee completed its task in 1833, and although its work did not involve legislative reform, it did produce a code that was the one authoritative compilation of Russian law.

Nicholas took a sharp turn to the right after the Polish rebellion of 1830. The unrest in Poland, which deeply resented domination by the Russians, was triggered by the revolutions in 1830 in the West. Not only were the Poles stimulated by the example of revolutionaries taking matters into their own hands in France, where the king was forced to abdicate, they were also appalled at the tsar's plan to use Russian and Polish troops to quell the disturbances there and in Belgium. An insurrection broke out in the Polish army in November and quickly spread to various parts of the country. The fighting was fierce and lasted about eight months, but in the end the Russian forces won, though the victory was not due solely to military superiority. To split the Polish opposition, Tsar Nicholas in May 1831 issued a *ukase* lightening the economic burden on Polish peasants, many of whom now became indifferent to the insurrection. This explains the peculiarity that peasants in the western borderlands of the empire enjoyed better conditions than those in the heartland.

Nicholas treated the defeated Poles with great severity. Many of the leaders of the insurrection were banished from their country, the land of about one-tenth of the nobility was confiscated and handed over to Russian generals and senior officials, and the Polish constitution was abolished. In 1832, the government in St. Petersburg issued the so-called Organic Statute that declared Poland to be an invisible part of the Russian Empire. The Statute also promised the Poles that they would retain their civil liberties and institutions of local government, and that they would be permitted to use the Polish language in their schools, courts, and civil administration, but under the newly appointed viceroy, Ivan Paskevich, who behaved as a virtual dictator, the promises were not kept. Paskevich treated Poland as a Russian province and pursued a firm policy of Russification. Thus, Russian and French, but not Polish, were to be accepted languages in higher administrative agencies. Russian became the language of instruction in secondary schools, and early in the 1840s the estates of the Catholic Church were secularized. Outraged by these repressive measures, the British press referred to Nicholas as 'the master of noble slaves, the ravisher of women, the destroyer of domestic happiness, the assassin of children . . . [and] a monster in human form'.

In Russia itself, the minister of education, Sergei Uvarov, who insisted that Russia must be viewed as separate from Europe, formulated what might be called the ideology of Nicholaevan reaction. In 1832, when he was still assistant minister of education, he circulated a memorandum to senior officials in the educational administration proclaiming it to be the obligation of all teachers to indoctrinate students in the 'spirit of Orthodoxy, Autocracy, and Nationality'. He went on to express his conviction that 'every professor and teacher, being permeated by one and the same feeling of devotion to throne and fatherland, will use all his resources to become a worthy tool of the government and to earn its complete confidence.' For the next two decades, Uvarov's formula was reprinted and elaborated upon endlessly in the Russian press as well as in journals, books, and textbooks.

The interpreters of Uvarov's trinity declared Russian Orthodoxy to be the only authentic religion, and Nicholas, convinced of the close link between God and Russia, regularly referred to the 'Russian God'. The autocrat, described as the kind, gracious, and benevolent father of the Russian people, was said to derive his power directly from God. The third term in the trinity, Nationality, was in many ways the most obscure. But from numerous writings on the subject certain critical features can be discerned. The proponents of the trinity believed that the Russian people were unique in their fervent devotion to autocracy and Orthodoxy and that their culture, especially their language, was superior to every other. Russian, it was claimed, was free flowing, noble, solemn, fresh, and melodious.

Uvarov urged schools to focus on the training of loyal, subservient subjects and believed that the lower classes should not receive any education that might lead them to cherish hopes of rising to a higher class. Thus, in 1827, the government decreed that peasants were to attend only primary schools, and after 1828 only the children of nobles and officials were to be admitted to gymnasia. The government also increased its control over institutions of higher learning. Insisting that he had the right to make professorial appointments and to dictate the curriculum, the minister of education made theology, church history, and church law compulsory for all students. The occupants of the new chairs in Russian and Slavic history were carefully chosen for their devotion to Russian nationalism, and their views echoed those of M. P. Pogodin, professor of history at Moscow University, who wrote, 'How great is Russia! How large is her population! How many nationalities it comprises! How immense are her resources! Finally, is there anything the Russian state could not do? A word – and a whole empire ceases to exist, a word – and another disappears from the face of the earth!' Increasingly, scholars or writers who wished to write in a more objective or nuanced tone were subjected to government censorship, which arbitrarily controlled the publication of books, journals, and newspapers.

In 1826, the government created the notorious Third Department (Department III of His Majesty's Own Chancery) for the purpose of collecting information on counterfeiters, religious sects, dissenters, and 'all happenings without exceptions'. Designed to prevent the organization of opposition movements such as the Decembrists, the Third Department quickly amassed enormous power, including the exercise of certain judicial functions. It consisted of two sets of agents: the gendarmerie, which was a uniformed military force that drew most of its officers from educated and well-established families and operated throughout the empire, and a large corps of secret informers who were instructed to keep an eye on every social group and to report on all signs of disaffection. The importance that Tsar Nicholas placed on the Third Department is evident from the fact that its director was considered a 'kind of prime minister'.

However, despite Russia's deserved reputation as a repressive police state, the police and the civil servants were not notably efficient, primarily because the government was niggardly in its appropriations for the security forces and the state bureaucracy in general. This generalization held true until the collapse of the empire in 1917. In 1796, the tsarist government employed one official for 2,250 subjects; in 1851, that had increased to one official for 929 subjects. But that was a much smaller ratio than in Great Britain and France, where in mid century the ratio was one to 244 and one to 208, respectively. In other words, in Western countries that were much less repressive than Russia, the state bureaucracy was about four and a half times larger per capita. Because the pay in Russia was extremely small, the authorities found it very difficult to attract able people. And among those it attracted, corruption was extraordinarily widespread. The endless stories of official venality and incompetence related by such writers as Nikolai Gogol reflected reality in all its sordidness and pettiness.

Still, the reign of Nicholas I was not all darkness. Despite his conservatism, Nicholas recognized that serfdom was an evil and he favored measures to improve the peasants' lot. But he did not advocate emancipation of the peasants, for fear that it would lead to a great catastrophe, by weakening the landowning class, the pillar of the autocracy, and by provoking an uprising of peasants dissatisfied with the conditions of their freedom. However, the tsar did appoint a series of secret committees, nine in all, to make proposals for lightening the burden on the serfs without, however, infringing the prerogatives of the serf owners. The committees faced an impossible task; they were being asked to square the circle.

General P. D. Kiselev, the minister of state properties, who had been sympathetic to the Decembrists, became the guiding spirit of the committees. He believed that emancipation was unavoidable and he also believed that freed peasants must be given adequate amounts of land. He could not persuade Nicholas to take such bold steps, but in 1842 the authorities did enact a law that allowed noble landowners to reach voluntary agreements with their serfs under which land would be transferred to the serfs in return for financial compensation. However, Kiselev did not succeed in specifying the amount of land to be transferred or the amount of the compensation; these matters were to be settled by agreements between the parties. Consequently, only 24,700 serfs received their freedom under this the most ambitious reform undertaken during Nicholas's reign. Other legislative measures touched on relatively minor issues: they forbade the sale of peasants without land by public auction in settlement of private debts and forbade nobles who did not own populated estates from buying serfs without land.

Kiselev was somewhat more successful in his attempt to improve the lot of state peasants,[3] because the reforms he proposed did not involve any limitations of the rights of noble landlords. Kiselev's goal was far-reaching; he favored the creation of a class of rural freemen who would be granted a large say in local organs of self-government. The government also attempted to equalize the freemen's land holdings and sponsored an elaborate 'welfare program'. Fireproof buildings were to be built in peasant villages, medical facilities were to be established, and an effort was made to promote temperance and education. During the eighteen years that Kiselev headed the Ministry of State Properties, the number of schools for state peasants rose from a mere 60 to 2,551 and the number of students from 1,800 to 111,000. These were modest gains and most peasants remained unenthusiastic about the reforms, in part because Kiselev, for all his progressive views, administered his department in a thoroughly bureaucratic, even tyrannical, manner. What was probably most important about the various measures he undertook was that they officially placed the issue of serfdom and the condition of the state peasants on the public agenda, but this cannot be considered a breakthrough.

The peasants were certainly not satisfied with the government's initiatives. Although no massive disturbances occurred, the period from 1826 to 1854 was far from peaceful. During those twenty-four years there were 712 incidents of unrest, during which peasants killed 173 landlords and bailiffs and tried to kill another seventy-five. During the eighteen years from 1836 to 1854 the government used troops on 132 different occasions to put down disturbances. It is worth noting that peasants tended to be most restless at times of political tension – for example, during the Decembrist Uprising in 1825 and the revolutions in the West in 1848 – which suggests that the rural population was aware of developments abroad and in distant places in the empire.

DOMESTIC DEVELOPMENTS

In the long run, the most significant development during Nicholas's reign was the emergence of the Russian intelligentsia, a group that came to exercise enormous influence on the course of Russian history. 'Intelligentsia' is a term that is not easy to define. Put simply, the members of this group were individuals – writers, philosophers, political activists, artists – who devoted their lives to intellectual pursuits, but that alone does not adequately describe them. The Russian intelligentsia were also individuals who took a critical stance towards the prevailing order, although they did not agree among themselves on how Russia should be changed. Not surprisingly, most of the intelligentsia in the first half of the nineteenth century came from the nobility, the best-educated social class in the country, but as the educational system expanded commoners also became part of the intelligentsia. Despite the authorities' belief that education bred disaffection, they realized that the expanding bureaucracy and professions could not be manned only by nobles, for the simple reason that there were not enough of them. This explains the rise in the number of students in Russian schools from 62,000 in 1800 to about 450,000 in the mid 1850s. Most of the pupils received only a rudimentary education, but nevertheless by the 1840s somewhere between fifteen and twenty thousand non-nobles could be considered part of the intelligentsia. Even then, the intelligentsia as a whole comprised only a tiny portion of the total population, but numbers alone do not tell the whole story. Ideas matter in history, and Russian intellectuals were imaginative, energetic, and resourceful in formulating and disseminating their views. The authorities realized very quickly that this group's ideas could influence the public and consequently watched their activities with the greatest anxiety. One of the central themes of Russian history from the 1830s to 1917 and beyond is the government's attempts to curb the intelligentsia.

The government's main weapon was tight censorship, but a few statistics will demonstrate that this weapon was not very effective. Between 1801 and 1826, enterprising citizens founded 129 magazines, a number that rose to 224 in the next thirty years. More to the point, Russian writers found ingenious ways of circumventing the censorship. Indeed, literature, one of the country's great achievements in the nineteenth century, was filled with allusions to current affairs, allusions that readers easily understood. Moreover, censors were not the most discerning judges of the likely impact of the written word. In 1872, for example, the censors permitted the publication of a Russian translation of Marx's *Capital* on the grounds that the work was so abstruse that it would attract little attention.

The concerns of the intelligentsia were wide ranging, but no theme received more attention than the destiny of Russia. Thus, Alexander Pushkin, a poet who did as much to shape the Russian language as Shakespeare did to shape English, warned that a political system that relied on repression could not count on a secure future. In one of his poems, 'The Dagger', he went so far as to advocate the assassination of tyrannical rulers. Vissarion G. Belinsky, a highly talented literary critic, insisted that it was the writer's obligation to be politically engaged, to champion progressive causes. He was enraged when Nikolai Gogol disavowed the widely held interpretation of his two great works, *The Inspector General* and *Dead Souls*, as criticisms of serfdom and bureaucratic corruption. Gogol claimed that these evils were not the consequence of the political system but of the moral failings of individuals. On the contrary, Belinsky argued, 'the most vital national questions in Russia today are the abolition of serfdom, the repeal of corporal punishment, and the introduction, as far as possible, of the strictest application of at least those laws which are already on the books.'

One of the more contentious debates among intellectuals developed with the rise of Slavophilism, to which I referred at the beginning of this book. First enunciated in the 1830s, Slavophilism was important because it posed in the starkest terms the different perspectives of the Westernizers such as Belinsky, who tended to look upon the West as a cultural and political model for Russia, and those who believed that Russian civilization was superior to every other and that as much of it as possible should be preserved. Slavophilism is also noteworthy because it influenced later political movements that stressed the merit of certain institutions unique to Russia. And it can be argued that in emphasizing the idea of Russia's unique mission in world history the Slavophiles facilitated the adoption by many intellectuals of Marxism, which also contains a strong missionary message.

In one way or another, the conflict between Western values and Slavic ideals confronted Russian intellectuals with difficult choices, and it was not uncommon for individual thinkers to modify their positions and even to move from one side to the other. A case in point is Alexander Herzen, a magnificent writer and activist who early in his career supported the goals of the Decembrists and believed fervently in the necessity of revolution in Russia. Persecuted for his views, he left Russia for the West in 1847, but the failure of the revolutions of 1848 led him to have doubts about the possibility of fundamental change in the West. The attachment to private property was simply too deeply ingrained in the culture of Western nations. He now concluded that the chances for socialism were much better in his native country because the commune had accustomed the Russian people to 'communal life' and egalitarianism. 'The Russian peasant', he wrote, 'has no morality save that which flows instinctively, naturally, from his communism; it is profoundly of the people; the little he knows of the Gospels nourishes it; the flagrant injustice of the government and of the landlords binds him all the more to his customs and to his commune.' Herzen never became a Slavophile; he should be seen, rather, as the first proponent of a strand in Russian thought that came to be known as *narodnichestvo*, which literally means 'populism' but is perhaps better translated as 'Russian socialism'. Eventually, his ideas were incorporated by the largest socialist movement in Russia, the Socialist Revolutionary party.

The founder of Slavophilism, Ivan Kireevsky, also began his career as an advocate of Russia's Europeanization. At that time he was critical of Russian Christianity for its failure to permeate Russian society and to shape the economy and civilization of the country. He also believed that Russia was uncultured and that only Europeanization could raise the country's culture to a desirable level. His views changed dramatically when he was in his thirties, as a result, it has been assumed, of his marriage to a deeply religious woman. Whatever the reason, Kireevsky now became a devout adherent of Orthodoxy and rejected the West in every respect. Western Christianity, especially Protestantism, had destroyed faith because it sought to prove that divine revelation was consistent with reason. He considered parliamentary rule unacceptable because it was based on materialism, rampant in the West. Westerners, he contended, sanctified private property and luxury and placed no value on the individual. By contrast, the Russian state had developed organically out of the commune, and as a consequence property was communal and the individual was highly prized. 'The Russian', he claimed, 'is spiritually unified' and needed no formal, legal guarantees for protection. Although Russians acknowledged that there were still imperfections in their society, they were basically at ease with themselves and satisfied with their lives. His overall conclusion, to which all the Slavophiles subscribed, was that Russia must become the spiritual leader of the world.

The intelligentsia, then, was a diverse group, but a group that had one thing in common: they wanted Russia to change. The authorities tried their utmost to rein in the critics – censored them, imprisoned them, exiled them – all to no avail. But, however influential and subversive, ideas alone would probably not have led to fundamental reform. In the end, it was the government's bumbling foreign policy in the early 1850s that exposed the frailties of Russia's economic, social, and political system and made reform the order of the day.

THE CRIMEAN WAR

Until the 1850s, Nicholas had been quite successful in handling foreign affairs. After the shock of the Decembrist Uprising, he had decided to focus on domestic issues and to shun as far as possible aggressive moves abroad. Whenever he did pursue a forward policy he calculated his options carefully and moved cautiously. This was true of Russia's involvement in Greek affairs at the time of the rebellion against Turkey (1821–9), of the various attempts to increase Russian influence in Turkey, and of the growing rivalry with Britain. This is not to say that Nicholas was oblivious to Russia's long-standing goal of gaining control over Constantinople and the Straits, which would turn Russia into a major naval power in the eastern Mediterranean. But he understood that such expansion was bound to alarm European nations, particularly Great Britain, which feared Russian designs on India. He therefore shunned aggressive policies in the region.

At first glance, the international crisis that erupted in 1853 into the Crimean War appeared to have been sparked by differences over a relatively trivial matter, the protection of Christians and Christian churches in Turkey, and more specifically in Palestine. Since pilgrimages to the Holy Land were made more frequently by individuals of the Greek Orthodox faith than of any other, the Christian sanctuaries there were largely supervised by the Orthodox Church. But in 1842, the French renewed their interest in the Near East and also began to make claims as guardians of the Holy Places. Louis Napoleon, who came to power in 1848, sought to follow the example of his uncle, Napoleon I, by enhancing France's influence abroad. In particular, the French government now demanded to be given the key to the great door of the Church of Bethlehem and the right to replace the Latin star marking the birthplace of Christ that Greeks had allegedly stolen in 1847. The Russians, on the other hand, warned the Turkish authorities that they would not tolerate concessions to the French. Unwilling to offend either the Russians or the French, the Turks at first prevaricated and then, in 1852, promised both sides that they would accede to their wishes, a duplicitous move that did not deceive anyone for very long. Enraged, in December 1852 Louis Napoleon put on a show of naval force in Turkish waters and forced the Turks to yield to his wishes.

At this point, Tsar Nicholas made his first major miscalculation. He mobilized two army corps in the expectation that Austria would come to his support. After all, in 1849, when Austria faced widespread domestic unrest, Nicholas had sent Russian troops to help the Austrian government put down the revolution. It was only natural, the tsar thought, that Austria would reciprocate now that Russia needed help. He also believed that a firm stance by him and his assumed ally would force Turkey to give in to his demands. He now called on Turkey to agree to a secret alliance with Russia that would guarantee not only the privileges of the Orthodox Church with regard to the churches but also grant Russia the right to act as protector of all Orthodox subjects (about two million) in Turkey. Not only Turkey but the European powers were appalled by Russia's demand, which they rightly considered to be a violation of Turkey's sovereignty. They feared that Russia's real goal was to establish a protectorate over Turkey. Great Britain urged Turkey to reject Russia's more extreme demands. When it did, the Russians invaded the Danubian principalities of Moldavia and Wallachia (in July 1853), though they were soon forced by international pressure to retreat from them. Both France and Great Britain came to

Turkey's aid; Prussia remained neutral and Austria adopted an anti-Russian stance, going so far as to occupy the very principalities that Russia had coveted. Naively, Nicholas was surprised and offended. 'Was not Schwarzenberg himself [the Austrian minister who died in 1852]', he told one of his subordinates, 'alleged to have declared that Austria would one day astound the world by the greatness of her ingratitude?'

Early in 1854, the war began in earnest with Russia ranged against Turkey, Britain, and France. Even though the Russians scored some victories at various stages of the conflict, the war proved to be a fiasco for all the belligerents but most of all for the Russians, who were unable to defend their own territory. The most intense battles were fought in the Crimea, and despite many blunders the Western generals succeeded in capturing Sevastopol (in September 1855), a major naval station on the Black Sea. This was a devastating blow, but it was not until four months later, when Austria threatened to enter the war if Russia did not immediately agree to negotiate peace on previously stipulated conditions, that the authorities in St. Petersburg decided to end hostilities and to attend a peace conference. Bad judgment and incompetence had characterized the Russian war effort from the beginning: the Christians in the Ottoman Empire did not rise up in arms; the existing railway lines were incapable of transporting in a timely fashion the men and ammunition to the war zone; Russia's weapons were much inferior to those of France and Britain; and the Russian commanders, some of whom were thoroughly corrupt, turned out to be even more prone than their opponents to make catastrophic blunders. Russian losses in men and equipment were horrendous; according to an estimate that includes deaths from disease, about 600,000 soldiers died during the three-year conflagration. There could be no doubt that Russia was in almost every respect a country that lagged far behind the rest of Europe.

Under the circumstances, Russia fared better than might have been expected at the Paris Peace Conference in 1856, although overall the final treaty did not please the government

and certainly not Russian nationalists. The allies did withdraw from all the Russian territory they occupied, but Russia
had to cede to Moldavia a strip of southern Bessarabia border-
ing on the Danube. Turkey retained suzerainty over Moldavia
and Wallachia, and all the signatories promised to respect the
territorial integrity of the Ottoman Empire and to refrain from
interfering in the internal affairs of Turkey, which, in turn, agreed
to establish religious and legal equality for all its subjects (including specifically all Christians). Finally, the delegates at the peace
conference agreed that the Black Sea would be neutralized; that
is, it would be open to merchant ships of all nations, but closed
to warships. Thus, neither Russia nor Turkey would be allowed
to operate its navy there, a restriction that would become a major
issue over the next half century.

Tsar Nicholas, who shared much of the responsibility for
the calamity of the Crimean War, was spared the humiliation
of having to sign the agreements reached at Paris. He died in
February 1855, leaving the task of coping with the aftermath of
the war to his son, Alexander II.

6

REFORM AND
COUNTER-REFORM, 1861–94

The year 1861 marked the beginning of what is often referred to as the 'Age of Modernization'. From that time until 1917 the authorities in St. Petersburg introduced a series of major changes in the country's social and political order and in its economy. There were some notable interruptions in this process, but the basic thrust was towards modernization. The primary, though not the sole, motive of the monarchy and the political elite was to reinvigorate the state, which appeared to be losing ground in comparison with other major powers. In a sense, the Russian monarchy was continuing a tradition of reform from above that could be traced back at least to Peter the Great early in the eighteenth century. But by the second half of the nineteenth century the ability of the ruler and the state to shape by themselves the course of events in the empire had declined. Increasingly, society – that is, groups other than the autocracy and the bureaucracy, such as the middle classes, the intelligentsia, the industrial proletariat, and the peasantry – played a role in framing the national agenda. Inevitably, the emergence of society as a significant political force led to sharp conflicts not only between it and the state but eventually also between various sectors of society. These conflicts became dominant themes in the history of Russia after 1861.

Tsar Alexander II, who ascended the throne in 1855 at the age of thirty-seven and came to be known as the 'tsar-liberator', was in many respects an unlikely person to be able to cope with such complexities, much less to emerge as a leader who would undertake bold initiatives. Neither very intelligent nor well educated, Alexander was brought up to admire the values of his father, Nicholas I, who cherished the principles of autocracy and official nationality. Nor was Alexander a decisive person. He rarely expressed his own views unequivocally and almost never provided vigorous leadership on the pressing issues of the day. He tended to rely heavily on advisers to set the agenda, but, since he retained in high office men with sharply different views on government policy, no one could be sure whether he would follow the advice of liberal or of reactionary officials. But in the end, the tsar seems also to have been a man with a realistic and pragmatic bent, and for a leader at a time of severe crisis that trait can be more telling than any other.

When Alexander assumed the mantle of autocratic power, Russia faced national humiliation of unprecedented proportions. The defeat of Russia on its own territory during the Crimean War had revealed that militarily, economically, and socially the country lagged far behind the West and that it stood in danger of being relegated to the status of a second-rate power. Much as he wished to retain the old order, the tsar concluded that he had no choice but to introduce far-reaching changes, though he always sought to minimize the impact of those changes on his auto-cratic authority and on the privileges of the nobility. His underlying motive in abolishing serfdom, the one institution more than any other that marked Russia as a retrograde country, was not humanitarian but thoroughly pragmatic. It had become clear that serfdom was undermining Russia's military prowess.

In the first half of the nineteenth century, the Russian Empire maintained the largest standing army in Europe, in all some two and a quarter million men. So large a force was considered necessary because of the long, exposed frontiers, the absence of a railway network enabling the rapid movement of troops from one region to another, and the lack of trained reserves. But even that huge army proved to be insufficient during the Crimean War because a sizable portion of it was stationed, for security reasons, in the Kingdom of Poland and along the Galician frontier. The government therefore drafted a large number of raw recruits, but it could not find enough men capable of serving as officers in the enlarged army. When Sevastopol, a major naval station on the Black Sea, came under threat, the high command could muster only 100,000 trained men for the city's defense. It also turned out that the Russian economy could not produce an adequate supply of equipment for the army. And when the war ended, Russia faced a serious fiscal crisis: in 1857 alone, the treasury had a deficit in excess of 75 million rubles, almost all of which could be traced to the increased outlay necessitated by the Crimean conflict.

The most plausible solution to the crisis was to emulate the practice of the European countries that maintained a relatively small standing army and a trained strategic reserve that could be called into action in time of war. But so long as serfdom existed such a course was out of the question. It would have meant training a large number of serfs in the use of firearms and military tactics and then discharging them without any guarantee that they would find productive employment. The potential threat to public order was so obvious that the government believed it had no choice but to adopt a more radical alternative, the abolition of serfdom.

But there were other reasons for adopting that alternative. The peasants themselves had made clear their desire for emancipation. During the thirty years of Nicholas I's reign, more than six hundred peasant revolts broke out. Most of them were relatively minor and could easily be contained, but increasingly Tsar Alexander II as well as many nobles came to believe that they had more to fear from inaction than from emancipation. As Alexander II put it in 1856, 'It is better to abolish serfdom from above than to wait until the serfs begin to liberate themselves from below.' It also dawned on landlords, especially in the regions where land was fertile, that it would be more profitable to cultivate it with hired, cheap labor than to retain a system of farming that was strikingly inefficient. In addition a growing number among the country's elite had reached the conclusion that serfdom was an inhumane institution that could no longer be tolerated. This humanitarian consideration may not have been the primary reason for the government's reforms, but it definitely played a role in the intensive debates about serfdom that engaged the bureaucracy and the intelligentsia for some five years from 1856 to 1861.

To appreciate the dimension of the problem posed by emancipation, consider the fact that in the United States at the time only about eleven percent of the population was enslaved and yet their emancipation created enormous controversy and many hardships that have left their mark to this day. The racial factor enhanced the complexity of the problem in the United States, but the far greater number of people that the Russian government had to deal with meant that emancipation would necessarily entail a fundamental reordering of the country's political, not to speak of social, institutions. About three-quarters of the roughly 74 million people in Russia were in bondage either to the state or to landlords. The lot of the landlord serfs, about fifty-five percent of all peasants, was in several respects not much different from that of chattel despite some feeble attempts by the government in the first half of the nineteenth century to place limits on the power of the landlord over his serfs.

The state peasants can best be defined as those who lived on state property that was administered by the treasury. Economically, they were better off than the landlord serfs, and the control that bureaucrats imposed on them was less harsh than that of the nobles. The common feature of the state peasants and landlord serfs was that all were tied to the land; they could not freely move from their place of abode.[1]

The question of serfdom was so sensitive that once the tsar had decided on abolishing the institution he moved with great discretion and sought advice from many individuals in the country's elite. He appointed a special 'Main Committee' to conduct its deliberations in strictest secrecy. It, in turn, was to receive advice on how to implement the reform in local areas from Provincial Commissions, which included both elected and appointed members. When all the information had been sifted, the projects that had been formulated were to be sent to an Editorial Commission in St. Petersburg charged with refining the proposals by taking into account the larger administrative, economic, and legal aspects of the recommendations.

Although the emancipation decree of 1861, which initially applied only to the landlord serfs – state peasants were emancipated five years later – was not nearly as far-reaching and generous as the peasants had hoped, it was a reform of the greatest importance. It began a process that by 1866 had changed the legal condition of the great majority of Russian subjects. It outlawed the sale of human beings and prohibited the arbitrary transfer of men and women from field work to house work; peasants were now free to marry whomever they wished, they could acquire property, become traders, and were granted the right to bring actions to court.

From the standpoint of the peasants, the principal drawback of the decree was that it did not give them enough land; at best, it offered them as much land as they had worked before the reform and in many instances they received less. The peasants were also forced to pay to the government redemption dues, which were calculated by capitalizing the *obrok* and the *obshchina* at six percent, over a period of forty-nine years. In the meantime the government gave the landlords interest-bearing bonds covering about three-quarters of the total value of the dues, which was in many instances more than the value of the land that was handed over to the peasants. In other words, contrary to a promise made by the authorities, the peasant had to pay for the redemption of his person.

The commune was not only preserved but strengthened. Most notably, the Assembly of the Commune took over the bulk of the public law powers previously exercised by landlords; it also supervised and guaranteed the redemption payments as well as the collection of the poll tax, and it issued the passports peasants needed if they wished to leave their area of residence even for a temporary period. These powers of the *mir* were in addition to the ones it had exercised before the emancipation.[2]

When the peasants became aware of the details of the emancipation decree, many were incensed. They had believed that they would be granted 'full freedom', which to them meant that they would be given, free of charge, all the land held by the landlords. The peasants, it must be stressed, had long been convinced that the land belonged to those who worked it. They also believed that the tsar, their 'father', wanted them to have the land and that only the self-serving landlords and bureaucrats had prevented the tsar's will from being carried out. Significantly, there were more peasant disturbances after emancipation than in the years preceding the reform: 1,176 in 1861, 400 in 1862, and 386 in 1863. The authorities responded forcefully, shooting many disturbers of the peace in the villages and flogging and exiling many others. By 1864 order had been restored; that year, the police recorded only seventy-five incidents of unrest in the countryside.

Over the next few decades, economic conditions for most peasants deteriorated. One reason for this was the sharp rise in the peasant population, which increased from fifty to seventy-nine million in the years from 1860 to 1897. The inevitable result was that the size of individual land allotments shrank from an average of 13.2 *desiatinas* (one *desiatina* equals 2.7 acres) in 1877 to 10.4 in 1905. The average tax on the peasants' land, moreover, was ten times as high as on the nobles' land. Agriculture remained extremely backward, in large measure because of the periodic repartition of the land, which discouraged innovation. In Germany, for example, one *desiatina* of land yielded 128 *poods* (one *pood* equals thirty-six pounds) of wheat in the summer and 104 *poods* in the winter. In European Russia, the comparable figures were sixty-four and forty-one *poods*, respectively. Periodic famines, caused by inclement weather, only added to the woes of the peasantry. Many statistics could be cited to demonstrate the wretched conditions in the countryside, but none is more telling than the following: the death rate in Russia was almost double that in Britain.

JUDICIAL, ADMINISTRATIVE, AND MILITARY REFORM

Emancipation was clearly the most important reform enacted by Alexander II, but it was not the only one. The tsar and many of his advisers recognized that the liberation of the serfs necessitated other reforms to persuade the nation that Russia was abandoning the most egregious features of arbitrary rule. In 1864, the government introduced a series of judicial reforms, which provided for open and public trials and a jury system, and eliminated the harshest forms of corporal punishment. Under the new dispensation, judges were to be irremovable, although their promotion still depended on the goodwill of senior government officials. The judicial reforms may be considered a first step towards the establishment of the rule of law, but they were not rigorously applied and were often superseded, especially after 1881, by various emergency decrees that allowed the authorities to punish so-called political criminals arbitrarily. Part of the problem was the administrators' unwillingness to give up methods of rule that had served them well, but it should also be noted that a jury system in a country with a woefully uneducated and unsophisticated citizenry is bound to encounter serious difficulties. A foreign observer reported that one jury returned a verdict of 'not guilty with extenuating circumstances', another settled a difficult case by casting lots before an icon, and several juries produced a verdict of 'not guilty' even when the accused made a full and formal confession during the trial. In a widely publicized case in 1878, a jury refused to convict Vera Zasulich, a revolutionary who had shot and wounded the military governor of St. Petersburg for having ordered the flogging of a political prisoner. The government now ordered the removal of all political cases from normal judicial procedures.

Another major reform introduced in 1864 created an entirely new system of local self-government. The measure provided for the election of local organs of self-government, known as *zemstvos*, at the county (*uezd*) and provincial levels. The elections were not 'democratic' as we understand the word. The population was divided into three classes, or colleges – nobility, townsmen, and peasants – and the number of representatives they could send to the *zemstvo* was based on the value of the property owned by each group. Also, the county *zemstvos* elected the delegates to the higher, provincial *zemstvo*, a further dilution of democratic principles. As a result, nobles and government officials, who represented a small minority of the population, were a decisive force in the organs of self-government. In 1865, for example, they constituted forty-two percent of the delegates in the district assemblies and seventy-four percent in the provincial *zemstvo* assemblies.

Nevertheless, the *zemstvos* were, as nearly all scholars agree, remarkably effective in improving general conditions at the local level. They played a decisive role in the construction and maintenance of roads and hospitals, they supervised local educational institutions, they encouraged economic development, they administered prisons, and they saw to the building of new churches. To carry out these functions the *zemstvos* employed a growing number of trained experts – doctors, veterinarians, agronomists, statisticians, teachers, engineers – who, known as the 'third element', had become by the end of the nineteenth century an influential force in public life. These *zemstvo* employees were overwhelmingly idealistic men and women who made considerable sacrifices to serve the public. By the early twentieth century, the third element numbered close to seventy thousand people, most of them sympathetic to liberal or socialist causes. Several leaders of the liberal parties that played a notable role in public life in the early twentieth century gained their first experience in public affairs in the *zemstvos*. To prevent the *zemstvos* from challenging the central authorities, the government had taken the precaution of prohibiting them from considering matters of national concern. But within a few decades it became evident that officials in St. Petersburg had deluded themselves in believing that authentic self-government could coexist with an autocratic system of rule.

It was not until 1874 that the tsar and his advisers settled on a reform of the military forces, the poor condition of which had been a major catalyst for the social and political changes in the first place. The decree reduced the period of service from twenty-five to six years, created a reserve and a militia, and introduced a more humane system of discipline. This appeared to be a system of universal military service, but it should be noted that men who held academic degrees enjoyed various privileges, such as reduced terms of service. Nevertheless, the military reform was a step in the right direction, but as would become clear in the empire's last two wars – in 1904–5 and in 1914–17 – it did not go far enough in transforming the army and navy into effective fighting forces. In another war, against a weak Turkey in 1877–8, Russia did emerge victorious, but here, too, the army did not perform with distinction.

CONSEQUENCES OF REFORM

Although the reforms of the 1860s and 1870s produced fundamental changes in Russian society, they did not come close to satisfying the aspirations and expectations raised by the discussions of reform in the 1850s. The peasants' dissatisfactions have already been noted, but, remarkably, even the nobility or *dvorianstvo*, the class whose interests the authorities were determined to protect, could not cope well with the consequences of emancipation. The nobles, after all, were the main prop of the autocracy even though they constituted a small and highly diversified group. According to the census of 1897, 1.5 percent of the population were either hereditary or lifetime nobles, among whom were rich and poor ones, liberals and reactionaries, those who spent most of their time in the large cities and those who remained in their country residences, and men who served in the civil service as well as a sizable number (about one-fifth) who became professionals of one sort or another. Moreover, about half of the privileged class was non-Russian, over twenty-eight percent of them being Polish, a national group that was subjected to extensive discrimination. This diversity helps explain the absence of political solidarity among the Russian nobility.

A large number of nobles found it extremely difficult to adjust to the emancipation of the serfs and to their own subsequent decline as a force in society, and this, in turn, accounts for the increasing political stridency of many of them. Until 1861 the nobility had performed important functions in the body politic. They exercised vast authority over the roughly forty-five percent of the peasants who were their serfs, manned the judicial posts in their districts, supervised the collection of the soul tax, and oversaw the recruitment of men for military service. A few nobles, moreover, owned large estates that yielded a surplus for the export market. No matter how the other social classes viewed these arrangements, they could not deny that the *dvorianstvo* discharged obligations useful to the state. After the reforms, however, the nobility lost much of its *raison d'être* and standing in society, though that was not the government's intention.

The most striking manifestation of the nobility's decline was its loss of land. Unable or unwilling to administer their estates on a capitalist basis, many nobles sold their land to townsmen or peasants. In the period from the Great Reforms until 1905, the nobility surrendered about one-third of its total land holdings. To appreciate the magnitude of the transformation in landownership, it should be kept in mind that in the 1860s the privileged classes owned half of all privately held arable land.

Economic trends played an important role in the nobility's decline. The severe agrarian crisis in the last decades of the nineteenth century, a worldwide phenomenon that caused a sharp drop in prices of major crops, hindered the development of large-scale farming in Russia. Moreover, most nobles never mastered the rudiments of scientific farming and made only the feeblest efforts to obtain up-to-date machinery.

In the last analysis, the nobles' inability to turn their estates into profitable ventures was rooted in their psychological disposition. Under serfdom, noble landlords had never been known for hard work, managerial skills, or frugality. Accustomed to receiving state handouts and dues as well as services from their serfs, they failed to develop the drive and initiative necessary for success in a market economy. The emancipation of the serfs made matters worse for the nobility, for now they had to fend for themselves under circumstances thoroughly alien to their experience.

By the 1890s the government was alarmed at the nobility's declining role in public institutions. So many nobles had fled the countryside that the supply of personnel qualified to hold positions of authority was seriously depleted. At times, not enough nobles could be found to fill all the seats to which they were entitled in the *zemstvo* assemblies. It has been estimated that in fifty provinces out of seventy-eight the *dvorianstvo* was no longer capable of exerting a measurable influence on local affairs. The government was at a loss as to how to reverse the trend.

Other classes did not and could not fill the vacuum, for the authorities, insisting on the maintenance of the autocracy and the privileges of the nobility, had failed to create institutions that might have provided adequate opportunities for emerging social groups to play a significant role in public affairs. Neither the peasantry nor the middle class nor the working class could find adequate legal outlets for self-expression. Increasingly, members of these groups turned to illegal political activities.

This development was in part the result of the gradual increase in the education of non-nobles. The newly educated, referred to as the *raznochintsy* (men of different ranks), tended to come from poorer elements of society such as priests, petty bureaucrats, artisans, and to some extent even peasants. They became part of the intelligentsia, which until now had consisted almost exclusively of nobles critical of the prevailing order. Although upper-class intellectuals often sympathized with the poverty and suffering of the masses, they had not experienced firsthand the miseries of the masses as had the *raznochintsy*, who demanded change with a fervor and stridency generally absent from earlier critics of the tsarist regime. The new mood that emerged in the 1860s gave Russian radicalism a particular stamp of impatience and even fanaticism.

That radicalism assumed various forms. The first was 'nihilism', a term coined by I. S. Turgenev in his novel *Fathers and Sons*. D. I. Pisarev was the leading spokesman of the nihilist movement – if it can be called that, for it was really more an attitude than a political ideology. Pisarev disdained traditional social and artistic values and such institutions as the family or established religions. He placed the greatest value on the natural sciences and utilitarian rationalism. Among his favorite aphorisms were 'What can be broken should be broken' and 'A shoemaker is more important than Goethe.'

Narodnichestvo (populism) had a much larger following among the intelligentsia. A movement that evolved out of the writings of Herzen (discussed in chapter 5), N. K. Mikhailovsky, and the radical anarchist M. A. Bakunin, Russian populism should not be confused with Western 'populism', which generally refers to popular, agrarian movements. The Russian populists (or *narodniki*) contended that the future of Russia rested with the peasants, whose long experience with the commune had turned them into instinctive supporters of communism. Uncontaminated by the values of Western institutions, which were based on the sanctity of private property, Russia could bypass capitalism altogether in its evolution towards socialism. Nikolai Chernyshevsky's *What Is to Be Done?* (published in 1863), a work of fiction that focused on the heroic revolutionary prepared to suffer endless hardships for the cause of socialism, was widely read and converted many alienated intellectuals to populism. Unlike Herzen, who towards the end of his life believed that socialism could be attained by peaceful means, Chernyshevsky thought that force would be necessary.

The means to be used to bring about fundamental change soon became one of the most vexing issues for opponents of the old order, which still enjoyed a considerable degree of support among the people. The failed attempt in 1866 by the populist Dmitrii Karakozov to assassinate Tsar Alexander fueled the debate, for the government made clear that it would respond to violence with repression: it tightened discipline in the schools and placed new restrictions on the press. Early in the 1870s, the opposition tried a different tack and this, too, proved to be unproductive. Idealistic young *narodniki* launched the 'Go-to-the-People' movement; hundreds of them moved to the countryside and lived with the peasants with the intention of teaching them to read and write as well as the rudiments of modern technology. But the ultimate goal of the young populists was to prepare the masses for revolution. To the agitators' despair, many peasants were baffled by the *narodniki* and suspected that they were interlopers trying to lead them astray. Some peasants even turned the visitors in to the police, who in the mid 1870s arrested a large number of them, bringing the well-intentioned project to a close.

In 1877, M. A. Natanson and A. D. Mikhailov organized a new movement, the Land and Freedom Society, committed to intensive revolutionary propaganda among the peasantry. But within two years, in 1879, the Society split, and the issue again was the means to be employed in the struggle against the old order. One group, the Black Partition, insisted on continuing the peaceful course of propaganda, on the assumption that recourse to violence, which it did not repudiate under all circumstances, would at this time be counterproductive. The other group, The People's Will, was led by Mikhailov, who insisted that only terror, directed especially at leaders of the government, including the tsar, could lead to a radical transformation of the social and political order by arousing peasants to revolution.

DEEPENING OF POLITICAL FERMENT

The growing unrest from below was not the only troublesome development facing the authorities in the 1870s. In 1877, Russia became embroiled in yet another conflict with Turkey, the fourth in the nineteenth century, over control of the Balkans, where large numbers of Christians were under the domination of the Turks. This time the Russian forces generally fought well, and in March 1878 the Treaty of San Stefano was imposed upon the Turks, radically changing the boundaries in the Balkans. Russia annexed southern Bessarabia and the important cities of Batumi in Transcaucasia and Kars in eastern Anatolia. Turkey was obliged to accept the full independence of Serbia, Romania, and Montenegro and the autonomy of Bulgaria, which became a principality dominated by Russia. However, Russia could not enjoy the spoils of victory for more than a few months. In July 1878, the great powers, most notably Austria-Hungary and Great Britain, forced the tsar to accept some important revisions of the Treaty of San Stefano. Although Russia retained the lands it had annexed, Bulgaria was substantially reduced in size and Austria-Hungary took control of Bosnia and Herzegovina. Once again, Russia was humiliated and many Russians were deeply angered at having been deprived of full victory after a war that had cost the country thousands of casualties.

The loss of face in the international arena occurred at a time of growing militancy from below. In the first of a series of attacks on senior officials, Vera Zasulich in March 1878 attempted to assassinate General Trepov, the police chief of St. Petersburg, and succeeded in wounding him seriously. When the revolutionaries early in August that same year killed General Mezentsev, the head of the Third Department, the government was so alarmed that it launched a special effort to secure the help of the educated public in fighting the terror. The government hoped that a strong denunciation of the terror by respected members of society would reduce if not stop the violence. It was a sign of the depth of disaffection in Russia that the zemstvos, composed largely of upper-class men, turned a deaf ear to the government. Several of the more liberal zemstvo officials went so far as to announce that they would not support the government's drive against terrorism until the people had been granted political rights.

In truth, quite a few of the most militant activists belonged to the privileged groups of society. Of the people either imprisoned or exiled during the five years from 1873 to 1877, 279 were young nobles, 117 were the children of non-noble officials, 197 were the offspring of priests, 68 were Jews, and only 138 came from peasant families. No doubt, terror alone could not succeed in overturning the tsarist regime, for the government could always find substitutes for the murdered officials and it could always step up repression. But the government's inability to put an end to the violence inevitably undermined public confidence in the authorities, a precondition for a successful revolution.

The terror also shook the self-confidence of the tsarist regime itself, which began to be unnerved by the boldness of the revolutionaries. Within a three-month period, from mid November 1879 to early 1880, they made two daring attempts to assassinate the tsar. In the second, Stepan Khalturin succeeded in planting a bomb under the main dining room in the Winter Palace, but it exploded before the tsar arrived for his meal. It did, however, kill eleven people. The political police, led by incompetent officers, were incapable of apprehending the terrorists. Indeed, their approach to the unrest – arbitrary crackdowns (between April 1879 and July 1880, 575 people were exiled and sixteen were sentenced to death) – only infuriated and emboldened the radicals. Increasingly, the tsar felt obliged to isolate himself from the people, and this seemed to belie the official ideology that the people loved their ruler. Instead of strolling outside, as he liked to do, he took his walks inside the halls of his palace. When he did venture outside he was heavily guarded and the blinds in his carriage were drawn. To many it appeared as though the powerful ruler of all the Russians had been reduced to the status of a hunted animal.

Early in 1880, Tsar Alexander decided on a bold change of course. He replaced the more conservative members of his government with moderates and appointed General M. T. Loris-Melikov as head of a 'Supreme Administrative Commission for the Maintenance of State Order and Public Tranquillity'. A few months later, when the commission was disbanded, Loris-Melikov became minister of internal affairs. The selection of Loris-Melikov for these important positions was in many ways an inspired move. A hero of the Crimean War and the Russo-Turkish war of 1877–8, he was highly popular. Moreover, as governor of the Terskaia region and as governor-general of Kharkov province he had shown that though he could be firm against perceived troublemakers, he understood the necessity of reform. On his appointment to the commission, he announced that he would not 'recoil from the most severe measures to punish those who are guilty of the criminal acts that are disgracing our society'. But, as his actions soon demonstrated, he also knew that the mailed fist alone would not suffice to restore order in Russia. And he knew how to exercise power. It has been plausibly argued that in 1880 and early in 1881 he wielded more power than any other official in the Russian Empire from 1855 to 1905.

To restore order, Loris-Melikov adopted a two-pronged approach. He ordered the police to crack down on the revolutionaries, which they did, but the leaders of The People's Will eluded them. At the same time, he abolished the Third Department of the Chancery, a department widely despised for its arbitrariness; he loosened the restrictions on the press; abolished the much-resented salt tax; and called on *zemstvo* activists to consider possible reform measures. Most important of all, he made clear that in his view some concession to popular participation in government would be necessary to calm the nation. It was a daring move, one that would not sit well with Tsar Alexander, who remained firmly committed to the principle of autocracy. This is not to say that Loris-Melikov proposed to replace the monarchical system with a democratic one. In a memorandum to the emperor, he went out of his way to assure the ruler that he did not envision a system of 'popular representation in imitation of Western patterns; not only . . . [is this] alien to the Russian people but . . . [it] could shake . . . [Russia's] basic political outlook and introduce troubles whose consequences are difficult to foresee.' Loris-Melikov's recommendations for political reform were, in fact, very modest. He proposed the creation of two Preparatory Commissions, one to focus on administrative–economic matters and the other on financial questions; both were to be chaired by 'a person endowed with the Sovereign's trust', although the commissions would also contain experts chosen by *zemstvos* and city councils. The two commissions would report to a body known as the General Commission, which would then formulate proposals on specific issues, but Loris-Melikov specified that this group would have the right to work only on matters presented to it by the tsarist authorities. The General Commission's final proposals would be sent to the State Council – an institution of tsarist appointees that served as a legislative advisory body – which would be expanded with the addition of fifteen persons elected by the public. Loris-Melikov's cumbersome scheme has often been referred to as a constitution, but it must be stressed that under it the emperor's power was to remain paramount. Yet its implementation would have marked a significant departure for Russia in that it provided for the participation of some elected representatives in the process of governing the country. It was an important move in the right direction, but not more than that.

Alexander sent Loris-Melikov's scheme for review to a group of eight dignitaries whom he himself appointed. The group expressed general approval of the proposal, but left it up to the monarch to decide whether to add elected members to the State Council. Convinced that political reform could no longer be avoided, Alexander approved the committee's report without changing the State Council's composition and scheduled a meeting on 1 March with the chairman of the Council of Ministers, Count P. A. Valuev, to prepare a final draft of the proposals for publication. The People's Will dramatically intervened and brought the reform process to a halt, leaving us to speculate on one of the more interesting 'might have beens' in Russian history.

The revolutionaries who had escaped the police dragnet had not lost heart. Led by Sophia Perovskaia, a small group continued to plan the tsar's assassination, and on the morning of 1 March

they threw a bomb at the monarch's carriage, which was returning from a military parade. Alexander was not hurt, but soon after
he stepped into the street to find out what had happened another
bomb was hurled at him and this one fatally wounded him. He
could barely utter a request to be taken to the palace before he
lost consciousness; he died shortly thereafter in his study.

The murder of the tsar sent tremors throughout Russian society. The defenders of the old order argued more vehemently
than ever that only force against the opposition could prevent
Russia from degenerating into anarchy. The non-revolutionary
opponents of the autocratic regime continued to believe in the
necessity of fundamental reform, but they now tended to speak
with muted voices. Emboldened, the government launched a
crackdown that greatly weakened the revolutionary movement,
which for at least a decade remained fairly quiescent. Perhaps
the most surprising reaction came from the masses, for whom
the revolutionaries claimed to be waging the struggle against
the authorities. Many lower-class people convinced themselves
that the Jews were responsible for the assassination – a Jewish
person, Jessie Helfman, was part of the terrorist group – and
must be punished for the crime. In the spring, summer, and fall
of 1881, marauders unleashed pogroms in some two hundred
villages and towns that left at least forty Jews dead, many more
wounded, and hundreds of women in despair at having been
raped. The destruction of Jewish neighborhoods in several cities
left thousands of people homeless.

Historians have been at odds over the origins of this wanton
killing and destruction.[3] Many have argued that the unrest was
instigated by the highest authorities in St. Petersburg to deflect
attention from the government. But it is now known that the
new tsar, Alexander III, who deeply disliked Jews, nevertheless ordered provincial governors to suppress the violence and
to protect the Jews. He feared that the pogroms might set off a
general social revolution. If the masses could plunder from the
Jews with impunity, why should they not also attack the estates
of the nobles? A significant number of revolutionaries initially

welcomed the pogroms, for precisely the same reason that the Tsar opposed them. All the major socialist newspapers in Russia except one carried articles hailing the pogroms as the first sign that the masses were bestirring themselves. Soon, however, most radicals realized that the peasants who attacked Jews did so not to promote the ideals of socialism but rather to give vent to their hatred of a minority whose way of life differed from theirs and whom they suspected of all sorts of evil machinations.

COUNTER-REFORM

Although the new ruler, Alexander III, opposed the pogroms, it should not be assumed that he was a man of liberal inclinations. On the contrary, he was a narrow-minded man, with limited intelligence, committed at all costs to maintaining the autocratic system of rule. He intensely disliked his father's reforms, which he believed had undermined Russia's traditional institutions that had guided the country to greatness. A man with a powerful build, he gave the impression, despite the awkward movements of his body, of a person with a strong will and a clear vision of how the nation should be ruled and how the country's power should be enhanced. But this was not a vision that Alexander had conceived on his own. He owed his political ideas to one of his tutors, Constantine Pobedonostsev, at one time a professor of civil law at Moscow University and from 1880 to 1905 chief procurator of the Most Holy Synod. Extraordinarily influential in affairs of state in the 1880s, Pobedonostsev set forth what can be described as the official ideology of pre-revolutionary Russia. Although not an original or systematic thinker, Pobedonostsev stated his views on society, politics, law, religion, and education in sufficient detail in his *Reflections of a Russian Statesman* that they can be presented as a coherent body of doctrines.

The essential premise of Pobedonostsev's political philosophy was that humankind was 'weak, vicious, worthless, and rebellious' and must therefore be held in check by coercive force.

Religion, too, was necessary to imbue the masses with the notions of obedience, industry, and virtue. The material conditions of the people did not interest him at all. He contended that the masses should be exposed to only a short period of education, during which they would master the rudiments of reading, writing, arithmetic, and religion and would be imbued by their teachers with the ideals of duty, sacrifice, obedience, work, and Christian love for one's fellow. To educate them more broadly and to teach them to think critically would only encourage them to seek to improve their economic conditions, and that would lead to conflict in society. Pobedonostsev disparaged industrialization because it would promote the movement of peasants to the cities, where they would come under pernicious influences. Order and stability were the chief procurator's highest goals. He never so much as mentioned the role of society in promoting justice, freedom, or the general welfare of the people.

In Pobedonostsev's political conception, the autocrat was the ultimate source of all state authority. He was vague in describing the sources of the tsar's authority, but suggested that it was based on divine right and also on what he called the 'national faith and national will'. Yet the tsar could not govern alone; he needed the support of the country's elite. Again, Pobedonostsev was vague on how the elite were to be selected, but suggested that there should be two criteria, merit and inherited wealth. Unlike the masses, the elite should be well educated so that they would be capable of making the critical decisions about the direction of the state. Both the autocrat and the elite were entitled to violate the law and even to 'smash institutions' if in their view the well-being of the state required it.

Pobedonostsev also believed that the church should be subordinate to the state and that in a well-functioning society there could be only one religion, a spiritual force that serves to bind together the people of a nation. He did not object to the ethnic minorities in the Russian Empire retaining their languages and customs, but he did insist that they should all adhere to Russian Orthodoxy. However, he doubted whether the Poles or the Jews could ever be won over completely to Orthodoxy. His prediction of how the Jewish problem would be solved was clear and simple: one third of them would convert, one third would emigrate, and one third would die.

Even a cursory examination of Tsar Alexander III's policies reveals the powerful impact of Pobedonostsev's views on the thinking of the man in the Winter Palace. On 14 August 1881, five and a half months after the assassination of Alexander II, the new ruler enacted a statute to enable the government to wage war against the opposition with a new weapon, the imposition of emergency regulations in any region of the empire. Widely applied during the last thirty-six years of the empire's existence even though it was initially enacted as a temporary measure, the statute has been called by Richard Pipes the 'real constitution' of the country. Its implementation demonstrated, perhaps more than anything else, that Russia was not a state based on law.

The statute provided for two kinds of special measures, 'Reinforced Security' (*Usilennaia Okhrana*) and 'Extraordinary Security' (*Chrezvychainaia Okhrana*). The first could be imposed by the minister of internal affairs or a governor-general acting with the minister's approval. The second could be imposed only with the approval of the tsar. Designed to facilitate the eradication of sedition, the statute was vague about what conditions would justify placing a region in a state of emergency, and gave the authorities in St. Petersburg considerable leeway in applying it. In addition to these emergency powers, the government could impose martial law on an area, which meant military rule, pure and simple.

The arbitrary power invested in local officials (governors-general, governors, and city governors) under the exceptional measures of 1881 was enormous. Under Reinforced Security, officials could keep citizens in prison for up to three months, impose fines, prohibit public gatherings, exile alleged offenders, transfer blocks of judicial cases from criminal to military courts, and dismiss *zemstvo* employees. Under Extraordinary Security, a region was placed under the authority of a commander-in-chief, who was empowered to dismiss elected *zemstvo* deputies and even to dissolve *zemstvos* completely, to suspend periodicals, and to close universities and other centers of advanced study for up to one month. Implementation of the exceptional measures depended largely on the inclinations of local officials: in some provinces they acted with restraint, whereas in others they used their powers to the utmost. Frequently, officials operating under the emergency rules exiled 'beggars, vagrants, and generally disorderly people'. There were times early in the twentieth century when sixty-nine percent of the provinces and regions of the Russian Empire were either completely or partially subjected to one of the various emergency codes.

In 1889, Tsar Alexander began to enact a series of counter-reforms that amounted to a major reversal of the reforms introduced in the 1860s and 1870s. Most important, he created a new post, that of land captain, and invested it with so much authority that the system of peasant self-rule, allegedly characterized by 'chaos and wild abuse', was greatly diluted. The Ministry of Internal Affairs retained ultimate control over the appointment of the land captains, who could nullify decisions of peasant assemblies and of communes, add items to their agendas, and remove peasant officials from their posts if they were considered to be 'unreliable'. The land captain could also void decisions of the canton courts and could on his own adjudicate certain civil and criminal cases. In creating the new office, the government had found a new way of blocking the peasants from gaining experience in self-government and in fulfilling the rights and obligations of citizenship.

The government took other steps to reduce the influence of the peasants in the body politic. In 1890, it issued a law providing for indirect election by peasants of *zemstvo* deputies and for a limitation on the number of deputies the peasants could elect (no more than 29.6 percent of the total number). The *zemstvos* themselves were also placed under new regulations: henceforth all elections and appointments of *zemstvo* officials had to be confirmed by provincial governors. Moreover, all decisions of *zemstvo* assemblies were subject to the approval of a governor or the minister of internal affairs. The Municipal Government Act of 1892 imposed similar changes on the franchise for urban *Dumas* (local legislatures) in cities and larger towns. The number of voters in St. Petersburg, for example, declined from 21,176 to 7,152.

In other spheres of public life, the government also pursued reactionary policies. It tightened the censorship of the press, it refused to uphold the principle of the irremovability of judges, and tried to do away with trial by jury. 'It is essential', the tsar contended, 'to get rid of this institution, in order to restore the significance of the court in Russia.' And the government made various efforts to reduce the number of students from the lower classes, already quite small, who attended high schools and universities. It raised educational fees and it encouraged educational administrators to sift out from the pools of applicants those who were likely to be 'politically unreliable'. At a time when only twenty-one percent of the population could read and write, the number of students in various types of high schools declined over a period of thirteen years (1882 to 1895) from 65,751 to 63,863. Jews were especially suspect and therefore placed under special restrictions. Not only were they ineligible to serve as deputies in the *zemstvos* and urban legislatures, but in 1887 the government set specific quotas on the number of Jews who could attend secondary schools or institutions of higher learning: in the Pale of Settlement, where most Jews lived, they could not exceed ten percent of the student body, and outside the Pale the figure was five percent. These measures not only negated the relatively liberal educational policies of Alexander II; they marked the first attempt in Russia to establish rigid quotas on the admission of students to educational institutions.

In 1894, Tsar Alexander III, only forty-nine years old, suddenly took ill with nephritis and died without having fully achieved his deepest aspiration, the transformation of Russia into a state along the lines envisioned by Pobedonostsev. True, Alexander had crushed the revolutionary movement and he had pursued a pacific foreign policy that enabled him to avoid costly foreign entanglements. It is also worth noting that he favored economic policies that promoted Russia's industrialization, a subject taken up in the next chapter. But it was not self-evident that he had created a new political order that would guarantee Russia the stability that he craved. It did not take long for the country to be embroiled in unprecedented social and political unrest. There is little doubt that Alexander III's policies, in going so forcefully against the currents of reform and liberalization, in the end did much to promote that unrest.

7

REVOLUTIONARY RUSSIA, 1894–1917

It would be hard to think of a man less suited to serve as auto-crat of a large empire in turmoil than Nicholas II, who ascended the throne in 1894. People acquainted with Nicholas were, in fact, alarmed at the prospect of his assuming ultimate author-ity. In October 1894, when it was clear that Alexander would not survive a serious illness, the minister of the navy, N. M. Chichaev, warned that the twenty-six-year-old Nicholas was 'a mere child, without experience, training, or even an inclination to study great problems of state . . . military service is the only subject that interests him . . . What will be the course of the ship of state under these conditions the Lord only knows.' Even a cursory examination of Nicholas's letters and diaries confirm the legitimacy of Chichaev's apprehensions.

A man of personal charm with strong religious convictions and deep affection for his wife and family, the tsar showed no serious interest in politics. In his diaries, he took pains to record how he spent his evenings with his family and his various sporting activities, going so far as to note the number of birds he bagged on his hunts. He could be deeply moved by such events as the loss of his favorite dog, Iman. 'I must confess,' he wrote in his diary on 20 October 1902, 'the whole day after that happened I never stopped crying – I still miss him dreadfully when I go for walks. He was such an intelligent, kind, and loyal dog!' Yet the great events of his rule – the wars with Japan and the Central Powers, the demands of liberals for a constitution, the industrial strikes, the violence of 1905, the breakdown of public order that year – received scant attention from him. He venerated his father's memory and believed that it was his 'sacred mission' to follow in his footsteps. Like his father, he felt he must be uncompromising in upholding the principle of autocracy, the only political idea for which he could muster any passion. On this issue he was much influenced by one of his father's favorite teachers, Pobedonostsev, whose retrograde ideas are examined in chapter 6.

Although moderately intelligent, Nicholas lacked the personal drive and vision to take charge of the government, to familiarize himself with the workings of the administration, and to instill a sense of purpose and direction in the ministers and bureaucracy. He was also a narrow-minded, prejudiced man, incapable of tolerating people who did not fit his conception of the true Russian. He especially disliked Jews and attributed his refusal to abolish restrictions on them to an 'inner voice' that told him it would be wrong to do so. Nor could he abide the intelligentsia, the one social group that, he believed, was not fully devoted to him.

Some people within the elite, prepared to give the new ruler the benefit of the doubt, thought that Nicholas might adopt policies more liberal than those of Alexander III. But Nicholas did not wait long before disabusing the optimists. Early in 1895 he told a delegation representing the nobility, the *zemstvos*, and the cities that they were entertaining 'senseless dreams' of participating 'in the affairs of internal administration'. He indicated that he intended to 'maintain the principle of autocracy just as firmly and unflinchingly as did my unforgettable father'.

But economic and social developments made it increasingly unlikely that he would be able to resist the pressures for political change. In the 1880s Russia had embarked on a new course, industrialization, and under the impetus of the dynamic S. Iu.

Witte, the minister of finance from 1894 to 1903, economic development proceeded rapidly. Witte promoted industrialization not because he believed that economic modernization was desirable in itself or because he wished to raise the standard of living of the Russian people; he wanted to transform the economy because that was the only way the country could maintain its status as a great power. As a political conservative, Witte believed that Russia could undergo economic modernization and still retain its ancient political and social institutions, a conviction he reluctantly abandoned during the revolutionary turbulence of 1905.

Always a major factor in the national economy, the state assumed an especially large role in stimulating industrialization. The government not only placed extremely high tariffs on foreign commodities and encouraged foreign investments and loans to Russian industrialists but also became directly involved in the economy. By 1912, when Russia was the fifth industrial power in the world, the state owned sixty-eight percent of all railways; by 1899 almost one-third of all metallurgical products were bought by the state; from 1903 to 1913 the government received over twenty-five percent of its income from its various holdings rather than from taxes. Another important characteristic of Russian industrialization was the prevalence of very large enterprises. In 1866, forty-three percent of the workers in the cotton industry were employed at plants with more than one hundred employees; in 1877, fifty-one percent; in 1894, seventy-two percent. The proportion of workers employed in factories with more than one thousand employees was three times as large in Russia as in Germany, generally considered to be the pacesetter in industrial concentration.

The concentration of industry facilitated both the formation of trade unions and the growth of political activism among workers, who, it must be stressed, constituted no more than 2.4 percent of the total population in the early twentieth century. The government's policies on the relations between workers and employers also contributed to restlessness among workers. The authorities insisted on transferring the allegedly benign, patriarchal relations between landlord and peasants to the industrial sector of the economy, where employers were to treat their workers with compassion but also with sternness if they did not follow the rules. The government claimed that their approach was entirely successful, and until 1905 it denied that there was any labor problem at all. Many senior officials knew better, but any public acknowledgement that the patriarchal relationship might not be applicable to the modern industrial setting was considered tantamount to denying the legitimacy of the social order under tsarism.

The system of disciplinary paternalism that prevailed in the factories was harsh. The Penal Code of 1845, for example, branded collective resistance to employers as illegal, punishable by fifteen to twenty years of hard labor, which meant that trade unions could not lawfully be formed to seek improvement in the grim conditions in factories. Until 1897, a working day of thirteen hours was the norm; that year, the working day was shortened to eleven and a half hours. Laborers, many of whom still returned for part of the year to their villages for field work, were generally housed in large, unsanitary barracks. Within the plant, the managers and owners treated the workers condescendingly: they addressed them in the familiar 'thou', searched them for stolen goods whenever they left the factory, and fined them for infractions of the strict 'Rules of Internal Order'. Workers deeply resented these humiliations, and during the revolutions of 1905 and 1917 their lists of grievances almost invariably included demands for polite treatment by factory officials.

By the late nineteenth century, it became apparent that Russian workers would not indefinitely accept their status of inferiority and that they would not remain docile. The most striking evidence for the change in mood was the growing strike movement. Between 1862 and 1869, only six strikes and twenty-nine disturbances in factories were recorded. By 1885, the annual number of such disorders had risen to twenty; between 1895 and 1904, that number was about 176. In 1902 alone, there were 550 strikes involving 138,877 workers. Dissatisfaction with economic conditions caused most strikes, but every time workers engaged in a work stoppage they contravened the law, which prohibited strikes, and thus they were also making a political statement. By 1905, a large number of the men and women who went on strike included specifically political demands in their list of grievances.

In the meantime, a small group of Russian intellectuals had founded a Marxist movement that claimed to represent the interests of the working class. The Marxists contended that Russia's development would be similar to that of Central and Western Europe. The country would be industrialized and would then undergo a bourgeois revolution by which the autocratic system would be replaced by a constitutional order dominated by the middle classes committed to capitalism. Eventually, when industrialization had reached maturity and the proletariat had become a powerful force, it would stage a second, socialist revolution. In 1898, the Russian Marxists formed the Russian Social Democratic Workers Party, which five years later split into Bolshevik and Menshevik factions.

The split occurred over the seemingly minor question of how to define a party member, but it soon turned out that the differences between the Bolsheviks (majoritarians) led by Vladimir Lenin (Ulyanov) and the Mensheviks (minoritarians) led by Iulii Martov and Pavel Axelrod touched on fundamental issues. Lenin, in keeping with views he had expressed in 1902 in his *What Is to Be Done?*, favored a highly centralized, elitist, hierarchically organized political party, whereas the Mensheviks stressed the necessity and desirability of broad working-class participation in the movement's affairs and in the coming revolutionary events. In short order, it also became evident that, although both factions subscribed to a revolutionary course, the Mensheviks tended to adopt more moderate tactics than did the Bolsheviks.

Less doctrinaire, but equally militant, was the party of Socialist Revolutionaries (SRs), who claimed to speak for the peasants. The heirs of the populists of the 1870s, the SRs formally created a political party in 1901 committed to the idea that, since most people in Russia had been exposed to the egalitarian principles of the commune, the country could attain socialism without passing through the stage of full-blown capitalism. The party advocated the transfer of all land to peasant communes or local associations, which in turn would assign it on an egalitarian basis to everyone who wished to earn their living by farming. Industry would be similarly socialized. Although the SRs insisted that the final goal, socialism, must be achieved by means of persuasion, they tolerated the 'Combat Organization', an independent organ of the party that carried out dozens of political murders. Political terror, many SRs believed, was necessary to bring about the dismantling of the autocratic regime.

Liberalism had also emerged as an organized force. Initially, as has been noted, people associated with the *zemstvos* advocated liberalization of the political system. They were joined in the late 1890s by a variety of liberal lawyers, doctors, writers, and professors. Highly articulate, these intellectuals soon exerted an influence on the national scene far out of proportion to their numbers in the population. Industrialists and businessmen in general were slower to take up the liberal cause; their economic dependence on the state made them politically cautious.

The liberals favored a fundamental reordering of society. They advocated the rule of law, the granting of civil liberties to all citizens, a sharp curtailment in the powers of the monarch, and the creation of a legislative body elected by the people. The journal they founded in 1902, *Osvobozhdenie*, and their underground organization, the Union of Liberation, formed in 1904, helped mobilize public opinion against the old order and thus set the stage for the first Russian revolution.

THE REVOLUTION OF 1905

Unwittingly, the government facilitated the growth of the opposition movement by bumbling into a catastrophic war with Japan

in 1904. Although the charge that the Russian government deliberately provoked Japan to stave off revolution has never been
proved and is probably unfounded, there can be no doubt that
elements within the tsarist government mindlessly pursued a
foreign policy in the Far East that the Japanese were bound to
regard as provocative. In the 1890s, Russia abandoned its generally cautious policy in the Pacific region and committed itself to
an assertive forward policy. Alarmed at Japan's emergence as a
strong, aggressive power as well as China's weakness, and eager to
promote Russia's economic development, the government in St.
Petersburg adopted various measures to extend its influence over
two regions also coveted by Japan: Manchuria, which was part of
China, and Korea, an autonomous kingdom under the suzerainty
of the Chinese emperor. Most importantly, the Russian government in 1891 decided to construct the Trans-Siberian Railroad.
Witte, who vigorously promoted the railway project during his
tenure as minister of finance, was interested primarily in the
economic exploitation of an area rich in resources and markets.
At the same time, he favored a cautious foreign policy that would
avoid needless provocation of other powers. Russian diplomats,
however, adopted an aggressive stance towards Japan and on
several occasions during the 1890s forced Japan to pull back
from positions on the mainland. These humiliations produced a
'paroxysm of public indignation' among the Japanese, who now
embarked on a program of massive rearmament.

Early in the twentieth century, hostility between the two
powers reached a climax. Japan had vastly expanded its economic
and political influence over Korea, whereas Russia had extended
its influence over neighboring Manchuria. When a Russian
speculator, A. M. Bezobrazov, received a concession from the
Korean government to cut timber on the Yalu and Tumen rivers,
the Japanese government became alarmed. To lower tensions,
it proposed an arrangement whereby Russia would be granted
predominance in Manchuria in return for Japan's predominance
in Korea, and in January 1904 the Japanese pressed St. Petersburg
for a speedy reply. When none was forthcoming, they decided on

a course of action they had believed to be unavoidable for some time. On 26 January they launched a surprise attack on Russian ships at Port Arthur and Chemulpo.

Once war began, it quickly emerged that Japan enjoyed enormous advantages. Its troops and naval forces were better trained, its intelligence services were more effective, and, unlike Russia, it did not face the enormously difficult task of having to transport reinforcements almost 4,400 miles over a railway system that was still quite primitive. From the moment of Japan's attack, Russia suffered one humiliating defeat after another, at sea and on land. As is generally true in the early stages of a military conflict, the public rallied to the government's support. But within a few months, as it became evident that the tsarist government had totally misjudged both the strength of the Japanese military as well as the prowess and competence of its own military, public opinion began to shift dramatically.

Many thoughtful citizens in Russia now questioned not only the wisdom of waging war but also the legitimacy of the entire political system. In the fall and winter of 1904–5, the liberals, who had held their fire so long as the government seemed to enjoy wide support, unleashed an extensive campaign (the so-called 'banquet campaign') for constitutional change. It was remarkably effective and marked the beginning of a nationwide assault on the autocracy that lasted two and a half years. Modeled on the famous banquets in Paris in 1847–8 that inspired a revolution throughout much of Europe, the campaign in Russia also had a clearly political focus and was therefore illegal. Sensing the depth of discontent, the government reluctantly allowed the meetings on the understanding that all the gatherings would be 'private'.

The rash of political meetings in conjunction with hearty meals – some thirty-eight in twenty-six cities – surprised society and seemed to suggest that the authorities had lost confidence in their ability to continue to rule without taking into account the wishes of the people. Never before had so many citizens, most of them from the educated classes, joined forces to give vent to their profound unhappiness with the state of affairs.

The banquets adopted various resolutions, but to one degree or another all contributed to mobilizing support for the demands of liberal activists. They called for civil liberties, amnesty for political prisoners, and a democratically elected constituent assembly.

The banquets were a prelude to the dramatic events on 'Bloody Sunday' (9 January 1905), which proved to be decisive in transforming what had been a peaceful campaign for reform by relatively small sectors of society into a national offensive against the old order that eventually enlisted the support of a huge number of workers, peasants, and national minorities. Ironically, even the procession of workers on that fateful Sunday had been intended as a peaceful affair. It was organized by Father Gapon, a mercurial and enigmatic figure. The workers and their families, numbering somewhere between fifty thousand and a hundred thousand, marched on the Winter Palace with a petition that amounted to a desperate plea to the tsar, still referred to as 'the father', to treat his subjects, as a matter of conscience, not as slaves but as human beings, and to institute reforms to lighten their burdens. In calling for a constituent assembly elected on the basis of democratic suffrage, civil liberties for all citizens, the right to establish trade unions, and an eight-hour working day, Gapon clearly aligned his followers with the political opposition that had turned increasingly vocal and militant in 1904. However, the petition did not demand the abolition of the monarchy or the introduction of socialism. Nor did it contain threats of violence.

Nevertheless, the government, out of fear, meanness, or simple stupidity, decided to disperse the procession, by force if necessary. When the marchers did not heed the officers' orders to disperse, soldiers began to shoot indiscriminately into the crowds, killing 130 and seriously wounding close to three hundred. The fury of the people in the streets was uncontrollable, as was the anger of citizens throughout the empire. Indeed, the massacre electrified public opinion in virtually every region of the country. It was widely believed that the tsar had lost the affection of vast numbers of people and that his authority and legitimacy had been greatly undermined. In this sense, Bloody Sunday was a pivotal event not only in the revolution but in the history of Russia.

The revolution now proceeded at a rapid pace. The industrial proletariat for the first time became a social and political force to be reckoned with by participating in massive strikes throughout the empire in support of wide-ranging demands. It is noteworthy, however, that none of the political parties of the left had played a significant role in preparing the procession. Bolshevik agitators who appeared at preparatory meetings for the purpose of radicalizing the crowds were shouted down and occasionally even hauled off the platform. Not until the spring and summer of 1905 did large numbers of workers become politicized; they now began to demand an end to the war and an end to autocratic rule. Even then, however, political activists did not exert a decisive influence over the mass protest movements, which were essentially spontaneous expressions of outrage against the authorities.

Within weeks of Bloody Sunday, virtually every sector of society was caught up in the turbulence: students at universities and high schools went on strike; disorders erupted in the borderlands where the minority populations resented the heavy hand of the Russian masters; peasants staged attacks on landlords' estates; middle-class people ignored the government's regulations on public meetings and censorship of the press; and on numerous occasions soldiers and sailors mutinied. It seemed as though the fabric of society was coming apart.

The government could not cope with the growing unrest. Instead of settling on a firm course of action, it alternated between strident assertions of the autocratic principle and half-hearted promises of reform, neither of which made much of an impression on most people. Had the government quickly made some far-reaching concessions, such as the establishment of the rule of law and the creation of an elected parliament with real powers, it might well have succeeded in separating the moderates and centrists from the revolutionary left within the opposition movement. But the tsar was unwilling to tamper with the institution of autocracy, and the result was a deepening of the revolution.

The high point came in October 1905, when a general strike brought the government to its knees. Unprecedented in scope, the strike was a spontaneous affair; no one planned it, no one organized it, and it spread rapidly. Although workers took the lead, they received the backing of the middle classes, who viewed the strike primarily as a weapon to wrest political concessions from the tsar. The opposition could act in unison because the political issue, the elimination of the autocratic regime, had assumed center stage. One city after another literally came to a standstill, and the government had no choice but to yield, especially since it was not sure that it could count on the army to obey orders to crush the strikes by force. On 17 October, the tsar reluctantly accepted the advice of Witte, who had just been appointed prime minister, to issue the October Manifesto, which promised civil liberties and the establishment of an elected legislature (*Duma*) with substantial powers. Most significantly, the tsar committed himself not to enact any law without the approval of the legislature. In conceding that he was no longer the sole repository of political power, Nicholas did what he had vowed never to do: he abandoned the principle of autocracy.

It was a great victory for the opposition. Had it been consolidated, the Russian Empire would have been on the road towards a Western-style constitutional state. For about seven weeks, from 18 October until early December, a period known as the 'Days of Liberty', the country enjoyed so much freedom that some observers considered the new conditions dangerous, because extremists would now be able to increase their support among the masses. The press could publish whatever it pleased, workers could form trade unions, political parties could be established, and they could freely publicize their programs. But the pessimists were prescient. It quickly emerged that the new order faced a series of intractable problems that the tsar and his followers, who believed that they had suffered only a temporary defeat, could not adequately deal with. On 18 October, one day after the issuance of the October Manifesto, large numbers of people, enraged at the government's surrender to the opposition,

violently and indiscriminately attacked Jews and anyone else
presumed to have been hostile to the old regime. Over a period of
about two weeks 690 anti-Jewish pogroms erupted, most of them
in the south-western provinces. Eight hundred and seventy-six
people were killed and between seventy thousand and eighty
thousand injured. In a few cities Jews lost property estimated
to have been worth more than a million rubles. Altogether, the
damage to property during the pogroms has been calculated to
be 6.2 million rubles. To one sober commentator it seemed that
'complete governmental anarchy' prevailed in Russia.

There has been much controversy about the origins of the
pogroms, the worst in Russian history up to that time, and about
the role of the authorities. It is known that on the local level,
officials and policemen either encouraged people to attack Jews
or looked the other way once the attacks began, but there is no
evidence that the unrest was orchestrated by the government in
St. Petersburg. In part, the violence can be traced to the rage of
those who feared that the demonstrations in favor of the manifesto signified the end of a social order in which they enjoyed a
special status that they wished to preserve. To a degree, then,
the violence from below was a spontaneous response by various groups determined to crush the opposition and to preserve
the old order. In addition, much of the reckless plundering and
beating of innocent civilians was the work of riffraff motivated
largely by prejudice and a craving for loot. But peasants, shop-
keepers, coachmen, janitors, and even some workers (though not
any who belonged to trade unions) also lent a hand, for much
the same reasons. For these people, however, another factor
played a role. They found unbearable the sight of multitudes of
ordinary Russians, among them many Jews and rowdy students,
celebrating their victory over the revered tsar, often by defiling
his portrait. For nine months the 'upstarts' had defied authority
more or less with impunity; now they had apparently succeeded
in bringing down the entire political system, and with it the hierarchical structure on which Russian society had been based. If
the autocracy could no longer restrain them, those who yearned

to maintain the old order, because they felt secure within it, would have to take the law into their own hands.

The government's failure to maintain order was not the only sign of its weakness. Throughout the country the soviets (councils of workers' deputies) that had appeared quite spontaneously as strike committees during the general strike vastly expanded their operations. The Petersburg Soviet, the most prominent in the empire, challenged the government's authority at one turn after another. It made its presence felt in particular during strikes, when it sent directives to government agencies such as the Post Office and the railroads, and entered into negotiations with the St. Petersburg City Council – and once even with Prime Minister Witte himself. The Soviet also sent numerous inquiries to government offices, and officials were often sufficiently impressed by the Soviet's authority to go to the trouble of answering. The Soviet also organized collections of money for unemployed workers and distributed thirty kopeks a day to adults and ten to fifteen to children. Moreover, it set up several inexpensive dining halls for the unemployed and their families. The boldest undertaking of the Soviet was the establishment of its own militia, numbering, according to some estimates, six thousand men. The militiamen wore special armbands and frequently interfered in police matters, going so far as to issue orders to policemen, many of whom were so confused by the troubled state of affairs that they gave in to the militiamen. A leading newspaper complained that there were really two governments, one led by Count Witte and one by G. S. Khrustalev-Nosar, the chairman of the Petersburg Soviet, and that no one knew who would arrest whom first.

The countryside also became restive during the Days of Liberty. From 23 October 1905 until mid November there were no less than 796 major and minor incidents of peasant unrest in 478 districts in the forty-seven provinces of European Russia and in parts of the Caucasus, the Baltic provinces, and Poland. The basic pattern of the disorders was similar to that of the earlier period: peasants cut down timber, refused to pay taxes, and took grain from estates owned by the nobility. In many regions agricultural workers staged strikes. But this new wave of the peasant movement was more violent than the one in the spring and summer. For example, in Tambov alone, buildings on 130 estates were burned down. It was also more common for peasants to seize land for 'temporary use', that is, until the State Duma, expected to meet soon, approved the seizures. Although violence against individuals also increased, it was still not widespread, in part because landlords made their escape before the arrival of marauding peasants. The peasant unrest subsided late in 1905, only to resume with renewed vigor in the period from May to August 1906. By the time the revolution ended in 1907, the empire had endured the most intense wave of agrarian upheaval since the Pugachev peasant rebellion of 1773–5. Total losses in European Russia alone amounted to twenty-nine million rubles.

The government could not always resort to its customary response to peasant unrest – massive force – because many men in the military services had themselves become unruly. These men chose to believe that the tsar's concession in granting the October Manifesto gave them license to ignore rules and regulations that they found burdensome. The manifesto itself made no reference at all to civil liberties for soldiers and sailors, but that was immaterial. The tsar had given in to the opposition, authority in the civilian sector had collapsed, and to men in the military it seemed as though they, too, were no longer bound by the old constraints. All told, 211 separate mutinies were recorded in the Russian army between late October and mid December 1905, though very few were accompanied by violence. In most of them, the men simply refused to obey orders, left their barracks, held meetings to discuss current affairs, and talked back to their officers. Although the elite corps, the cavalry and Cossacks, were virtually untouched by mutiny, one-third of all infantry units experienced some form of disturbance, and the navy was so riddled with disorder that the government feared that it could no longer be relied upon to carry out its mission. The minister of war, General Rediger, thought that the country was threatened with 'total ruin'. However, the government was never totally bereft of loyal troops, and in the end it could count on enough of them to restore order in the military and the country at large.

OUTCOME OF THE REVOLUTION

The last gasp of the radical phase of the revolution took place in December 1905, when workers in Moscow, under the leadership of the Bolsheviks and other revolutionaries, staged an uprising that triggered the bloodiest domestic strife of the revolution. Perturbed by a wide-ranging police crackdown, which included the arrest on 3 December of the Executive Committee of the Petersburg Soviet and two hundred of its deputies, the radicals in Moscow decided on a desperate attempt to overthrow the government by initiating a rebellion in the hope that it would quickly spread throughout the empire. At first, it seemed as though the insurgents might be able to seize the centers of government authority in Moscow. Some eighty thousand workers went on strike in support of the uprising, the economy ground to a virtual standstill, and, surprisingly, the troops were withdrawn from the streets, apparently out of fear that they might not be reliable in hand-to-hand combat. But it soon turned out that Admiral F. V. Dubasov, who had been appointed governor-general of Moscow late in November, would not be reluctant to use all the force under his command – some six thousand soldiers, two thousand policemen, and a division of gendarmes – to crush the rebels. On 10 December, he ordered the use of light artillery to dislodge the revolutionaries from their strongholds. It was the first time that such heavy weapons had been used in a domestic disturbance and, predictably, this aroused profound anger even among people unsympathetic to the insurgents. Within five days the government prevailed, though at a terrible price. One thousand and fifty-nine Muscovites, most of them civilians not involved in the fighting, were killed. Of these, 137 were women and eighty-six were children. Twenty-five policemen and nine soldiers lost their lives.

To consolidate their victory, the authorities unleashed a crack-down not only in Moscow but in other regions of the empire. The government's most devastating and brutal weapon against the radicals was the punitive expedition, an organized attack on individuals believed to be hostile to the government by small groups of specially selected troops in regions either controlled by radicals or in a state of unrest. The idea behind the punitive expeditions was not only to root out unrest but to intimidate the population by publicly, quickly, and ruthlessly punishing partici-pants in disturbances or people suspected of having participated in them. It was, in short, a form of state terror directed at its own citizens. There is no hard evidence of the total number of victims of this campaign. According to one estimate, between December 1905 and late May 1906, 1,170 people were killed in the Baltic region, admittedly one of the more turbulent parts of the empire. Not surprisingly, the government's repressive policy proved to be effective. Within about four months, the revolutionary movement was in retreat everywhere, incapable of holding the line against the authorities.

Yet the government did not seek to turn back the clock to 1904. It allowed the election of the State Duma to go forward and, on the whole, it was a fair election in which some twenty to twenty-five million citizens participated. Convinced that the peasants were still loyal to the tsar, the government had devised complicated procedures that assigned to them about forty-two percent of electors who made the final choice of Duma deputies. The landowners were assigned close to thirty-three percent of the electors, the town dwellers more than twenty-two percent, and the workers two and a half percent. This worked out at one elector for every two thousand landowners, thirty thousand peasants, and ninety thousand workers, and four thousand other subjects living in the cities. But the government had completely misjudged the mood of the people. The overwhelming majority of the deputies belonged to parties in opposition to the prevailing order. The newly formed Octobrist Party, which expressed satis-faction with changes in the political system introduced by the

October Manifesto, elected only thirteen deputies, the extreme right not one. The Kadets, or Constitutional Democrats, who favored a parliamentary system of government, were the largest single party with 185 deputies and dominated the proceedings of the first and second Duma.

It was predictable that a Duma with this complexion would not be able to cooperate with the tsarist regime, which still held the upper hand. The Fundamental Laws of 1906 stipulated that despite the existence of an elected parliament the tsar retained the power to appoint the cabinet as well as the right to veto measures adopted by the legislature. Moreover, he controlled the administration of the empire, determined foreign policy, commanded the military forces, and had the right to impose martial law or states of emergency on regions beset by unrest. Separately, Nicholas had changed the composition and authority of the State Council, giving it coequal powers with the Duma, whose competence was thus severely circumscribed. Once the Duma met, on 27 April 1906, the relationship between it and the government quickly turned acrimonious. There were many conflicts between them, but two were the most critical in sealing the fate of the legislature. First, the Duma offended the government by unanimously calling for political changes of the most fundamental kind, changes that would have transformed the country into a constitutional monarchy with paramount authority vested in the Duma. Then the Duma further enraged the government by considering several measures to deal with the agrarian issue, all of which, to one degree or another, called for compulsory alienation of privately owned land and its distribution to land-hungry peasants. The prime minister, I. L. Goremykin, a reactionary of limited ability, never took the Duma seriously and instructed his ministries not to attend any of its sessions. When the Duma refused to yield on its demands, the government dissolved it. It had existed for only seventy-two days and had held only forty sessions.

The Kadets protested vigorously. They met in Vyborg (Finland) and issued a call for passive resistance, but the response of the Russian people was muted. Exhausted from a year and a half of

turbulence, confronted in many cities with the threat of unemployment, the masses in the summer of 1906 were much more
reluctant to defy the authorities than they had been in 1905.
Moreover, an effective campaign of passive resistance requires
extensive preparation and organization. Surprisingly, the Kadets
did not seem to realize this, for they had done virtually nothing to
prepare the ground for an organized response to the dissolution.
They simply assumed that the masses were still in a militant and
activist mood.

But within a few months it turned out that the government,
too, had miscalculated badly. It had assumed that a new election
for a second Duma, held under the same electoral procedures,
would yield a more pliant legislature. In fact, the membership
of the second Duma, which began its meetings on 20 February
1907, was much more radical than the first. True, the moderate
Octobrists increased their strength from thirteen to forty-four,
and the extremists on the right, without any representation in
the first Duma, elected ten deputies and could count on
the support of some fifty-four from other small groups. But the
number of left-wing deputies jumped from 111 to 222. The
parties of the center suffered a serious decline: the Kadets and
their adherents won ninety-nine seats.

The clashes between the government and the legislature that
had plagued the first Duma recurred, but there was one important
difference. The government was now led by an able and vigorous
man, P. A. Stolypin, a former governor of Saratov who had displayed
considerable skill and toughness in dealing with the opposition and
who had a vision, conservative to be sure, for the restructuring of
the country. He was also an eloquent orator capable of more than
holding his own in debates with the opposition. He made what
were perhaps his most memorable pronouncements during heated
debates with the left. On one occasion he accused them of seeking to 'paralyze the government . . . [with attacks that all] amount
to two words addressed to the authorities: "Hands up." To these
two words, gentlemen, the government must respond, in complete
calm and secure in the knowledge that it is in the right, with only

two words: "Not afraid."' On another occasion he taunted the left with the words 'They need great upheavals, we need a great Russia!' When he decided that this Duma, like the first one, took stands on the agrarian issue and on political change that made cooperation with it impossible, he unceremoniously dissolved it again (on 3 June 1907), but this time he fundamentally changed the electoral law by depriving many peasants and minorities of the vote, ensuring the election of a conservative Duma. This marked the end of the revolution of 1905.

On the surface, the failure of the revolution seems puzzling. Never before had any European revolution been spearheaded by four popular movements, the middle class, the industrial proletariat, the peasantry, and national minorities. If the opposition was so pervasive, why was the government able to survive? One important reason was that the various sectors of the opposition did not act as a unified force, did not simultaneously attack the old order. Each one of the defiant groups acted more or less independently, which diluted the pressure on the government. When several movements (workers, professional groups, and some industrialists) did coalesce in October 1905, the government had no choice but to make far-reaching concessions. But the disagreements between liberals and socialists, to mention only one source of conflict, were too deep for prolonged cooperation between them. The liberals by and large did not favor a republic or socialism. Nor did they support violent methods of struggle against tsarism. And when the radicals took up arms late in 1905, the army, though plagued by disorder, in the end proved to be a reliable instrument for repressing unrest in the cities and the countryside. Finally, in 1906, foreign governments strengthened the tsarist regime by advancing substantial loans to it.

STOLYPIN'S REFORMS

Although the revolution had been defeated, the Russia of 1907 was different in several important respects from the Russia of

1904. The very existence of an elected legislature, whose approval was necessary for the enactment of most laws, diminished the powers of the tsar and the bureaucracy. The landed gentry, the business class, and the upper stratum of the peasantry, all of whom continued to participate in the election of the Duma, now exercised some influence in public affairs. Moreover, trade unions and various associations of cooperatives remained active, and censorship of the press and other publications was much less stringent. In short, Russia had taken a modest step away from autocracy and towards the creation of a civil society.

Well before dissolving the second Duma, Stolypin had launched his reform program. Although he did not shy away from repression, he contended that it alone could not restore order and establish a stable and prosperous society. His single most important reform, with which his name has always been identified, sought to transform the agrarian sector of the Russian economy, still the source of income for over eighty percent of the population. For some time, Stolypin had argued that the elimination of the commune was necessary to overcome economic backwardness and to stimulate economic growth. He was certainly not the first to make this point, but he was the first to translate abstract ideas about agrarian reform into reality. Stolypin's interest in eliminating the commune was not dictated only by a desire to improve the economy. He was convinced that the planned changes in the countryside would affect the peasants' attitudes on a whole range of issues, fundamentally altering the outlook of most of the people in Russia. The most critical problem, according to Stolypin, was that the peasants were wholly lacking in civic spirit; they did not respect the laws and they had no developed sense of civic obligation. In short, the peasants were not yet 'citizens' in the full meaning of the word. His goal, Stolypin stressed, was to transform them into citizens by giving them a stake in society, by making them realize that order and discipline were in their interest. 'Private peasant ownership', he wrote in a memorandum he submitted to the tsar in 1905, 'is a guarantee of order, because each small owner represents the nucleus on which rests the stability of the State.' Though radical in overturning an established institution, Stolypin's reform was designed to serve a conservative purpose, that is, to turn the peasantry into a force that would favor political stability.

Stolypin began the process of agrarian reform in August 1906 with the announcement that the government would make available for sale to peasants a modest amount of land from the state, the tsar's personal holdings, and the properties of the imperial family. Then, a *ukase* enacted by the government on 5 October provided for an extension of civil and personal rights to the peasants, narrowing the distinction between them and other classes and thereby conferring many of the attributes of citizenship on them. Peasants were now permitted to work in administrative agencies of the state, to attend educational institutions without prior permission from the commune, and to retain ties with their village communities if they entered the civil service or some other profession. But by far the most significant reform was embodied in the *ukase* of 9 November. It permitted every head of a peasant family who held land in a commune to claim it as private property. The precise conditions for the transfer would have to be worked out, but the communal assembly could no longer as a matter of law prevent such transfer. In addition, the *ukase* of 9 November made it easier for peasants to bring about consolidated ownership of the strips into which the land was divided. Until the reform, a unanimous vote of the communal assembly was needed before any consolidation could be enacted; now an affirmative vote by two-thirds of the assembly sufficed. The *ukase* was enacted under Article 87 of the Fundamental Laws, which permitted the government to rule by decree when the Duma was in recess; such a decree, however, became a dead letter if it were not confirmed by both houses of the legislature within two months after they reconvened. Article 87 was meant to allow the government to enact laws only in an emergency, and many within the opposition rightly contended that Stolypin was abusing his authority in resorting to it to enact measures that should have been considered by the Duma.

The implementation of the reform was bound to be complicated and slow. For one thing, many peasants out of sheer inertia rejected the very idea of seceding from the commune. Many others, committed to the principle of egalitarianism, feared that the new law would inevitably produce greater inequalities in the villages. Personal and social considerations also militated against the success of the reform. Women, especially those whose husbands spent large parts of the year working in distant cities, felt comfortable with the social life in the village and feared the isolation that would invariably accompany secession from the commune. They would have to live on farms far removed from their previous neighbors. But there were other practical impediments that slowed down implementation of the reform. It was extremely difficult for the land organization commissions set up by the authorities to decide which land was to be given to the separator: they had to take into account such matters as access to roads, wells, and the drainage system, and they had to decide how to divide lands of widely different quality into equitable plots.

An unqualified judgment on the effectiveness of Stolypin's agrarian reforms is difficult to make. His most ardent admirers claim that because of the outbreak of World War I and the revolution of 1917 the reforms could not be fully implemented and that it is therefore unfair to belabor these reforms for failing to change Russia's political landscape. But an examination of the reform process indicates that it was very slow to begin with and had become markedly slower well before 1914. The number of applications for secession reached its high point in 1909 and declined sharply thereafter. Some 508,000 households left the commune in 1908, 580,000 in 1909, and 342,000 in 1910. In 1913, the number shrank to 135,000. By 1914, only twenty percent of the peasants had obtained ownership of their land, and fourteen percent of the land had been withdrawn from communal tenure. Strip consolidation developed at an even slower pace. By late 1916, only 10.7 percent of the peasant households in European Russia worked land that was enclosed. On the other hand, Stolypin's contention that his reform was not designed to benefit only or primarily the richer peasants was substantiated. The main beneficiaries were peasants with average-sized holdings, who proved to be most eager to take advantage of the new law. Nonetheless, the process of privatization and consolidation would have taken many years to reach even a majority of the peasants. Whether in the meantime political stability, Stolypin's goal, could have been achieved remains an open question.

Stolypin himself did not supervise the implementation of his reform for very long. In September 1911, he was assassinated by a troubled man whose motives remain unclear. The assassin had been an informer for the secret police and had also expressed his support for the Socialist Revolutionaries. To this day, historians differ over whether he was serving the revolutionary or tsarist cause or acting purely on his own.[1] In any case, Stolypin's death brought to an end the last major effort under tsarism to reform the social and political order. Stolypin had tried to modernize the country in various ways, but his success was limited. He did expand public education and he managed to introduce measures to provide accident or illness insurance for certain categories of workers (about twenty percent of the country's workforce). But his efforts to liberalize religious laws to make the state more tolerant of minorities, to improve the efficiency of local governments, and to lift some of the restrictions imposed on the Jews all came to naught. The opposition of the ultra-conservatives among the nobility and the failure of the tsar to back him up proved to be his undoing.

Stolypin's successor as prime minister, V. N. Kokovtsov, showed little interest in reform, and, in any case, he was not a strong leader capable of implementing measures that disturbed the status quo. In dealing with defiant citizens his government did not take to heart the lessons of 1905. Early in 1912, troops fired on a crowd of about five thousand strikers at the Lena gold mines in eastern Siberia, killing some two hundred and wounding many more. The minister of internal affairs, A. A. Makarov, declared that the soldiers could do nothing but shoot at a crowd that was marching towards them. 'That', he said, 'is how it has been and that is how it will be in the future.' This callous reaction of the government to the massacre enraged many Duma deputies and society at large. The massacre triggered increased militancy in the labor movement, which manifested itself in victories by the Bolsheviks over the more moderate Mensheviks in several important labor union elections. And in 1914 there was an upsurge in industrial strikes. Thus, Tsar Nicholas faced what turned out to be his severest challenge, war with Germany, without having come to grips with the social, political, and economic problems that kept society dangerously fragmented.

WORLD WAR I

The results of the First World War (1914–18) are indisputable: horrible human and economic devastation, the collapse of monarchical rule in three major countries (Russia, Austria-Hungary, and Germany), significant changes in national boundaries, abiding hatreds between the victors and the defeated. Moreover, there is little doubt that neither communism nor National Socialism would have triumphed in Russia and Germany, respectively, had it not been for the suffering and despair generated by the war. The causes of the war, however, are not so evident. In the spring of 1914, no responsible leader in Europe wanted to lead his country into military conflict, much less into a conflict that would be worldwide. In a sense, at the crucial moments in July and August of that year, the leaders of the major countries were the captives of policies that their predecessors had followed over the preceding few decades.

After Bismarck unified Germany in 1871 and annexed Alsace-Lorraine, relations between Germany and France were bound to be extremely hostile. To isolate France and to prevent Germany from having to fight a two-front war, Bismarck pursued two policies, which became the backbone of his overall foreign policy: he formed a strong alliance with Austria-Hungary and he maintained good relations with Russia. To remain on good terms with the two powers in the east was not easy, since Russia and Austria-Hungary were rivals for influence in the Balkans. But Bismarck, a genius at diplomacy, managed it with remarkable success. In 1890, however, the new kaiser, Wilhelm II, decided, very rashly, on a new course. An erratic and aggressive man, Wilhelm dismissed Bismarck and changed the country's foreign policy in drastic ways. He ended the friendly relations with Russia and after a few years in office embarked on a provocative program of naval construction and colonial expansion. Great Britain, deeply troubled by the emergence of a new and aggressive naval power, established close ties with France, which had already formed an alliance with Russia (in 1894). By the early twentieth century, then, Europe was divided into two strong groups: the Triple Alliance (Germany and Austria-Hungary, joined in 1882 by Italy) and the Triple Entente (Great Britain, France, and Russia). All the countries in the two alliances devoted an increasing portion of their wealth to strengthening their military forces.

Alliances by themselves do not cause wars; they simply shed light on how nations at any particular moment view their national interests. But in times of crisis, when nationalistic passions run high, alliances often influence politicians by encouraging them to think that they have a stronger hand than they really have. The crisis of 1914 began on 28 June, when Archduke Franz Ferdinand, the heir to the Habsburg throne in Vienna, and his wife were assassinated in Sarajevo, the capital of Bosnia, a province populated largely by Slavs that Austria-Hungary had annexed in 1908. Vienna was convinced that Serbia wished to gain control over Bosnia as part of its plan to establish a new state, Yugoslavia, which would incorporate all Southern Slavs. For the Austro-Hungarian Empire, composed of several minorities, such a development was anathema, since it would most likely lead to the unraveling of that multinational state. After receiving a blank check from Germany to deal with the crisis, Vienna took a provocative and aggressive step. It sent an ultimatum to Serbia demanding not only the suppression of all anti-Austrian agitation in Serbia but also the participation of Austrians in the govern-ment's crackdown. No sovereign government could accept such conditions, and Serbia was no exception. On 28 July, Austria-Hungary declared war on Serbia.

Ideology as much as anything else dictated the policy of Russian statesmen during the international crisis. Long the protector of 'her little Slav brother', Russia, the country's elite widely believed, could not stand aside and allow fellow Slavs to be subjugated. Still, in response to a final plea from the kaiser to avoid any irrevocable action, Tsar Nicholas rescinded an order he had given for general mobilization and ordered, instead, a partial mobilization directed only at Austria-Hungary. But when his generals and his foreign minister, S. D. Sazonov, advised him that, since there were no plans for a partial mobilization, he should revert to the original order, Nicholas complied, setting off a chain reaction. Germany quickly followed suit in ordering mobilization of its forces, as did France. After some hesitation, Great Britain entered the conflict on 4 August on the side of France and Russia, mainly because it feared German domination of the continent. A serious incident in one relatively remote area of Europe had triggered a world war that no one had expected or wished for.

This brief account of Russia's slide into war suggests a certain inevitability about it all, as if there were no attempts to avoid a conflagration. In fact, P. N. Durnovo, a former minister of inter-nal affairs and an uncompromising reactionary, sent a memoran-dum to Tsar Nicholas in February 1914 warning that a European war would be prolonged and would surely provoke a social revo-lution with shattering consequences for the old order. He urged the tsar to realign the country's foreign policy by establishing close ties with Germany, a move that would enable Russia to avert war. Events would soon demonstrate that Durnovo was an insightful man.

Initially, the war, greeted by most people with a show of patrio-tism, went well for Russia. Its armies scored some victories when they attacked eastern Prussia and Galicia in an effort to help the French, who faced the brunt of the German army advancing across Belgium into France. But the Russian successes were short-lived. As soon as the Germans had assembled an army in the east, they routed the Russians in the Battle of Tannenberg (27–9 August 1914), inflicting heavy losses on them: some 300,000 casualties and the destruction or capture of 650 guns. In Galicia, the Russian successes lasted longer, in part because the Austro-Hungarian army was inefficient and beset with severe problems of low morale. Many Ukrainians and Czechs who had been recruited felt little loyalty to Austria-Hungary and voluntarily surrendered to the Russians, who occupied Galicia. But in May 1915 the German army turned its attention to this area and quickly defeated the Russians once again, driving them out of Poland.

It had now become clear that the Russian Empire's economic and social backwardness as well as its incompetent political and military leadership precluded success in the war. The tsar's first mistake was to appoint his uncle, Grand Duke Nicholas Nikolaevich, as commander-in-chief, responsible directly to him. The grand duke was very handsome and popular among the troops, but he himself admitted that he did not know how to run the military. He lasted in his exalted office for only one year, at which point the tsar made an even worse appointment. He himself took over as commander-in-chief. Not only did he know even less than his uncle about warfare, he would now be held directly responsible for the military's failings. And he did not have an adequate corps of officers on whom he could rely for sound advice. Most of the senior officers had moved up the ladder not because they were able men but because they had served loyally, though without distinction, for many years. They also tended to be excessively concerned with advancing their own reputation and often acted mindlessly without coordinating their plans with other senior officers. To make matters worse, many rank-and-file soldiers were illiterate and clueless about Russia's goals in the war. The government's talk about the need to wage war out of brotherly love for the Serbs did not resonate with them. Nor did

the promises of the Allies in 1915 and 1916 that at the conclusion of the war Russia would be given Constantinople and the
Straits and some regions in Asiatic Turkey.

Naively, the government believed that the key to military
success would be the creation of a huge army that would be
able to overwhelm the enemy simply by virtue of its size. One
year after the beginning of hostilities, Russia had mobilized no
less that 9.7 million men. But there were not enough officers
and non-commissioned officers to lead so large a force. At the
same time, the country lacked facilities for training the new
recruits, many of whom had to wait in miserable barracks for
months before they began their training. When they were sent
to the front, they often did not have the necessary equipment or
enough food. It happened more than once that when groups of
infantrymen were ordered to advance against enemy positions
only the men in the front rows carried guns. Those in the rear
lines were expected to pick up the guns of comrades who had
fallen in battle. It was thoroughly demoralizing and many surrendered to the enemy without fighting. By late 1915, Russia had
endured several defeats and had been forced to give up nearly
all the conquered lands. More ominous still, German troops had
penetrated deeply into the Russian Empire and could not be
dislodged.

In domestic affairs, the government also stumbled badly.
Because the army swelled to fifteen million, one-third of the
population of working age, industry had to employ people without
adequate skills, which lowered productivity at a time when there
was a desperate need for military hardware. Large agricultural
estates, the main suppliers of food products for the market, also
faced a shortage of labor. The railway system, not very efficient
to begin with, broke down, in part because many of the lines in
the west were under enemy occupation. In addition, the railway
companies could not repair all the engines that broke down. Nor
could they replace them with new ones. Between 1914 and 1917
the number of functioning railway engines declined from twenty
thousand to nine thousand. Increasingly, it was impossible to

ship all the available food supplies to the large cities, and the shortages of staples became widespread early in 1917, despite the introduction of rationing in 1916. People widely disregarded the government's system of rationing, and prices shot up at a dangerous pace, posing serious hardship for most citizens.

The empress urged Nicholas to cope with the mounting crises by being 'more autocratic'; utterly irrelevant advice, for he had no idea how to deal with the nation's problems. Increasingly, as the magnitude of the military defeats and casualties became apparent, people blamed the tsar himself for incompetent leadership. The losses were staggering. All in all, 650,000 men lost their lives, over 2,500,000 were wounded, and more than 3,500,000 either became prisoners of war or were missing. The last figure is especially noteworthy because it indicates the extent to which soldiers surrendered to the enemy rather than fight. The tsar tried to deal with the growing decline in confidence in the government by dismissing ministers who had demonstrated their incompetence, but the men he appointed to replace them were as incompetent as their predecessors. The 'ministerial leapfrog', as one conservative Duma deputy called the frequent changes in personnel, highlighted the bankruptcy of the old order.

So did the amazing influence at the highest level of government of Grigorii Efimovich Rasputin, an unkempt and semi-literate monk whose rise to prominence in late imperial Russia is one of the more bizarre indications of the degenerate state of Russian politics. Not much is known about Rasputin's early life beyond the simple fact that he was born in 1872 in the province of Tobolsk, 250 miles east of the Ural mountains. As a young man he gained a reputation for horse stealing and lust, and in the early 1890s he married, and sired three children. Neither marriage nor fatherhood restrained his search for sexual adventures, but his wife apparently did not mind. 'He has enough for all,' she explained.

At some point, Rasputin underwent a religious experience of sorts. He then joined an illegal mystical sect and disappeared from Siberia. For a few years he adopted the lifestyle of the *stranniki*, ascetic wanderers who traveled the country and lived off charity. After two pilgrimages to Jerusalem, Rasputin showed up at the religious academy in St. Petersburg in December 1903. The monk Illiodor, who met him at the time, remembered him as a 'stocky peasant of middle height, with ragged and dirty hair falling over his shoulders, tangled beard, and steely-grey eyes, deep set under the bushy eyebrows, which sometimes almost sank into pin points, and a strong body odor'. Illiodor and other clergymen, impressed by Rasputin's declaration that he wished to repent for his sins by serving God, helped him get settled in St. Petersburg.

Somehow, Rasputin persuaded dignitaries that he could perform miracles. He first demonstrated his skills by curing a dog beloved by the Grand Duke Nicholas Nikolaevich. Late in 1905, Rasputin was introduced to the tsar and tsaritsa, and immediately captivated the royal couple by stopping the bleeding of their only son, Alexis, who suffered from hemophilia. Apparently, Rasputin achieved the feat by means of hypnosis, and there is evidence that such a procedure can work. In any case, the tsarina immediately concluded that Rasputin 'was a holy man, almost a Christ'. She also interpreted his appearance at the court as a sign of the mystical union between the peasants and autocracy; a man of the people, she reasoned, had come to save the dynasty.

Rasputin conducted innumerable affairs, often with ladies close to the imperial court who were convinced that God revealed himself in his words and that his 'kisses and embraces sanctified each of his faithful disciples'. Some men actually felt honored to be cuckolded by the lascivious monk. However, many people in St. Petersburg society, including respected political leaders, were scandalized and publicly denounced Rasputin as a 'fornicator of human souls and bodies'. None of this bothered the empress, who relied on him more than ever when she played a major role in determining domestic policies during the tsar's long absences at the front. Early in 1916, for example, the empress urged Nicholas to appoint the incompetent Boris Stürmer as chief minister because he greatly valued Rasputin and 'completely believes in [his] wonderful, God-sent wisdom'. Unfortunately for Russia – and for himself – Nicholas heeded the advice.

Appalled by this embarrassing and harmful state of affairs, several archconservatives took it upon themselves in December 1916 to assassinate Rasputin. Prince Felix Yusupov, who was married to one of the tsar's nieces, organized a conspiracy and then invited the 'Holy Devil' to his home for a party. The host plied Rasputin with poisoned wine and cakes, which the monk devoured with few ill effects. Yusupov then fired several shots into the monk and with the help of the other conspirators dumped him in the Neva river. The conspirators had hoped that the murder of Rasputin would be a signal to conservatives to join a movement to save the monarchy. But it was too late. The people of Russia were now thoroughly disillusioned with the war and refused to tolerate any longer the hardships it had caused.

THE REVOLUTION OF 1917

The Duma, composed largely of moderates and conservatives, had lost patience with the government as early as July 1915, when a sizable number of deputies, including liberals and some conservatives, formed a 'Progressive Bloc' to urge the authorities to install a competent government that would enjoy the confidence of the people and respect the rule of law. The bloc specifically did not call for any constitutional changes, and yet the tsar ignored it, a snub that heightened political tensions. In one of the more dramatic moments in the history of the Duma, Pavel Miliukov, leader of the Kadets, delivered a speech in November 1916 in which he listed one after another of the government's failings and asked, provocatively, whether these were the result of folly or of treason.

At the same time, there were increasing signs that the mood of the people had turned sour. Initially, in 1914, few workers went on strike, but in 1915 there were some one hundred strikes involving about 550,000 workers, and the numbers continued to climb in 1916. In January and February 1917 there was a new upsurge in labor unrest in protest against declining living standards and the persistent food shortages (including bread). The government's policy of drafting strikers of military age and sending them to the front or keeping them in the factories as soldiers only served to embitter workers even more.

Russia was now teetering on the edge of a convulsion, but no one, not even the most committed radicals, sensed that the country was about to undergo a revolutionary upheaval. In a lecture to young workers in Zurich in January 1917, Lenin predicted that his listeners would have the good fortune of witnessing the 'coming proletarian revolution'. But he was pessimistic about his own chances of playing a role in such an event: 'We of the older generation may not live to see the decisive battles of this coming revolution.'

As it turned out, in 1917 Russia underwent two revolutions, quite different in their evolution, their mass support, and their ultimate goals. The first erupted spontaneously. On 8 March, International Women's Day, thousands of women in St. Petersburg left the breadlines to join strikers from the Putilov works who were demonstrating against the government with banners that featured a political slogan, 'Down with the Autocracy'. The police easily dispersed the marchers, but one day later a much larger demonstration, estimated at 200,000 people, appeared in the center of the city. It still seemed to be an unthreatening event, even though, ominously, the Cossacks now refused to charge the crowd. On 10 March, the crowds in the streets were even larger and the tsar, increasingly nervous, ordered the troops to fire at the marchers. As the army began to carry out this order it seemed as though the demonstrations would peter out. But then, on 12 March, one regiment after another not only refused to shoot but went over to the revolution. Moreover, no one stopped the workers who broke into military arsenals and seized forty thousand rifles. V. M. Rodzianko, the president of the Duma, realizing that the regime was on the verge of collapse, urged Nicholas to introduce reforms in a last effort to prevent a national disaster. The tsar, as short-sighted as ever, dismissed the advice: 'That fat Rodzianko has written me some nonsense, to which I shall not even reply.'

A few hours later it was clear that the government had lost control of St. Petersburg, and as unrest spread to other cities the tsar came under intense pressure from political dignitaries to abdicate, which he did on 15 March. A dynasty that had ruled Russia for some three hundred years and had claimed to govern by divine right collapsed after only a few days of unrest and with remarkably little bloodshed. All in all, about thirteen hundred people were killed or wounded. The disintegration of the old order had proceeded so rapidly because the support for it had simply evaporated. As the monarchist Duma deputy V. V. Shulgin, no friend of the demonstrators, noted, 'The trouble was that in that large city [St. Petersburg] it was impossible to find a few hundred people who felt kindly towards the Government. That's not all. The Government did not feel kindly towards itself. There was not a single Minister who believed in himself or in what he was doing.'

The critical task now was to establish a new center of authority that would be recognized by the people as legitimate. On 12 March, even before the tsar's abdication, Duma deputies, who had remained in the parliament building despite Nicholas's order proroguing the legislature, formed a committee to restore order and act as an unofficial government. Four days later this group declared itself the 'Provisional Government' and issued its program, which was thoroughly liberal and democratic. The Provisional Government established freedom of speech and unionization, it promised to grant an amnesty to political prisoners, to abolish all social, religious, and national restrictions, to hold a democratic election of a constituent assembly that would decide on the form of a new government, and to create committees to make recommendations on the agrarian question. Finally, the new government promised to continue the war, by far its most controversial decision.

At the very moment that the Provisional Government came into being, a rival center of authority, the soviets, appeared in St. Petersburg and soon thereafter in many other areas of the country. Chosen haphazardly by workers and soldiers, the soviets were dominated by Mensheviks and Socialist Revolutionaries and enjoyed the confidence of the politically active masses. The leaders of the Petersburg Soviet acknowledged the Provisional Government as the legitimate authority, but they did so half-heartedly and on some major issues they adopted stands at variance with those of the government. It soon became evident that without the full support of the Soviet the government could not enforce its will. As a result, there emerged what came to be known as 'dual power'. On the one hand, the government was formally charged with running the country but it could not by itself exercise political power. On the other hand, the soviets, the repository of political power, refused to assume any responsibility of government.

The leaders of the soviets, all socialists, had plausible reasons for refusing to participate in governing the country. Convinced that Russia was ripe only for a bourgeois revolution, they feared that their assumption of power would push moderates into the counterrevolutionary camp, endangering the revolution. In addition, the Petersburg Soviet's leaders lacked confidence in their ability to administer the machinery of government. Although they did not intend to cripple the government, their stance inevitably produced a situation that can only be described as political paralysis. Effective government is not possible in a country where there are two foci of authority, each with its own concerns and goals.

Conflicts between the Petersburg Soviet and the Provisional Government broke out soon after the collapse of tsarism. The first major clash occurred over Order No. 1 that the Soviet issued to the troops on 14 March. This abolished saluting when off duty, prohibited harsh treatment by officers of men under their command, and called for the election of committees in all army units. Although the committees were ostensibly to obey the orders of the Provisional Government, they were also directed to do so only if the orders of the authorities did not conflict with those of the Soviet. The purpose of Order No. 1 was to prevent the use of the military for counterrevolutionary purposes, but it was bound to undermine discipline in the military services, already very fragile.

But the principal source of conflict between the government and the Soviet was the war, which by now was extremely unpopular and which profoundly affected all major facets of national life. It increasingly became clear that if the war could not be ended quickly, the government would not be able to cope with any of the pressing problems facing the country: redistribution of land, creation of a constitutional order, and revival of the economy. And so long as the government could not make progress in these critical areas, it could not attract the popular support it needed to survive.

Yet the Provisional Government refused to extricate Russia from the war. One may reasonably question the wisdom of the new leaders' inaction on this score, but it must be recognized that they faced difficult choices. The government feared that abandoning the Allies and concluding a separate peace would lead to Europe being dominated by the Central Powers, which were ruled by monarchs who could be expected to be hostile to the democratic order now established in Russia. The government also believed that it had a moral commitment to France and Great Britain to continue the military struggle until the enemy had been defeated. But it must also be noted that some members of the Provisional Government (in particular the foreign minister, P. N. Miliukov) harbored less lofty motives. They wanted Russia to remain in the war in order to annex Constantinople once the Central Powers had been defeated.

The soviets and their supporters on the left, distressed in particular over Miliukov's stand, favored determined action by Russia to bring the war to an end. They urged all the belligerent powers to enter into negotiations for peace on the basis of the formula 'No annexations, no indemnities'. The Provisional

Government, however, could not be budged from its position. On the contrary, it assumed that a democratic Russia would be able to appeal to the army and people to make greater efforts to win the war. On the orders of Alexander Kerensky, the exuberant minister of war, the Russian army launched a major offensive in Galicia early in July. Initially, it scored some impressive victories, but after twelve days the Germans and Austrians counter-attacked and quickly mangled the Russian army, which did not put up much of a fight. Discipline simply collapsed. In a desperate attempt to restore morale, the government reinstated the death penalty in the military services, but it was of no avail.

THE REVOLUTION DEEPENS

No initiative that the Provisional Government undertook worked to stem the descent into the abyss. It was V. I. Lenin's genius to sense, before anyone else, the utter helplessness of the authorities and the futility of all their efforts. In Switzerland when the revolution erupted, he immediately tried to return to Russia, but a glance at the map will reveal the difficulties he would encounter. However, officials in Germany concluded that it would be to their advantage to have him and a few dozen other socialists in Russia stirring up trouble. Swiss socialists arranged to have Lenin and thirty other exiles cross Germany in a sealed train. On his arrival in St. Petersburg on 9 April, Lenin discovered, to his dismay, that even the leaders of his own party (including, incidentally, Stalin) favored a policy of conditional support for the new regime, though they were trying to apply pressure on it to extricate Russia from the war. Rejecting this approach as totally misguided, Lenin offered a radically new strategy that amounted to a complete repudiation of the Soviet's policies. He called for an end to support for the government, urged troops at the front to fraternize with Austrian and German soldiers, and proclaimed the imminence of the proletarian stage of the revolution. Lenin wanted the Bolsheviks to commit themselves publicly to the creation in the very near future of a 'commune state' based on the soviets.

Even to his closest colleagues in the Bolshevik party Lenin's scheme seemed to be utterly fantastic, and many wondered whether their leader had in fact lost touch with reality. But he persisted and used all his considerable skills to persuade his colleagues that his strategy and tactics were the right ones. As it became clear that the country was disintegrating, his prognosis appeared not to be unrealistic. The peasants, impatient with the inertia of the government, seized land, and no one could stop them. In the cities, workers took over factories after expelling the owners and managers. Local soviets assumed control over local government. National minorities broke away from the central authorities by proclaiming either autonomy or independence. Finally, the army was breaking up; soldiers, eager to end the war and take part in land seizures, deserted en masse (some two million men in the course of 1917). The Provisional Government promised reform and appealed to the population not to support these mass movements, but not many took seriously the promises or the appeals. It seemed as though the government was merely marking time.

Prodded by Lenin, the Bolsheviks eventually supported all the mass movements that were breaking down society, even though land seizures by peasants, workers' control over factories, and the collapse of authority ran counter to their long-term goals of a state-controlled economy and a highly centralized political order. Ever the opportunist, Lenin urged his comrades to follow the masses to achieve his immediate goal, the seizure of power.

As early as mid July, when news reached the capital that the offensive in Galicia had stalled, it appeared that in St. Petersburg at least Lenin could count on wide support for his plan. Militant soldiers, sailors, and workers staged an armed uprising to pressure the Soviet into seizing power. The Bolsheviks, believing the time was not yet right for frontal attack on the Provisional Government, initially hesitated to take part in the uprising and even tried to restrain the rebels. But when huge masses (estimated at 500,000 people) appeared in the streets carrying banners on which was inscribed the slogan 'All power to the Soviets', Lenin decided to support the action. There were some bloody clashes, but the government had too few reliable troops to stop the activists in the street, who almost certainly could have taken over the capital had Lenin been more decisive, even though the Soviet remained unwilling to take power, for reasons already noted. To calm the impatient demonstrators in the streets, the Soviet sent Victor Chernov, the leader of the Socialist Revolutionaries and known as a radical, out into the street to explain why a seizure of power was inadvisable at that moment. He was met by an angry mob, who, after searching him, accused him of being 'one of the people who shoots at the people'. One sailor shook his fist and shouted, 'Take power, you son-of-a-bitch, when it's given to you.' It was a dramatic scene not forgotten by the Bolsheviks. The government sought to punish the leaders of the demonstration by arresting them, but many, including Lenin and his close associates, went into hiding. The uprising had failed in its immediate goal, but it had revealed, once again, the weakness of the Provisional Government.

The government was further humiliated two months later, during a bizarre four-day episode known as the Kornilov Affair, which has justifiably been called the 'prelude to Bolshevism'. The two main protagonists in this affair were Alexander Kerensky, appointed prime minister on 20 July, and General Lavr Kornilov, whom the former had appointed supreme commander-in-chief at a time of grave military crisis. A relatively young and dashing officer (he was forty-seven), Kornilov had demonstrated great valor (some thought in a reckless way) in battles against the enemy and had dramatically escaped from an Austrian prison in 1916. Once the revolution had succeeded in overturning tsarism, his main concern was to revitalize Russia's fighting force. When he became commander-in-chief, he immediately let it be known that he intended to be his own man. He accepted the post on condition that he would be responsible 'to his own conscience and to the people at large', which was a peculiar demand for a general, who would normally be expected to be subordinate to his civilian superiors. Kerensky overlooked Kornilov's unusual behavior because he needed a commander-in-chief capable of restoring the fighting spirit of the army. But early in September a series of incidents seemed to suggest that Kornilov wished to take power and to crush the revolutionaries. Even now the origins and implications of Kornilov's actions are still murky and it is still not clear whether Kerensky initially conspired with Kornilov to establish a military dictatorship and then pulled back, or whether Kornilov simply imagined that he had the prime minister's support.

In any case, when Kerensky dismissed him, Kornilov ignored the order and then appointed General Krymov as commander of the 'Savage Division' of Cossacks, which began to advance on the capital. St. Petersburg seemed defenseless and Kornilov appeared to be unstoppable. Strangely, however, Kornilov's rebellion was suppressed without a single drop of blood being spilled. The general did not reckon with the listlessness of his troops nor with the effective opposition of the workers. The Soviet executive immediately organized workers for a defense against what it denounced as a counterrevolution. The most effective measures were taken by the Railway Bureau, an office set up by the Soviet. It called on workers to cripple the lines of communication and the system of transportation. Tracks at stations were blocked with coaches, and in three places the track was actually torn up, causing endless delays. As a consequence, some army detachments loyal to Kornilov were sent in the wrong direction and when they realized what had happened, it was too late. Also, continuous streams of agitators were sent to the soldiers, and they persuaded the troops not to do Kornilov's bidding and to remain loyal to the Provisional Government. The rebellion quickly fizzled out. General Krymov committed suicide, and Kornilov and some of his supporters in the army resigned.

But for the Provisional Government it was a pyrrhic victory. For one thing, the military services became even more demoralized, since many rank-and-file soldiers lost what little faith they still had in their officers. On the other hand, the Bolsheviks became militarily much stronger, for in its anxiety to create a fighting force against Kornilov's advancing troops, the Provisional Government had permitted indiscriminate arming of workers. As a result, the first units of the Bolshevik Red Guard were formed and soon mushroomed into a force of 25,000 people, none of whom gave up their weapons after the affair ended. Moreover, it was widely whispered that Kerensky had been in accord with Kornilov over the necessity of a dictatorship and had betrayed him under pressure from the soviets. And because a number of leading liberals had expressed sympathy for the Kornilov movement, it became impossible for the parties of the center to continue cooperating with each other within or outside the government. A concerted effort to stop the revolutionary left was now quite unfeasible. The Bolsheviks reaped the first concrete advantage from the Kornilov Affair on 13 September, when they achieved, for the first time, a majority in the Petersburg Soviet. Five days later the same thing happened in the Moscow Soviet. Fear of counterrevolution had produced a decisive shift to the left among the working class. Late in September, Lenin declared that the moment had come for the Bolsheviks to seize power. He was certain that 'we will win *absolutely* and *unquestionably*.'

THE BOLSHEVIKS SEIZE POWER

Goaded ceaselessly by Lenin, the Bolsheviks now made extensive preparations for the second revolution, which in some important respects would be quite different from the first, so-called 'bourgeois', revolution. It would not be a spontaneous outpouring of masses of people in the streets of St. Petersburg but a carefully planned seizure of power by at most a few thousand men and women. Its goal would be not a democratic and liberal political order but socialism, regardless of whether the prerequisites that Marxists had always claimed were necessary prevailed in Russia. But in one respect the November and March revolutions were similar. Both succeeded without encountering much resistance.

Early in 1917 and later that year Russia was politically prostrate. So deep was the public despair and apathy that neither the tsarist regime nor the Provisional Government could muster the necessary support to retain authority. Ousting Kerensky's government, as Lenin noted early in 1918, was 'extremely easy'. Within hours, after the Bolsheviks made their move, they controlled the major centers of power in St. Petersburg. It is worth noting that the Bolsheviks throughout the Russian Empire commanded a membership of only about 200,000 people, and the proletariat, in whose name the revolution was staged, numbered perhaps three and a half million out of a total population of 150 million.

On 8 November, one day after taking power, Lenin announced a series of policies that he knew would receive wide acclaim. First, he came out in favor of the Socialist Revolutionary land program; property rights of the nobility would be eliminated and lands in rural regions would be placed at the disposal of Land Committees and district soviets of peasants' deputies for distribution to the peasants. Lenin explicitly justified the abandonment of the Bolshevik land program of nationalization on the grounds that it was now necessary to demonstrate to the peasants that their land hunger would be satisfied and they were no longer subservient to the landlords. With this one move, Lenin assured himself of at least the temporary support or neutrality of the peasants, still the overwhelming majority of the population.

Lenin also immediately introduced workers' control in industry and in commercial and agricultural enterprises, abolished distinctions and special privileges based on class, eliminated titles in the army, and issued a decree outlawing inequality in wages. Perhaps most important for the survival of his government, he quickly initiated negotiations with Germany to end the war. That turned out to be a difficult process, but in March 1918 the Bolsheviks signed the Treaty of Brest-Litovsk and thus extricated Russia from the war against the wishes of the Allies. But the treaty imposed extraordinarily harsh conditions on Russia, depriving the country of some twenty-six percent of its arable land and twenty-seven percent of its population. Many

of Lenin's comrades raised strong objections to the treaty, but
Lenin insisted on accepting Germany's terms. He was convinced
that the treaty would not remain in force for long because the
proletariat in other countries would soon follow the example
of Russian Marxists and seize power. Once the revolution had
triumphed throughout Europe, relations between states would be
harmonious, Lenin contended, and the Treaty of Brest-Litovsk
would be abrogated.

Although the months immediately following Lenin's seizure
of power have often been depicted as the idealistic phase of the
Russian Revolution during which the leadership was guided
by the principles of equality and popular rule, some Bolshevik
actions caused sympathizers to raise their eyebrows even then.
For one thing, Lenin made clear that he wanted a monopoly
of power for his party, even though it represented only a small
minority of the Russian people. He also suppressed newspapers
opposed to the new regime, ostensibly as a temporary measure
until the new order was firmly consolidated.

Most ominously, on 20 December 1917, the Cheka, the security police, was established to protect the revolution, which it did
by arresting and often shooting opponents of Bolshevism without
regard to due process. When members of his own party protested
the actions of the police, Lenin attacked them as 'narrow-minded
intellectuals' who 'sob and fuss' over the Cheka's 'mistakes'. He
further declared that 'When we are reproached with cruelty, we
wonder how people can forget the most elementary Marxism.'
Nikolai Bukharin, a leading figure in the Bolshevik party, justified
the terror during the early years of communist rule with a quota-
tion from St Just, one of the militants of the French Revolution
of 1789: 'One must rule with iron, when one cannot rule with
law.'

Many would succumb to government-sponsored terror, but
in the early period of the revolution no act of violence was as
dramatic as the murder of the tsar and his family in July 1918.
A year earlier the family had been moved to Ekaterinburg (later
Sverdlovsk), a city on the border of Europe and Asia, and placed

under house arrest. Apparently because the Bolshevik hold on power was at the time highly precarious – Ekaterinburg itself was then in danger of falling to forces trying to overthrow the new regime – Lenin ordered local communists to kill the entire family and their staff. It may well be that Lenin viewed the murder both as a means of rallying support for the Bolshevik government and as a warning that the authorities would resort to brute force to remain in power.

Still, the elections to the constituent assembly, planned by the Provisional Government, had been allowed to proceed late in November 1917. The Bolsheviks received 23.5 percent of the votes, 9.8 million out of 41.7 million. The lists of delegates for the constituent assembly had been drawn up before the Bolshevik seizure of power and may therefore not have fully reflected the will of the people. However, it is clear that Lenin was no admirer of democratic procedures. On 26 December 1917, he published an article in *Pravda* in which he declared that 'A republic of soviets is a higher form [of government] than the customary bourgeois republic with its constituent assembly.' He also let it be known that the constituent assembly, which was to meet early in January 1918, would have to accept 'Soviet power . . . the Soviet constitution'. Otherwise, 'a crisis in connection with the constituent assembly can be solved only by revolutionary means.' The assembly was allowed to meet, but when it became clear that the delegates were not well disposed towards the new regime, Bolshevik sailors armed with rifles dissolved it by force. This was, in the words of the historian E. H. Carr, the final 'tearing asunder of the veil of bourgeois constitutionalism'.[2]

The true test of Lenin's leadership came in the years from 1918 through 1921, when he faced civil war, foreign intervention, peasant unrest, and violent protests by revolutionaries who had been among his most dedicated supporters. Lenin's ability to overcome all these challenges is a true mark of his political and ideological tenacity as well as his tactical flexibility.

8

THE SOVIET UNION UNDER LENIN AND STALIN

Rarely in the history of any country has one man cast so long a shadow as V. I. Lenin has over Russia. The basic contours of the communist system fashioned by Lenin remained intact for about seventy years. Not only was he indispensable in bringing Bolshevism to power, but he created the ideology of Bolshevism, he inspired and guided the organization of the communist movement, and he, more than anyone else, shaped the Soviet system of rule during the first six years of its existence. Anyone who examines the profound changes that Russia underwent after 1917 in its economy, political institutions, and legal order, in the government's policy towards religion and the national minorities, and in the country's moral climate invariably encounters the hand of Lenin. This is not to say that every domestic policy of Soviet leaders after Lenin's death in 1924 followed in detail the lines set down by the architect of the revolution or that Lenin would have acted precisely in the way his successors did. But for over six decades Soviet leaders considered Lenin's teachings to be sacrosanct and persistently invoked his name to justify their policies. And they spared no effort in disseminating his doctrines. It has been estimated that in 1990 there were no less than 653 million copies of Lenin's writings in 125 languages in the Soviet

Union, which one wag believed was 'perhaps the only area of abundance achieved by communist efforts'.

Whichever policy Lenin pursued, and sometimes he shifted from one to another rather abruptly, he never lost sight of his final goal, socialism, and no matter how precarious his government's hold on power, he never contemplated giving up. He was always certain that he was right and that his opponents were not only wrong but perverse in holding on to their position. As one of his contemporaries who knew him well put it, in speaking with Lenin one had the feeling that he had a piece of paper in his pocket with the truth written on it.

His zigzags were especially conspicuous in his attempt to cope with Russia's crumbling economy. In the cities, there was a real danger of starvation because of a severe shortage of grain, a consequence of both the war and the reluctance of peasants to sell their produce at the prevailing, very low prices. Industrial production had declined by more than two-thirds, leaving many workers unemployed and therefore without the wherewithal to buy the food that was available. Moreover, the transportation system had deteriorated to such an extent that in some regions of the country products could not be shipped to markets. To deal with the mounting crisis, the government in June 1918 introduced a series of radical measures known as 'War Communism', the central feature of which was the creation of a state monopoly over all grain. On the government's initiative, village committees of the poor peasants were formed to requisition the grain from well-off peasants, by force if necessary. As an incentive to the committees, their members were promised a share of the grain they seized as well as a share of the industrial goods available for the villages. The ideological underpinnings of War Communism were clear: it brought class warfare, often accompanied by ghastly outbursts of violence, into the countryside.

In November 1918, the government nationalized trade and established a network of state cooperative stores authorized to distribute goods. Because of the pervasive shortages, a system of rationing was introduced. Two months later, the government nationalized all banks and began to print money at a feverish pace to pay for its expenditure. The predictable result was rapid inflation, which prompted the government to replace the system of monetary taxation with a system of taxation in goods. Workers' control in factories, which had been approved in November 1917, remained in force, even though industrial production declined at an alarming rate, by 1920 to about thirteen percent of the 1913 level. Meanwhile, by the second half of 1918, about twenty-eight percent of all wages were paid in kind and in three years this rose to ninety-four percent. Russia now in effect had a barter economy, which continued to deteriorate because the peasants, rather than turning their crops over to the committees of the poor, decided to reduce output. Within four years of the revolution, agricultural production had declined to fifty-four percent of the 1913 level. It has been estimated that in the years from 1918 to 1920 over seven million people died of malnutrition. Many citizens living in cities returned to the countryside; Moscow and St. Petersburg, to cite but two examples, lost about half their population. But the Bolsheviks could claim some positive results from War Communism: they secured control over the so-called 'commanding heights' of the economy, that is, over heavy industry, transportation, banks, and foreign trade. And they gained some administrative experience, which would serve them well in the future.

In addition to the economic crisis, Lenin had to contend with growing political and military opposition to his regime. For about three years, from 1918 to late 1920, a brutal civil war raged in the country, and to many observers at the time it seemed highly unlikely that the Bolsheviks would be able to retain power. Arrayed against the communists were a wide range of political parties, former officers of the imperial army, and nationalists who wished to secure independence from Russia. In the summer of 1918, small contingents of soldiers from France, Britain, Japan, and the United States landed in Russia and, although the major aim of the British and French was to restore the eastern front against Germany, they also helped the Whites, as the anti-Bolshevik

forces were known. Japan landed troops in hopes of seizing territory, and the United States did so to check the Japanese. The
main consequence of this ill-advised and ill-conceived foreign
intervention was to enable Leninists to claim that they were the
true patriots because they were defending Russian soil against
the foreign invader.

The Whites scored some impressive victories against the
communists and in the summer and fall of 1919 seemed to be on
the verge of capturing Moscow and St. Petersburg, but in the end
they failed to dislodge the new government. Too often involved
in fierce squabbling among themselves, and politically inept,
the Whites were incapable of arousing wide support among the
people. Moreover, their forces were dispersed in the territorial
periphery of the country, where the economy and the transportation system were especially underdeveloped. The Whites never
managed to create a unified force that could launch a concerted
attack on the government in Moscow. On the other hand, the
Bolsheviks controlled a compact area in the center of the country, where the systems of communication and transportation
were more efficient. With their land program, described in chapter 7, they succeeded in turning the peasants into a neutral, if
not friendly, force. Perhaps equally important, Leon Trotsky, the
minister of war, was highly effective in organizing and inspiring
the Red Army, which quickly became a potent fighting force. It
not only inflicted major defeats on the Whites; in 1920, it also
managed to fend off the Poles, who had marched into Kiev in an
attempt to restore the Polish frontiers of 1722.

By the spring of 1921, the Reds had defeated the Whites
and had reestablished a semblance of order in most of what
had been the Russian Empire. But there were important losses.
Finland, Estonia, Latvia, Lithuania, and Poland became independent states, Romania annexed Bessarabia, Poland took parts
of Belorussia and the Ukraine, the Japanese held on to some
lands in the Amur region, Georgia remained independent, and
there continued to be pockets of resistance to the communists in
Bukhara (Central Asia). Still, the Leninists could now be said to

have consolidated their power and so could turn their attention to the economy, which remained thoroughly enfeebled.

THE TENTH PARTY CONGRESS

Major decisions on reviving the economy were taken at the Tenth Party Congress in March 1921, which in several respects marked a turning point in the history of Bolshevism and of Russia. There is little doubt that Lenin intended to chart a new course at the congress, but before the meetings began an unexpected and dramatic development strengthened his resolve to change direction. A sizable number of sailors, who had been among the most fervent supporters of communism, staged an anti-government uprising in Kronstadt, a naval base seventeen miles west of St. Petersburg. Motivated in part by news of industrial unrest in the capital and, probably more so, by the hardships of peasants, the sailors issued a series of demands to the communist authorities: they called for new and free elections of the soviets, freedom of speech for workers, peasants, anarchists, and Left Socialist Revolutionaries, recognition of the right of workers and peasants to form associations, and the liberation of all socialist political prisoners. On 2 March, the insurgents created a Provisional Revolutionary Committee to press for the implementation of their demands, none of which could be legitimately considered reactionary. Nonetheless, in calling for new elections the rebels challenged the legitimacy of the Bolshevik system of rule. Pointing to that demand, the government denounced the insurgents as counterrevolutionaries, and then launched a savage attack on the fortress in Kronstadt and crushed the uprising. Hundreds and perhaps thousands of rebels were executed without trial. The Communist Party throughout the country rallied around the government, although outside Russia some supporters of the Leninist experiment were shaken by the brutality.

Lenin now made several pronouncements at the congress on the organization of the Communist Party that proved to be fateful. Although Lenin had been the first among equals within the Bolshevik leadership, and although he had long favored a highly centralized party, he had tolerated some political disagreement and had allowed individuals to express their personal views. But now that the leadership faced a serious political challenge and was about to embark on a new economic program, Lenin put an end to the relative freedom to discuss political issues. On the second day of the Tenth Party Congress, he declared that the time had come to 'put a lid' on all opposition to his program. He insisted that it was pointless to reproach him for advocating such a course, for it followed 'from the state of affairs', by which he presumably meant that the Bolsheviks were politically too weak to allow freedom of speech. A few days later, the congress, at Lenin's urging, adopted by very large majorities a resolution dissolving all 'groups with separate platforms'. Those who refused to abandon 'factionalism', as it came to be called, would be expelled from the party by the Central Committee. The provision on expulsion, which remained secret until 1923, became a powerful weapon for the silencing of any opposition to the leadership. It marked a very significant step towards the formation of what has been called the 'communist autocracy'.

Lenin's new economic program, also announced at the Tenth Party Congress, marked a decisive shift away from the highly centralized and coercive policies embodied in War Communism, which had been a major cause of economic disintegration since 1918. But the abandonment of War Communism had for some time been advocated by the Mensheviks, long a rival of the communists for working-class support. Under the circumstances, Lenin found it inconvenient to allow the Mensheviks to continue operating as a political party. People might ask why the Mensheviks, who, it now turned out, had been right all along, should not be permitted to exercise power. To forestall such embarrassing queries, the Bolsheviks stepped up the repression of the Mensheviks and soon also of other non-communist socialist parties.

In introducing what came to be known as the 'New Economic Policy' (NEP), Lenin sought not only to revive industry and agriculture but also to grapple with the political tensions caused by the growing split between the peasants and the workers. There were signs that the goodwill that Lenin had gained in 1917 with his pro-peasant policies was disappearing. Peasant uprisings, which had increased at an alarming rate in the fall of 1920 and became especially intense in Tambov, did not end until 1924, despite the government's extensive use of force against the insurgents. To appease the peasants and revive the economy, Lenin was prepared to make concessions to them and to a lesser extent to industrial entrepreneurs and workers, even to the point of abandoning War Communism, but he would not give up his ultimate goal, the establishment of socialism.

The main features of the NEP can be easily summarized. Most important, the government abolished compulsory requisitioning of agricultural products and, instead, imposed a tax that in 1922 was set at ten percent of the peasants' crops. The peasants could then sell the remainder of their produce on the free market and pocket the profits. The peasants were also permitted to hire labor and to lease land, which, however, they still could not buy or sell. In another break with War Communism, the government reintroduced a currency and created a state bank that conducted its business along traditional lines. By 1924, all taxes in kind were replaced by a tax in cash and the barter economy came to an end.

Industry was divided into two sectors. On the one hand, the state retained ownership of about 8.4 percent of all enterprises, but these comprised all the large ones that together employed about eighty-four percent of the labor force. On the other hand, small enterprises could be owned by individuals, and within a few years over eighty-eight percent of all enterprises fell into this category, but these employed only about 12.5 percent of all industrial workers. Although progress was not always smooth, within a few years the economy revived to a remarkable degree. By early 1928, the output of many branches of industry equaled that of 1913, the last year before the decline that set in during the war. Agricultural production also increased greatly, and the standard of living of most people more or less returned to the prewar level, which was not exactly high but was much better than during the grim years from 1917 to 1921. It has been estimated that if so-called 'socialized wages' such as health benefits, state insurance schemes, and educational scholarships are taken into account, urban workers were actually better off in 1927 than they had been in 1913.

STRUGGLE FOR POWER

In the meantime, the political landscape had changed fundamentally. Early in 1924, Lenin, the undisputed leader of the country, died after a series of debilitating strokes. The death of a tsar in imperial Russia generally provoked anxiety about the views and abilities of the new ruler, but ever since 1825 the succession at least had been clear-cut and no one was in doubt about who the new ruler would be. The constitution of 1918, never taken very seriously by Lenin, described the Marxist principles that would guide the administrations of the state and guaranteed the vote to all except the bourgeoisie, but beyond that did not specify how the political leadership would be selected. Late in 1923, when he was already incapacitated, Lenin seems to have realized that the Bolshevik party and the country would face a crisis of leadership after his death. He drafted a testament, in which he passed judgment on prominent men in the national leadership and found all of them wanting. He was so negative in his judgments that every effort was made to conceal the document, and it came to light in the West only because Max Eastman, an American writer then sympathetic to communism, smuggled it out of the country. Lenin regarded Trotsky, his right-hand man since 1917, as the most gifted man in the Central Committee but also as too self-confident and too interested in the 'purely administrative side of affairs'. He thought that N. I. Bukharin was 'the most significant theoretician' but weak in dialectics. Lenin reserved his sharpest barbs for J. V. Stalin, whom he considered to be too concerned with amassing power, which he did not always use wisely. Lenin also warned that Stalin was 'too rude' and suggested that he be removed from the very important post of general secretary of the party. If that were not done, Lenin warned, there would be a split among the party leaders. In making this last point, Lenin proved to be uncannily omniscient.

For four years, the leaders of the Soviet Union engaged in a brutal struggle for power that they liked to portray as essentially a conflict over profound ideological issues touching on the interpretation of Marxism and Leninism. It was that to some extent, but the endless intrigues and constantly shifting alliances suggest that it was even more a conflict over who would inherit the mantle of Lenin and become the undisputed leader of the socialist cause. In terms of achievements, prominence, and ability, the most likely successor to Lenin would appear to have been Trotsky, a powerful orator, a highly effective military leader during the civil war who had also demonstrated a capacity for brilliant and original thought in the arcane area of Marxist thought. But he could not restrain his arrogant behavior and, despite his acute intelligence, he was not a talented politician capable of persuading colleagues to accept him as their leader. Moreover, he was a Jew and it seemed unlikely that the Russian masses would be willing to be ruled by him even though his religious background was totally unimportant to him.

Trotsky's main rival, Stalin, seemed unqualified for other reasons: he was not an intellectual with a deep understanding of Marxism, he was not known as an innovator, and he certainly was not a charismatic personality. But he was extremely shrewd and knew how to ingratiate himself among members of the communist bureaucracy. He carefully cultivated contacts at all levels of the party, never tired of listening to people with complaints, and never gave the impression of harboring great personal ambitions. His obscurity made him in many ways an ideal person for leadership in a political movement that derided the role of individuals and emphasized the critical importance of social forces in history. Not to be overlooked is the fact that during Lenin's lifetime

Stalin accepted party positions that the more colorful and brilliant men shunned. He was the commissar of nationalities, the commissar of the workers' and peasants' inspectorate, and in the Politburo, the real government of the country, he took on more of the day-to-day tasks of the party than anyone else, tasks that the intellectuals scorned as drudgery. In 1922, he was appointed general secretary of the Central Committee, whose function it was to coordinate the work of the numerous branches of the committee. In that post, Stalin set the agenda of the Politburo and then supervised the implementation of its decisions. The general secretary also was in charge of the appointments and promotions of party functionaries. It soon became a position of enormous power and within a few years the general secretary of the Communist Party in the Soviet Union and in every other country with a Communist Party became the preeminent leader of the movement. Stalin never relinquished the title, even when he was the undisputed ruler of Russia.

In 1923, while Lenin was still alive but greatly weakened from his strokes, two Politburo members, G. E. Zinoviev and L. B. Kamenev, formed an alliance with Stalin, giving the three, known as the 'triumvirate', a majority that could administer the country. Zinoviev and Kamenev worked with Stalin not because they favored his rise to power but because they wished to stop Trotsky from attaining the top post in the party. It did not even occur to them that Stalin viewed himself as a candidate for that post. Ideological differences did not surface until 1924, when the triumvirate charged Trotsky with subscribing to three heresies: he advocated the theory of permanent revolution, he failed to understand the revolutionary potential of the peasantry, and he rejected the doctrine of 'socialism in one country'. The latter doctrine, most vigorously advocated by Stalin, was a clear deviation from classical Marxism, which had always maintained that socialism could triumph only on a worldwide basis. Indeed, Zinoviev and Kamenev initially adopted the doctrine only because they believed that Stalin had come up with a clever weapon in the increasingly bitter conflict with Trotsky.

But Stalin was dead serious. He insisted that Russia was so rich in raw materials that it could on its own proceed to build socialism. Close examination of Stalin's and Trotsky's position on this question shows that they were not all that far apart. Trotsky also believed that Russia should adopt policies that would move the country towards a socialist order, but he contended that the process of creating a fully developed socialist society could not be completed in one country alone. Even though Stalin conceded that to complete the process of building socialism in Russia alone would take a long time, he had devised a doctrine that resonated widely among the people who followed politics. It was a shrewd doctrine bound to appeal to a population that had endured terrible hardships and was therefore inclined to clutch at any suggestion that their sufferings were not in vain, that if they persisted they would be able to reach the ultimate goal of an affluent and egalitarian social order.

Step by step, the triumvirate pressed its campaign against Trotsky, who early in 1925 felt obliged to resign as commissar of war. Now that Trotsky's political power had been undermined, Stalin turned his attention to Zinoviev and Kamenev by forming an alliance with other members of the Politburo against them. He kept shuffling his alliances and it took him until 1929 to emerge as the ultimate leader of the Communist Party and the state. When on the tenth anniversary of the revolution, on 7 November 1927, Trotsky and Zinoviev led a peaceful procession separate from the official one, both men were immediately expelled from the party. Early in 1929, the Politburo adopted Stalin's recommendation that Trotsky be expelled from Russia. Other opponents or presumed opponents of Stalin were also driven from their positions of authority. Several of them abjectly renounced their views, pledged loyalty to Stalin, and thus gained readmission to the top echelons of the party, where, however, they remained for only a few years. Trotsky never renounced his views and for eleven years traveled from one country to another – several refused to give him refuge – before settling down in Mexico, where in 1940 Stalin's henchman murdered him in cold blood.

On Stalin's fiftieth birthday, 21 December 1929, it became clear that his triumph over his rivals would usher in a form of personal rule remarkable even in a country accustomed to the ritualistic glorification of the tsars. Unlike Lenin, who in 1920 insisted on a relatively modest celebration of his fiftieth birthday, Stalin approved of an elaborate campaign that has been called a 'symbolic celebration' of him as the 'party's new *vozhd*' (leader). In numerous articles the press referred to him as Lenin's worthy successor and he promised 'to devote to the cause of the working class, the proletarian revolution and world communism, all my strength, all my ability and, if need be, all my blood, drop by drop'. Within a few years he was glorified as almost a sacred figure who was infallible, the repository of ultimate wisdom in all fields of endeavor, a kind and gentle man who ranked with Marx and Lenin as a theorist of Marxism and who cared deeply about his people. But what his program would entail was not yet clear. He had not articulated his views during the struggle for power and over the preceding five years he had gravitated from one position to another depending on the perceived political requirements of the moment. But it soon became clear he and his close advisers were committed to a series of policies that would amount to nothing less than a second Bolshevik revolution, a revolution from above that would transform Russia perhaps even more radically than had Lenin's in 1917.

REVOLUTION FROM ABOVE

The new revolution, initiated in 1928, was designed to deal with the economic and social consequences of Lenin's New Economic Policy. Although Russia at the time was better off than it had been for close to fifteen years, it still was a predominantly agrarian country and the concessions of 1921 to capitalism seemed to suggest that socialism was but a distant dream.

Under the NEP large-scale industry had made considerable progress, but it remained a tiny sector of the economy. Moreover, for some time, the left within the Politburo had argued that the peasants were becoming so powerful economically that they would soon be capable of undermining the Soviet system of rule by threatening to withhold agricultural products from urban centers. The only way to counter the leverage of the countryside was for the government to spur rapid industrialization, which would provide Bolshevism with a solid base of support and would turn Russia into a modern state militarily capable of defending itself against capitalist countries still bent on destroying socialism. The proponents of this position favored the establishment of collective farms to increase agricultural production rapidly and to free up labor needed in industrial areas. An underlying assumption of the leftists was that revolutions in the West remained possible, and that the program they favored would encourage communist parties in industrially advanced countries to make renewed efforts to gain power.

On the other hand, the rightists in the Politburo, led by Bukharin, contended that a policy of rapid industrialization was feasible only if private businesses were heavily taxed to pay for the creation of new factories. In an economy that was already shaky, that would cause serious disruptions. Bukharin's proposal was to let the private sector continue to operate on the profit principle. He adopted the provocative slogan of the nineteenth-century French prime minister François Guizot, generally regarded as the spokesman par excellence of bourgeois interests, who urged entrepreneurs to 'enrich yourselves'. Bukharin believed that socialism would still be safe in Russia because the communists would continue to control industry, banking, and the system of transportation. He also believed that in the West capitalism had been stabilized and that therefore there was little likelihood of socialism spreading in the foreseeable future.

In 1928, Stalin, who during the struggle for power had posed as a moderate, sided with the left and came out for a radical restructuring of the economy. The chief proponent of 'socialism in one country' since 1925, he now feared that the countryside, led by the 'rich' peasants (*kulaks*, as they were known in Russian), would soon be strong enough to turn Russia back to capitalism. Was this fear justified? In 1927 there had been a decline in the amount of grain shipped to urban centers, but this does not seem to have been the result of a political decision by the peasants to undermine socialism. Most of the agricultural surplus came from middle and poorer peasants, who together constituted about eighty-seven percent of the rural population and who were now living better by consuming a larger share of their total produce than in previous years. That was why less food was being sent to the cities. Nor did the *kulaks*, long derided by the Bolsheviks as particularly dangerous villains, have enough economic power to shape the nation's economic system. They made up only 3.9 percent of the rural population and could hardly be considered truly wealthy. They were better off than most peasants in that they owned larger plots of land and some draft animals and equipment and often leased land from poorer peasants. But in 1927, they produced only thirteen percent of the total amount of grain, which was hardly enough to give them the clout necessary to determine the shape of the national economy.

Yet in some respects the Bolsheviks had reason to be nervous about developments in the countryside. They had not been able to impose their political will on the villages, where traditional peasant institutions continued to play an important role in the lives of the vast majority of the people. For example, in many regions the age-old commune was still a center of administration, more active than the local soviets. A report to the Fifteenth Party Congress in 1927 indicated that, whereas the communes and various other informal peasant organizations had a budget of eighty million rubles, the 2,300 soviets in the countryside disposed of only sixteen million rubles. At the same time, *kulaks* were accepted by the peasants as the leaders of local social organizations and this did not sit well with administrators selected by the Communist Party. The authorities in Moscow were also troubled by the fact that despite their campaign in favor of atheism, religious observance was rising in the countryside. In 1928 alone, 560 new associations of Orthodox believers had been formed, and in the Ukraine the number of priests had risen sharply.

A final consideration for Soviet leaders in their drive to modernize the national economy was the belief that war with the Western powers was a real possibility. In 1927, a war scare became acute because Great Britain had broken off relations with the Soviet Union in retaliation for the help that the Bolsheviks had given British workers during the general strike of 1926. But the more one studies the economic upheaval unleashed by Stalin in 1928, an upheaval that lasted for at least a decade and caused an unprecedented degree of suffering and dislocation, the harder it is to avoid the conclusion that at bottom Stalin's motivation was ideological. He was determined, once and for all, to abolish private property in the means of production and to turn the entire population into employees of the state. The grandiosity of the scheme and the single-mindedness and ruthlessness with which it was pursued suggest that the revolution from above launched in 1928 was the brainchild of a man, or group of men, obsessed with a vision that they were determined to pursue regardless of human cost.

A few statistics about the Five Year Plan, as the new initiative was called, will indicate the scope of Bolshevik ambitions. Within a mere five years, by 1932–3, total industrial production was to rise by 235.9 percent. Electric power was to be quadrupled, the output of coal was to double, and the output of pig iron was to triple. Moreover, industrial production was slated to become more efficient: costs would be reduced by thirty-five percent but wholesale prices would be reduced by only twenty-four percent, and the difference – eleven percent – would be applied to investments, for the most part in heavy industry. Such an ambitious plan required a major increase in the industrial labor force and a large increase (of about 150 percent, it was estimated) in the food supply. The Soviet leadership planned to achieve their goal in the agrarian sector by initiating a policy of collectivization, the merging of individual farms into collectives known as *kolhkozy*. The collectives were expected to be much more efficient than small private farms, and Soviet leaders planned to move the excess manpower to the cities.

Although the government vowed to implement the policy of collectivization on a voluntary basis, once it was in full swing, in mid 1929, that commitment became a dead letter. For it turned out that only the poor peasants, slightly over twenty percent of the total village population, stood to benefit from the new policy and only among them was there strong support for it. Nearly all the others were passionately attached to their land, as peasants have always been in all countries at all times. Huge numbers of Russian peasants resisted the authorities with every weapon at their disposal, and it is no exaggeration to say that class warfare spread to almost the entire countryside. Rather than give up their belongings, peasants would destroy their livestock, eat to capacity, and then give away or burn what they could not consume. In many instances, they also destroyed their equipment and burned their crops. The point was to reduce to a minimum what the state would be able to confiscate. In many villages, troops charged with enforcing the directive on collectivization were met by peasants refusing to leave their land. The soldiers responded by surrounding the villagers and then firing their machine-guns into the crowds, killing large numbers. Another form of coercion was to exile recalcitrant peasants to distant places such as Siberia. During a two-year span from 1930 to 1931, about 400,000 households (roughly two million people) were forcibly deported from the countryside. The disruptions in the villages greatly reduced agricultural output and caused widespread famines.

Russia paid a staggering price for Stalin's agrarian policy. According to conservative estimates, some five million villagers lost their lives during the five-year collectivization drive. Moreover, by 1933, the number of horses in Russia had declined by one-half, the number of cattle by one-third, and the number of sheep and goats by one-half. Midway in the process, in March 1930, Stalin himself acknowledged, in a famous article entitled 'Dizziness with Success', that the process had proceeded too rapidly and stated that force should not be used to compel peasants to enter the collectives. He blamed the excesses on low-level functionaries in the Communist Party. Within two months, about six million peasant families out of fourteen million left the collective farms. But a few months later, the government reapplied pressure on peasants to give up their private farms and by 1932 about sixty percent of all families were once again in collectives. To maintain control over the workforce in the countryside, the government instituted a system of internal passports. Only those who received such a passport could move to another part of the country. This meant that the peasants were bound to the land on which they worked, a throwback to the serfdom of the pre-1861 era.

The government did make some concessions to the peasants. Instead of forcing them into the preferred type of collective, the state farm (sovkhoz), in which peasants worked full time on the commonly held land, it gave them the option of entering a kolkhoz, in which the peasants divided their working time between their own small plots and the land under control of the collective. Most collectives fell into the latter category. Ironically, this two-fold arrangement not only deviated from the principles of socialism but also demonstrated the effectiveness of economic incentives. Peasants would work leisurely during the sixty to one hundred days they devoted to the collectivized land and would preserve their energy for their own plots of land, the proceeds of which they could sell directly to consumers. Although only three percent of all the land was under private cultivation, that sector produced roughly a third of the country's food. During the next six decades – for as long as the Soviet Union existed – agricultural productivity remained very low, as did the quality of food products. And since the transportation system was primitive, a high percentage of the produce rotted before it ever reached the market.

In the industrial sector, progress was more impressive, though not nearly as great as Soviet leaders claimed. Within four years, rather than the anticipated five, the country could boast of having developed entirely new industries that produced tractors, automobiles, agricultural machinery, and airplanes.

Whereas, in 1928, industrial output amounted to forty-eight percent of the country's total output, in 1932, it amounted to seventy percent. But there were major setbacks. Again, the cause of the failures could be traced to the confusion resulting from the incredible speed with which the government sought to reach its goals. In some regions, managers of newly constructed factories often discovered that machines they needed were not available. Elsewhere, machines turned out to be available for factories that were not built to accommodate them or where the manpower capable of running them was not at hand. In general, skilled labor remained in short supply. It was one thing to bring men and women from the countryside to the cities to work in industrial plants. But it was quite another matter to transform peasants, used to working hard but accustomed to being masters of their own schedules, into disciplined operatives in a factory, where workers on an assembly line are dependent on the prompt completion of tasks by their colleagues.

To imbue factory employees with the necessary work habits, early in the 1930s, the government introduced a rigid system of discipline. For example, factory managers controlled the issuance of ration cards, which until 1935 were required for the purchase of food and manufactured goods. Workers dismissed from their jobs for one or another reason would lose their card and might also lose their place of residence, which was under the control of the enterprise. After 1932, factory managers were directed to dismiss and deprive of their housing any workers absent from their job without good reason for just one day. The growing intrusion of the state in the affairs of the citizens was an integral aspect of Stalin's revolution from above and thus marked the beginning of a new political system, totalitarianism.

TOTALITARIANISM

The term 'totalitarianism' has come under considerable criticism. Many scholars consider it a term of opprobrium coined during the Cold War as a weapon with which to stigmatize the Soviet Union. In fact, the word was already in use in the 1930s and the person who popularized its usage was none other than Benito Mussolini, the Fascist dictator of Italy. Mussolini was proud to be striving for the establishment of totalitarianism in his country, by which he meant a polity in which the state seeks to control every facet of economic, social, and political life. In this sense, Russia under Stalin became totalitarian, for the government sought to secure total control over national institutions and over the people's affairs, private as well as public, even though it did not fully succeed in achieving its ultimate goal.

A brief sketch of Stalin's system of rule in the 1930s will demonstrate this. But first it may be instructive to touch upon another vexing issue in modern Russian history, the relationship between what are now known as Stalinism and Leninism. Put differently, was Stalinism a mere continuation of Leninism, or did the two represent quite different polities? Scholars who take the latter position argue that Lenin was far more pragmatic and tolerant and much less ruthless than Stalin. They also argue that Lenin would probably have continued the New Economic Policy and almost certainly would not have embarked on so radical a program as the Five Year Plan and collectivization. There may be some merit to this line of reasoning, but it should not be forgotten that Lenin resorted quite freely to terror during his period in power and that War Communism, his creation, was also an extraordinarily harsh social and political system. Moreover, throughout the eleven years of Bolshevik rule before Stalin's ascendancy there was no legal order in the Soviet Union. The best evidence for this is the Criminal Code of 1922, which adopted the essence of Lenin's draft of a statement on governmental discretionary power. It stated that any action – be it merely propaganda, agitation, or support of anti-communist organizations – by a citizen 'helping in the slightest way that part of the international bourgeoisie' that is committed to overthrowing the communist system is 'punishable by death or imprisonment'. So vague a formulation is a citizen's nightmare and a policeman's dream. There can be little doubt that Lenin's legacy, ideological as well as institutional, helped pave the way for Stalinism. The terror, the absence of a legal order, and rule by a hierarchically organized party not only facilitated Stalin's rise to power but also constituted central features of both Leninist Bolshevism and Stalinism.

And yet it cannot be denied that Stalin's 'excesses' went well beyond those of Lenin and hence it is appropriate to consider the Stalinist polity of the 1930s distinctive. In its determination to control society from above it marked the apotheosis of totalitarianism, unmatched at the time by any other regime. Stalin was the paramount leader, or dictator, without whose approval no major initiative was undertaken, but even he had to rely on a vast apparatus to implement his directives and to maintain order. The Soviet system had three pillars that kept it functioning for several decades: the Communist Party, the secret police, and what might be called the system of incentives.

The Communist Party, an elite organization, or the 'vanguard' of the proletariat, never numbered more than about ten percent of the adult population, and the core of the party, the functionaries who were full-time employees, was a smaller group of about 200,000 (in the 1950s). The party's members were chosen with the greatest care. Children in kindergarten belonged to the Little Octobrist movement; at the age of nine they joined the Young Pioneers and at fourteen they could, after careful screening, be admitted into the *Komsomol*, in which they generally remained until the age of twenty-six, when a decision would be made about admission into the party as full members. It was a long process designed to weed out those who were insufficiently committed to the cause or who were insufficiently energetic to carry out the numerous tasks of party members. They were expected to serve as models for the rest of society (by avoiding hooliganism and heavy drinking), to agitate among the masses to support the party's decisions, to help recruit new members and to indoctrinate them, to energize the masses to fulfill the various economic plans, and to maintain a watchful eye on mismanagement or laxity in workplaces. They also had to adhere to the principle of 'demo-cratic centralism', the central organizational tenet of the party, which stipulated that the decisions of the higher party units were absolutely binding on the lower ones.

The highest organ, the Politburo, chose its members by co-optation, not election, and its directives had to be carried out without reservation. The lower party members could discuss how best to implement the directives, but they were not free to debate the substance of the directives. By the 1930s, the party had a strong foothold in every sector of society – the economy, military services, media, educational institutions, high as well as low culture, even associations devoted to sports. Moreover, the higher a person's position in any of these sectors the more likely it was that he or she would be a member in good standing of the Communist Party. To serve the party was not easy by any means: members had to devote much of their time after work to endless meetings and were required at all times to be vigilant and to report any sign of indifference or hostility to the regime among their colleagues.

But rewards for loyal and energetic party members, especially those who rose to the upper reaches of the organization, often referred to as the 'nomenklatura', were substantial. They would receive faster promotions in their places of work, more spacious apartments, attractive summer homes in the country, admission for their children into the best schools, and access to special medical facilities and special stores that stocked products not available to the general public. Among industrial workers a system of differential pay was established in the mid 1930s, creating a hierarchy within the alleged mainstay of the regime, the prole-tariat. This began with a public relations campaign about the feats of a coal miner, Alexei Stakhanov, who during one night in August 1935 mined 102 tons, far above the normal amount of 7.3 tons, in a six-hour shift. Stakhanov was said to have been so productive not only because he worked harder but also because he had devised more efficient methods of mining. The authori-ties did not reveal that Stakhanov had been especially well rested and well fed before his performance. Nonetheless, the government now decreed that in order to encourage greater productivity workers would be paid on a piecework basis, which led to wide discrepancies in income. There is little doubt that the various incentives, the second pillar of the Stalinist system of rule, help explain that system's durability.

But no less important was the third pillar of the Stalinist system, the secret police. In tsarist Russia, the secret or political police devoted itself to protecting the autocratic order, often by extra-legal means. In communist Russia, its task was to protect first the revolution and then the socialist order, but it adopted means that in ruthlessness and scale far surpassed those of the tsarist police. The Soviet secret police had numerous names over the years – Cheka, GPU, OGPU, MVD, NKVD, and KGB – but for several decades its principles remained essentially unchanged: that the revolution was the supreme law and that whatever was done in its name was justifiable; that the counterrevolutionary forces were intransigent in their opposition to socialism and would do all in their power to undermine the Soviet Union. Eternal vigilance and terror against actual or presumed enemies were therefore necessary. Institutionalized by the 1930s, terror was so pervasive that even when it was not being applied everyone knew that the machinery of terror existed and could be applied whenever the authorities considered it necessary. Not a single sector of society escaped the vigilance of the secret police, always on the alert for the slightest expression of discontent with the government.

STALINIST TERROR

Political terror reached its highest level after an incident that is still shrouded in mystery. On 1 December 1934, Leonid Nikolaev, an unemployed man with a troubled past who apparently was a party member with oppositional views, assassinated Sergei Kirov, the party boss in Leningrad widely believed to be Stalin's heir.

It has been charged that Stalin was behind the murder – the evidence is inconclusive though circumstantially strong. Be that as it may, on the very day of Kirov's murder the Central Executive Committee of the Communist Party announced a crackdown on its presumed opponents. The committee issued a decree that stripped anyone accused of anti-government terror of virtually all rights for a legal defense, and a few hours later it issued another decree, which was distributed only to officials in the police and the party. This stated that the investigations of people accused of anti-government terrorism should be carried out more expeditiously (within ten days), and that once a verdict of guilty had been reached those sentenced to death should be executed immediately. There was no provision for an appeal or for a petition for clemency. Then, exactly three weeks after Kirov's assassination, the government announced that Nikolaev was part of a conspiracy that sympathized with the views of Zinoviev, who had at one time been Stalin's ally against Trotsky but had at various times wavered in his support of the dictator. There was a trial of sorts (in secret) of fourteen alleged conspirators, all of whom were sentenced to death. On 29 December, barely four weeks after the murder, Nikolaev was executed.

This was only the beginning of what can be called Stalin's second war against his own people – the first was carried out under the banner of collectivization. On 16 January 1935, the secret police arrested Zinoviev and Kamenev and some other activists who had at one time belonged to the opposition to Stalin. They were to be put on trial for having secretly fomented opposition, for lying when they had repented of past political deviations, and for having 'indirectly' influenced Nikolaev's decision to kill Kirov. These people, too, were tried in secret and then sentenced to imprisonment. It was an ominous event because it was the first time that individuals who had been loyal and distinguished members of the Communist Party were formally accused of criminal conduct and were then put on trial.

A year later, in 1936, the Stalinist leadership undertook a vast purge of the party to rid it of what were called 'hidden enemies'. Such purges were repeated over the next couple of years and it has been estimated that all in all about 800,000 were expelled from the party. In mid August 1936, Zinoviev and Kamenev, among others, were subjected to another trial, this time accused of having formed a 'terrorist center' guided directly by Trotsky. They all confessed and were immediately shot. Early in 1937, there was yet another trial of former party leaders and this time the charges were even more serious. The men in the dock were said to have conspired with Japanese and German officials to dismember the Soviet Union. They, too, confessed. A few months later, several military leaders, most of whom had rendered distinguished service to the Soviet Union, were secretly tried for having committed sabotage for Germany and Japan. It turned out that a hotel in Copenhagen where the conspira-tors were supposed to have met with foreign contacts had been razed some years before the alleged 'meeting'. The notion that so many leaders of Russian communism and the Soviet military had been spies and traitors is utterly unbelievable. They were dedi-cated to the party and thoroughly patriotic.

A few statistics will reveal the scope of Stalin's war against his own people. According to information released by the Soviet government after Stalin's death, about half the entire officer corps of the army (35,000 men) were arrested, including three out of five marshals, thirteen out of fifteen army commanders, fifty-seven out of eighty-five corps commanders, 110 out of 195 division commanders, 220 out of 406 brigade command-ers, all eleven vice commissars of war, seventy-five out of eighty members of the Supreme Military Council, ninety percent of all generals, and eighty percent of all colonels. The number of people in high positions in the civilian sphere who were charged with crimes against the state is equally astonishing: over 1,100 out of 1,966 voting and non-voting delegates at the Seventeenth Party Congress in 1934; seventy percent of the 139 members and candidates of the Central Committee of 1937. Many of the accused were shot. As already noted, many lower-ranking party members were purged and then either executed or sent for long periods to one of the corrective labor camps (part of the Gulag),[1] where conditions were ghastly. A large number of ordinary citizens too were shipped off to these camps for minor infractions of regulations or for no reason except that they were suspected of counterrevolutionary sympathies.

It is not known exactly how many ended up in the camps, but there is no doubt that the number ran to millions. Even the most conservative estimate is that in January 1953 there were 5,221,880 citizens in various camps, colonies, and 'special settlements'. Other estimates that cannot be dismissed put the figure closer to ten or twelve million. No one disputes that the security forces, which administered the Gulag, were the single largest employer in the Soviet Union. It is also difficult to determine how many were executed or died because of the horrendous conditions in the camps, but, again, the number was huge. Respected historians have suggested that if one adds up all the people who died as a result of official policies (including Stalin's agrarian polices from 1919 to 1932) a figure of fifteen to twenty million is not unreasonable.[2]

At least two questions about the terror are worth pondering. Why did people who were obviously innocent confess to the crimes with which they were charged? It must be stressed that although the show trials were among the more striking events of the 1930s and have received a great deal of attention from historians, only a handful of people actually made confessions. It used to be assumed that these men, all of them dedicated to communism, had agreed to confess as a last service to the party. They were allegedly prepared to sacrifice themselves in order to save the revolution, which was threatened by deep political divisions within the Communist Party. If those divisions had been made public, the people would have become disillusioned and would have abandoned the party. Moreover, the accused might also have thought that they could serve as scapegoats for the failings of communism and for the terrible hardships that the people were enduring. But information found in Soviet archives opened only recently makes it clear that the men who caved in to their captors had been subjected to various forms of physical torture and also mental torture such as threats to their families. They were probably incapable of acting as autonomous human beings.

The second question is even more complicated and certainly more important to students of history. What possessed Stalin to unleash violence against his own people on such a vast scale? To say that he was insane is unconvincing because we know that on many occasions during the 1930s and 1940s he made rational decisions on weighty issues. He surely was a deeply insecure and sadistic person, but these are not necessarily the traits of a man who has lost the power to think rationally. He was also a man obsessed with power, and it is possible that he feared that once the Five Year Plan had ended in 1933 the party would no longer consider it wise to keep him in power. Or it may well be that Stalin, who had become paranoid, instinctively sensed that under totalitarianism, which demands total subordination of the citizen to the state, everyone was potentially disloyal for the simple reason that total subordination is ultimately intolerable. Under such circumstances, the leader would believe that he could be fully secure in the exercise of power only if all citizens were so terrorized that they were rendered incapable of independent behavior.

In the course of 1938, the purges of party members ended, as did mass arrests of citizens. A fair number of inmates in the labor camps were released and some secret police officers were now sent to jails and labor camps, where, it has been reported, they met people they had interrogated only months earlier. Nikolai Yezhov, the sinister head of the secret police, was replaced by Lavrenti Beria, who, initially at least, gave the impression of being less ruthless. Beria had Yezhov arrested and it seems that in 1939 Yezhov was executed. But neither Stalin nor his subordinates repudiated the four-year campaign of terror, although they did concede that there had been excesses, which they blamed on traitors and Trotskyites trying to make a political comeback. Still, it was clear that the party had changed direction, most probably because it had concluded that the terror was causing irreparable damage to the country and perhaps even to the party itself. Fear of state institutions and distrust of almost everyone had become so prevalent that there was a real danger that the social bonds holding society together would disintegrate. There is also evidence that it was becoming more difficult to find individuals willing to replace the party members who had been purged; people were simply afraid of assuming positions of responsibility, and this was bound to harm the economy at a time when rapid industrialization was still the order of the day.

EVERYDAY STALINISM

The everyday life of the citizens of the Soviet Union in the 1930s was extraordinarily grim, and not only because of the terror. For one thing, shortages of essential goods, including bread, a staple at every Russian meal, were widespread. In recently opened archives, a scholar found a letter sent to Stalin in the late 1930s by a housewife from the Volga region, who complained: 'You have to go at two o'clock at night and stand until six in the morning to get two kilograms of rye bread.' In Alma-Ata in 1940 there were huge lines for bread and '[o]ften, going past these lines, one can hear shouts, noise, squabbling, tears, and sometimes fights.' Other foods such as meat, milk, butter, and vegetables, as well as salt, soap, kerosene, and matches were also often difficult to obtain. The shortages of clothing were perennial, and the garments that were on sale were of shoddy quality. Citizens who wished to mend their clothing could not find thread, needles, or buttons.

Living conditions were another burden of daily life. The average living space of Muscovites in 1940, for example, was slightly over four square meters. It was not uncommon for three or four families to share one communal apartment, which had one kitchen and one toilet. It was also not uncommon for couples who were divorced to continue living in one room because no other space could be found. In Magnitogorsk in Siberia, early in the 1930s, ninety-five percent of the workers at a new industrial enterprise lived in barracks. In 1933, Dnepropetrovsk, a city of almost 400,000 inhabitants in the Ukraine, still lacked a sewage system, electric lighting, and running water. Many smaller provincial towns had no paved roads and only the most rudimentary public transport services. Hooliganism and criminality were so widespread in the 1930s that citizens in many cities found it dangerous to walk in the streets.

Given these circumstances, it is remarkable that the Soviet people were able to rise to a severe challenge early in the 1940s – war with Germany. Ideologically, Adolf Hitler and the Nazi party had posed a clear threat to communism ever since their rise to power in Germany in 1933. Marxism and Judaism were, in Hitler's view, Germany's greatest enemies and he vowed to crush both, although in his many political campaigns and in his writings he did not indicate precisely how he would achieve his two-fold goal. During much of the 1920s, the Soviet Union and Germany, the two pariahs after the end of the First World War, had collaborated on several matters. In the Treaty of Rapallo (1922) the two countries committed themselves to improving trade relations, and shortly thereafter the Soviet Union secretly agreed to allow the German army to conduct various training exercises on its soil in return for an annual fee and for providing training to Russian soldiers. When Hitler became chancellor the Bolsheviks believed that his regime would not last long and that his reactionary policies would in the end help the cause of communism. He would embark, so the Stalinists claimed, on a highly reactionary program that would antagonize the working class, who would be radicalized to the point of staging a successful revolution against Nazism. It did not take the Soviet leadership long to recognize the flaws in their analysis.

By the mid 1930s, it was clear that Hitler had crushed the working-class movement in Germany and that Nazism posed a potential threat to the left and to democracy in other countries, most notably in Spain, and, even more ominous, that

Hitler had expansionist ambitions that could be harmful to the Soviet Union. By the late 1930s, the Western powers and the Soviet Union sought a unified policy to stop the expansion of Nazism, but the distrust between them was too great. Statesmen in Great Britain and France feared Germany but they also feared the spread of communism, which after the brutalities of Stalin's industrialization and collectivization seemed to be more menacing than ever. On the other hand, Stalin suspected that the leaders of the West were prepared to strike a deal with Hitler against the Soviet Union. In the end, Stalin calculated that Germany was the lesser danger to his country, and on 23 August 1939, he signed the Nazi–Soviet Non-aggression Pact, an agreement that struck many people, among them ardent radicals, as a horrendous betrayal of all that was decent. The pact gave Hitler a free hand to attack Poland and several secret provisions stipulated that after Poland's defeat Eastern Europe would be divided between Germany and the Soviet Union. Finland, Estonia, and Latvia were placed in the Russian sphere of influence and the Russians were also given carte blanche to annex Bessarabia. On 1 September, Hitler attacked Poland, and three weeks later, after the country lay prostrate, the secret provisions went into effect. Great Britain and France, sensing that Hitler's appetite for conquest was insatiable, declared war on Germany, thus initiating the Second World War.

Over the next two years, Hitler scored one military victory after another and became the master of Central and Western Europe. The one major power in Europe that he could not subdue was Great Britain, which inflicted such severe blows on the German air force during the Battle of Britain in the summer and fall of 1940 that Hitler gave up his plans to conquer the island. Instead, he turned his attention to the east. Despite extensive evidence that Hitler was massing troops in the east, and despite many warnings from Winston Churchill and others that Germany was on the verge of attacking the Soviet Union, Stalin looked the other way. He simply would not believe that Hitler would betray him. When, on 21 June 1941, Stalin was told that a deserter

from the German army had informed Russian border guards
that the German army would attack early on the morning of
22 June, Stalin dismissed the report as an obvious provocation
and ordered his commanders to be on the alert but not to take
any action. When the German attack came, precisely as the
deserter had predicted, Stalin fell into a state of shock, utterly
paralyzed, and for about seven days he was incapable of running
the government.

The German army was unstoppable. In armor, in strategy
and tactics, and in determination, it easily outclassed the Soviet
army. In the Ukraine, the Germans were aided by the defection to their side of hundreds of thousands of soldiers as well
as civilians who believed that life under the conquerors would
be preferable to rule by Stalin. In one month, the German army
under General von Bock's leadership advanced five hundred
miles before encountering major resistance. In mid October,
the German army stood at the gates of Moscow, and for four
days, from 15 to 19 October, Stalin suffered another nervous
breakdown. By that time, the Germans had gained control over
territories in which sixty million Russians (about thirty percent
of the total) lived and that contained two-thirds of the country's
coal reserves and three-quarters of its iron ore. The Red Army
had suffered staggering losses: thousands of Russian tanks, guns,
and airplanes had been destroyed or captured and the number of
casualties endured during the first four months of the war ran to
over three million.

Remarkably, after the second nervous breakdown, Stalin
became a highly effective leader of the nation at war. He appealed
to the patriotism of the people, invoking many of the symbols of
Russian nationalism, and he also mastered military strategy and
tactics and supervised the reorganization of the army and the
restructuring of industry for the manufacture of military equipment. He quickly established close relations with Great Britain
and later with the United States, both of which sent large amounts
of supplies to the Soviet Union. He was also helped by Hitler,
who, it now turned out, was not the infallible leader his earlier

diplomatic and military successes had suggested. One of Hitler's biggest mistakes was to treat the Ukrainians, potential allies, as racial inferiors and thus to convert them into mortal enemies who within a year of the invasion began to subject German troops to savage partisan attacks. By October 1942, partisan units were active in seventy-five percent of the forests behind the German lines, and a year later no less than ten percent of all German troops in the Russian war zone were bogged down fending off the partisans. Nor had Hitler learned any lessons from Napoleon's defeat in 1812. The Russian winters were once again a trap; the German army was not properly outfitted to withstand the bitter cold and German armor could not move with its usual speed in the snow, or in the mud after the thaw. The Germans had conquered vast stretches of European Russia, but they failed to capture the two most important cities, Moscow and Leningrad, and in their drive into southern Russia they badly overextended their lines of communication. In the end, Hitler also misjudged the morale and fighting ability of Soviet soldiers. Sometimes, it is true, Stalin used hardfisted methods to make sure that the soldiers would not flee from battle (such as placing machine-gunners behind the front lines to keep an eye on the troops), but once the people became convinced that they were protecting the motherland many fought with remarkable bravery.

The greatest test of battle began in the fall of 1942 outside Stalingrad, an industrial city of some 500,000 inhabitants on the right bank of the Volga river in the south-eastern region of European Russia. In itself, the city was not all that important militarily, but Hitler was obsessed with its capture mainly because of its name. He apparently believed that its fall would be a devastating psychological blow for the Russians, who, however, put up a determined defense of the city. It soon emerged that the Germans had miscalculated in launching the attack and Wehrmacht generals urged Hitler to withdraw from Stalingrad to more secure lines, but the Führer ignored them. In fact, he dismissed his chief of the general staff, Franz Halder, and ordered General Friedrich Paulus, in command of the Sixth Army, to persist in the attack; under no circumstances was he to retreat or to give up. For four months the battle raged, the fiercest in the entire war, and on 31 January 1943, Paulus, surrounded by Soviet troops and short of food, ammunition, and winter clothing, had no choice but to surrender. It was Germany's single greatest military defeat and proved to be a turning point in the war. The war dragged on for another two and a half years, but it was now obvious that Hitler had made a fatal mistake in attacking the Soviet Union in the first place.

STALIN'S LAST YEARS

The Soviet Union's contribution to the defeat of Nazi Germany did much to enhance the stature of Stalin and of the country at large, and for decades the experiences of the war were regarded by many citizens as the most challenging and uplifting in their lives. But the price had been horrendous. It has been estimated that over eight million soldiers died and more than fifteen million civilians lost their lives. In European Russia, perhaps as many as 25 million people lost their homes because of the devastation wreaked by the German military. The production of grain fell by two-thirds and production of consumer goods fell almost as much, and yet Stalin would not abandon his failed, prewar economic policies. During the war the government had tolerated some private farming, but now it ordered the land to be returned to the collectives. As for shortages in consumer goods, a few statistics tell the story. In the immediate postwar years only 63 million pairs of leather shoes were produced annually as against 211 million in 1940. Steel production declined by one-third, oil by forty percent, and wool fabrics by over fifty percent.

Many Russians hoped that their sacrifices and heroism would prompt their leader to relax the controls, economic and political, he had imposed on the country in the 1930s. It was a hope Stalin quickly dashed. In his first major speech of the postwar era, on 9 February 1946, Stalin announced that in view of the imperialist danger that continued to threaten Russia the country would have to endure at least three or four more Five Year Plans so that the Soviet Union would be able to face 'all contingencies'. An American diplomat who listened to the speech in the home of an older Russian recalled that at the end of the speech his host 'put his head down on his folded arms on the table as he heard' Stalin's words. It seemed to the listener to mark 'the end of hopes for a better life in the postwar period'. The man's anxieties were justified. Stalin wasted little time before returning to the harsh policies of the 1930s.

The first victims in the postwar period were the large number of Russians who had spent some time abroad during the war either on official assignments or as prisoners of war. The Soviet authorities feared that these citizens had been contaminated by alien ideas on economic matters or the advantages of civic and political freedom. On their return to the Soviet Union, therefore, they were closely interrogated by the secret police and many of them were sent to labor camps. A fair number of the returnees suffered a worse fate: they were shot soon after they set foot on Soviet soil. Entire groups of ethnic minorities were shipped to the Gulag because some among them had collaborated with German troops. In 1947 and 1948, an anti-Semitic campaign, inspired by the government, led to the arrest of Jewish writers and artists. Under A. A. Zhdanov, the secretary of the Central Committee in charge of ideological matters, all the controls of the 1930s were reimposed on literature and the arts, forcing creative men and women to echo the party line in whatever works they produced. Economic policy, too, returned to the prewar pattern, which meant an emphasis on heavy industry to the neglect of consumer goods. The battle cry was to overtake the West in economic production and to produce as quickly as possible an atomic bomb, which the United States had developed during the war and had used against Japan to end the conflict. In part because of the bomb, the United States had become a superpower. Russia, too, had to achieve that status no matter what the cost.

Relations between the Soviet Union and the West had improved during the war but the two sides never fully overcame their distrust of each other. The communists were enraged at the failure of the West to open a second front in 1942 and 1943 against the Germans and believed that Churchill and Roosevelt had deliberately delayed an attack to allow Germany and Russia to bleed each other to death. Meanwhile, Churchill and to a lesser extent other Western leaders continued to believe that Stalin was determined to export revolutionary socialism. Stalin contended that all he was interested in after the war was a security sphere in Eastern Europe to protect Russia against future attack. But once Stalin gained a foothold in Poland, East Germany, Romania, Bulgaria, and eventually Hungary and Czechoslovakia, he imposed upon these countries regimes – known as 'people's democracies' – that closely resembled the totalitarian system of the Soviet Union. Churchill, for many years a Cassandra about communism, in a famous speech in Fulton, Missouri, in March 1946, asserted that 'an iron curtain has descended across the continent' that stretched 'from Stettin in the Baltic to Trieste in the Adriatic', and urged cooperation between the United States and Britain to nip in the bud any 'temptation to ambition or adventure', a clear reference to what he believed to be the expansionist dreams of Stalin. The speech marked the official beginning of the Cold War, a bitter conflict that lasted forty-four years and for the most part was confined to economic, political, and military rivalries between the communist/totalitarian world and the capitalist/democratic world. Although each side was protecting its national interests as it interpreted them, ideology also played a critical role in the conflict. The two sides represented two fundamentally different worldviews: one upheld the principles of free enterprise, personal freedom, popular participation in government, though it is true that these principles were not perfectly implemented; the other upheld the principles of one-party rule, public ownership of the means of production, state control over all institutions, and economic and social egalitarianism, though here, too, the principles were not perfectly implemented.

As Stalinism per se breathed its last, it behaved true to form. Ever since 1947, the Soviet leadership had fomented anti-Semitism, a prejudice that had surfaced as official policy from time to time since the 1920s. Now, however, it was more intense than ever, probably as a result of growing sympathy among Russian Jews for the newly created state of Israel. Initially, the Soviet Union had favored the establishment of the Jewish state, but when it became clear that Israel would not become a Soviet outpost in the Middle East, Stalin's attitude changed abruptly. Probably, he also feared that if Jews were permitted to express support for Israel it would be very difficult to prevent other minorities from supporting national movements of their own. Whatever the reason, the government now applied rigid quotas on the admission of Jews to institutions of higher learning, closed the Yiddish theater in Moscow, ordered the arrest of numerous people prominent in Yiddish culture, and denounced Zionists as traitors. Most ominous of all, in January 1948, the famous Yiddish dramatist Solomon Mikhoels was murdered, almost certainly on Stalin's orders.

Four years later, there were rumors, widely credited, that Stalin intended to send all the Jews in the country – about 2.3 million – to Siberia. Then, in January 1953, the government announced that thirteen doctors, most of them with Jewish-sounding names, had been arrested as wreckers and terrorists who had used medical procedures to murder several prominent leaders, including Andrei Zhdanov, and had also planned 'to wipe out the leading cadres of the USSR'. The authorities put much of the blame for the doctors' successes in their nefarious work on the security police, who allegedly had not been sufficiently vigilant in rooting out the enemies of communism. Many in the Soviet elite now feared that Stalin intended to stage a new purge of party activists and that the charges against the doctors were simply a pretext for such a cleansing of party ranks.

But the country was spared another convulsion. On 5 March 1953, the seventy-three-year-old Stalin unexpectedly died. As so often in the long history of Russia, the death of a ruler provoked questions about foul play. Perhaps it is because people in Russia tend to attach God-like qualities to their rulers that they do not readily accept the possibility of a natural death even for a man like Stalin, who was old, in poor health, and had suffered a stroke some years earlier. It must also be conceded that Stalin inspired deep antipathies, and some of his subordinates could have wished for his speedy end. Nonetheless, despite some mysterious circumstances surrounding his last hours of life, the evidence is not compelling that he died from other than natural causes.

9

REFORM, STAGNATION, COLLAPSE

For thirty-eight years Soviet leaders sought to come to grips with Stalin's legacy, by no means a simple matter for adherents of Marxism-Leninism. There could be no doubt that Stalin had achieved many of the goals set by the Bolsheviks in 1917: he had imposed a form of socialism on Russia by completing the transfer of ownership in the means of production to the state, and he had modernized the country, transforming it into a predominantly industrial and literate society. Moreover, in leading the country during the Second World War and the successful testing of an atomic bomb in 1949, he had achieved something well beyond Lenin's dreams in 1917. He had guided the Soviet Union into the ranks of the great world powers, turning it into a rival of the United States in military strength and influence around the world.

But these achievements came at a heavy price. The government devoted vast financial and human resources to the military services to the neglect of the civilian sector, which remained underfunded, poorly administered, and shot through with corruption. As a consequence, the standard of living of the vast majority of people, very low to begin with, lagged far behind that of other industrialized countries. Furthermore, in the immediate postwar period, the heavy hand of the dictatorship was not relaxed and the fear that the security forces might at any moment unleash a new wave of terror produced a mood of apathy among the people, many of whom lost confidence in their government and the ideology that supposedly guided it. In the summer of 1953, there were signs that this mood was turning into outright hostility towards the authorities in Russia itself and in some of the satellite countries. Revolts broke out in several slave labor camps (probably the bloodiest one in Vorkuta), and there was serious unrest in the Czech city of Pilsen and, on an even larger scale, in East Germany. Overwhelmed by the problems they faced, Stalin's successors floundered, alternating between reform and liberalization, on the one hand, and a tightening of controls over society, on the other. Neither approach succeeded. Within twenty-five years of Stalin's death, it was becoming increasingly evident that the socialist experiment was not fulfilling its promises of material progress and social harmony. In the end, in 1991, it collapsed even faster and with less bloodshed than had tsarism in 1917.

The leaders who succeeded Stalin quickly settled on a course of extensive reform, but because of their ideological commitments and their fear of losing power altogether they proceeded cautiously. They avoided any initiatives that might undermine economic and political institutions. In any case, before they could tackle basic problems the leaders had to decide on Stalin's successor as head of the party and therefore of the country. As had been true after Lenin's death in 1924, there were no rules for deciding the succession. The leaders announced that political power was to be in the hands of a 'collective leadership' of five men (G. M. Malenkov, L. D. Beria, V. M. Molotov, K. E. Voroshilov, and N. S. Khrushchev) and the new rulers went to absurd lengths to demonstrate that they were equals. When they left their various cars on returning to their offices at the Kremlin from an official function they would make sure that all the doors opened simultaneously. But this was merely an outward show of comity designed to persuade the public that all was well in the highest circles of government. For several years the leaders were in fact engaged in a fierce struggle for power. At first, Beria seemed to have outwitted his rivals, but even though he vowed to press for extensive reforms he had been too closely associated with the worst excesses of the Stalin era to be acceptable to senior officials. At the end of 1953, Beria disappeared under mysterious circumstances. It is still not clear whether he was killed in a shootout in the Kremlin or secretly executed in the cellar of the police headquarters. He was the last Soviet leader who physically disappeared immediately upon losing his political post. That, alone, was significant progress.

Although nominally a collective leadership now governed the country, two men, Malenkov, the prime minister, and Khrushchev, the first secretary of the Central Committee of the Communist Party, were the dominant figures, but soon they fell out. Before they quarreled, however, the leaders had agreed that relaxation of the police regime was essential not only to calm the nation but also to provide themselves with protection against the security forces. Within weeks of Stalin's death they announced a limited amnesty for prisoners in labor camps, declared that the Doctors' Plot had been based on false information extracted from suspects who had been tortured, and promised to replace Stalinist arbitrariness with a system that came to be known as 'socialist legality'. In 1955, Khrushchev emerged as victor from endless intrigues at the highest levels of authority, but it took him another couple of years to remove his chief rivals from the center of power in Moscow. In another demonstration of the new political culture, the losers were not liquidated or sent to jail. Malenkov was appointed director of a hydroelectric power station in Kazakhstan, and several other high officials were given similar demotions.

DE-STALINIZATION

Khrushchev was the first post-Stalin leader to rule the country for an extended period (about eight years) and to leave a lasting and significant mark on Soviet history. Born in 1894 into a peasant family, Khrushchev joined the Communist Party in 1918 and advanced steadily through the ranks; by the late 1930s he occupied the position of first secretary of the Ukrainian party organization. Intelligent and sharp-witted, he was also a gruff and boisterous man given to expressing himself in earthy language. A firm believer in communism, and highly ambitious, he had faithfully carried out Stalin's orders. There is evidence that he had qualms about some of them, but at the time he never voiced any reservations. His explanation for his silence is revealing. At a meeting chaired by Khrushchev when he was head of the government, someone raised the question of why no one had opposed the crimes of Stalin. 'Who said that?' Khrushchev asked sharply. No one spoke up. 'There's your answer; then, too, we were all scared.'

But once he became the 'First' in the Presidium, to use the Russian designation, he launched a policy of de-Stalinization, one of the most momentous and dramatic turns in Soviet history. Khrushchev did not, it must be emphasized, wish to dismantle the dictatorial system of rule or to abandon the goals of Marxism-Leninism, and there is still some question about his motives in undertaking the campaign against Stalinism. It may be that he did not know the full extent of the terror until 1954 and that he was genuinely shocked when he learned the details of Stalin's crimes. It also seems likely that he realized that the mass terror had adversely affected the economic and social life of the country, because it had inhibited people from assuming responsible positions or from taking initiatives in their work. At the same time, Khrushchev probably sensed that his unmasking of Stalinist crimes would be political dynamite and would greatly add to his stature. Whatever the reason, at the Twentieth Party Congress in February 1956 he delivered a four-hour, strictly secret speech in which he spelled out in amazing detail the horrors of the 1930s and 1940s, for which he blamed Stalin, accusing him of what now became a cardinal sin, 'the cult of personality'. Despite his candor, Khrushchev went out of his way to stress that the evils of the 1930s were an aberration that did not affect the essential correctness of Marxism-Leninism, the viability of the Soviet system of rule, or its superiority to every other form of government. The congress, he declared towards the end of his speech, 'has manifested with a new strength the unshakable unity of our party, the cohesiveness around the Central Committee, its resolute will to accomplish the great task of building communism'. The delegates all rose and greeted these comments with 'tumultuous, prolonged applause'.

Nonetheless, the delegates to the congress were taken aback by Khrushchev's speech, not only because they apparently had not known the magnitude of the terror but also because they feared that the revelations would destabilize the country. In short, the speech was a bombshell; what made it especially gripping and frightening was the description of the terror that Stalin inspired even in his closest associates. Khrushchev told the congress that N. A. Bulganin, a member of the Politburo, the highest political body in the country, had once confided to him that no one felt secure in visiting Stalin: 'It has happened sometimes,' Bulganin revealed, 'that a man goes to Stalin on his invitation as a friend. And, when he sits with Stalin, he does not know where he will be sent next – home or to jail.' The Soviet leadership took all sorts of precautions to prevent the publication of Khrushchev's speech, but within days a translated version of it appeared in the *New York Times*, and copies of it also circulated among party activists and the intelligentsia in the Soviet Union. There is reason to believe that Khrushchev was not displeased by the publicity, even though it provoked a considerable amount of soul-searching among communists within the country and, perhaps even more so, abroad.

The policy of de-Stalinization took various forms. Within a few years, most of the inmates of the Gulag (some four and a half million) were released, many citizens – according to some estimates between eight and nine million – who had been falsely accused of crimes were rehabilitated, and the security police became considerably less visible, though it did not by any means close down its operations. In various ways the government relaxed its controls, which amounted to what came to be known as a 'thaw'. Writers such as Alexander Solzhenitsyn, Vladimir Dudintsev, and some others were able to publish their works even though they exposed unseemly aspects of Soviet reality. In the graphic arts and in cinema, the government was also more tolerant of newer forms of expression, and there was a flowering in both these fields. But the authorities limited the scope of the thaw. Thus, Boris Pasternak could not publish his novel *Doctor Zhivago*, which was critical of the Bolshevik Revolution, in the Soviet Union and sent it abroad for publication, for which he was punished by not being allowed to accept the Nobel Prize for literature in 1958. Periodically, Khrushchev would rave and rant against writers who seemed to him to be insufficiently supportive of Soviet institutions and values. At times he could be scathing in denouncing art he did not like, especially works by modernist and abstract painters.

For the Russian people, the end of the worst features of the Stalinist terror was welcome, as it was for foreign communists. According to Moscow wags, when Yugoslavia's Marshal Tito visited the mausoleum that contained the mummified figures of both Lenin and Stalin, he saluted the structure with a hand over one eye so that he could see Lenin but not Stalin. The campaign against Stalin's cult of the individual reached its highest and most bizarre point at the Twenty-Second Party Congress in 1961. On that occasion, D. A. Lazurkina, a longtime party member who had spent many years in a forced labor camp, strode to the platform and, after announcing her great reverence for Lenin, whom she always 'carr[ied] in [her] heart', announced that she had consulted with Ilych (Lenin) and he had said to her, 'It is unpleasant for me to be side by side with Stalin, who brought so many troubles upon the party.' The congress promptly passed a resolution acknowledging that it was 'inappropriate to retain the sarcophagus containing the coffin of J. V. Stalin in the Mausoleum', citing his 'serious violation of the behests of Lenin, his abuse of power, his mass repressions against honest Soviet

people, and other actions in the period of the cult of personality'.
The next day, Stalin's body was removed and reburied in a place
behind the mausoleum near the Kremlin wall.

In economic affairs, too, Khrushchev was a reformer. Since
1953, Soviet leaders had sparred with each other over how to
stimulate the national economy. Several critical questions were at
issue: Should the government continue to emphasize the development of heavy industry or should it put greater stress on agricultural products and consumer goods, still in very short supply?
How much of the national budget should be devoted to the military build-up, considered necessary in light of the tensions associated with the Cold War? These issues were debated against
a backdrop of a sluggish economy, the consequence of Stalin's
misguided economic policies, the devastation caused by the
Second World War, and a terrible famine in 1946–7 caused by
an especially harsh drought. The income of farmers in 1949, for
example, amounted to about fifty percent of the 1928 level, and
by 1953 it had gone up to only sixty percent of that level. In industry, the recovery in the immediate postwar period proceeded more
rapidly, but there were still serious shortages. In 1951, the shoe
industry still produced less than one pair of shoes per person and
the quality was very low indeed. Knitted garments also remained
in short supply, and refrigerators and television sets were considered a luxury that the vast majority of citizens could not afford
until the late 1950s. Careful studies have revealed that, in 1953,
most people in the Soviet Union probably lived in poverty or on
the edge of poverty.

Khrushchev proposed several policies to improve the economy. From mid 1953 he advocated an increase in the production of wheat in south-east Russia, west Siberia, and Kazakhstan,
and early in 1954 he advanced the so-called virgin and idle
land program, which called for the cultivation of tracts of land
hitherto idle and land that had not been tilled for five years or
longer. It was to be a mammoth undertaking that would lead to
the cultivation of some thirty-two million acres of land in such
widely different regions as the north Caucasus, the Volga, west

Siberia, north Kazakhstan, east Siberia, and the Far East. Faced with considerable resistance to his plan, Khrushchev launched an intensive campaign in newspapers, party journals, and public meetings to promote the scheme. He finally got his way and the government organized the move of over 300,000 young men and women to the new farms, but the problems the pioneers encountered were daunting. For one thing, as scientists had warned Khrushchev, the warm winds from Central Asia tended to erode the soil in the steppe, making it risky to count on a steady run of good harvests in Kazakhstan, where much of the virgin program was being implemented. Moreover, in many places the authorities had failed to make adequate preparations for the newcomers, some of whom, forced to live in tents, gave up and moved to more hospitable regions of the country. All in all, Khrushchev's agrarian policy had mixed results. There was an increase in the grain supply but not enough to solve the perennial shortages. A solution of the basic problems in Soviet agriculture would have required abandonment of the collectives and the innumerable regulations imposed on peasants. For example, a peasant who wished to slaughter a cow needed the written permission of no less than seven people. Abandonment of state control, a basic principle of Stalin's agricultural program, was unthinkable for Khrushchev.

For the industrial sector, Khrushchev proposed reforms that were almost as bold as his agrarian program. In February 1957, he recommended the dissolution of the ministries in Moscow that supervised industry and their replacement by about one hundred councils operating in local regions of the country. He argued that administrators and managers would be in a better position to make decisions on industrial priorities if they were in closer touch with the enterprises. It seemed to be a sound idea, but by itself it did nothing to increase productivity or to rationalize the pricing system, which was chaotic and generally impeded productivity (see below). But Khrushchev believed that socialism as he knew it was the best economic order ever devised by humankind and that it greatly surpassed capitalism, for which he had nothing but contempt. This explains his frequent boasts that the Soviet Union would in the not too distant future have a much more productive economy than the West – at one time he stated that this would happen no later than 1981. It also explains his boast, addressed to the West in 1957, that 'We will bury you.' Widely interpreted at the time as a threat to physically destroy the West, it actually was meant to convey his certainty that socialism would outlive capitalism.

To a growing number within the political elite, Khrushchev appeared to be a man who flitted from one reform to another – only a few of the more prominent ones have been mentioned here – without a clear and sound vision for the country. He alienated many party activists by frequently shifting around or dismissing administrators he believed were not energetic enough in implementing his policies. Only a year and a half after he had reached the highest position in the party, in June 1957, several members of the Presidium, soon to be known as the 'anti-party group', conspired to oust him from office. The ensuing intrigues are among the more bizarre political events in recent Soviet history. It was clear that the conspirators had the votes in the Presidium to sack Khrushchev, but the first secretary would not give up. He told the Presidium that, since he had been elected by the Central Committee, it alone had the authority to dismiss him. In the meantime, Khrushchev's supporters had begun to alert Central Committee members throughout the country of the impending coup and urged them to rush to Moscow. In an inspired move, Marshal G. K. Zhukov sent planes to bring them to the capital. Some members had already forced themselves into the meeting room by banging on the door to gain admission, to be joined soon by another three hundred brought in on military planes. The Central Committee then voted to retain Khrushchev in office, motivated apparently by a desire to continue his policies (which gave individual Central Committee members more influence than ever before) and by a fear that his defeat might restore the authority of the dreaded security police.

FOREIGN POLICY UNDER KHRUSHCHEV

Khrushchev was a dynamic leader, but he was also erratic, bombastic, crude, even boorish, and he was willing to take drastic steps to get his way. These traits frequently manifested themselves in his foreign policy, in the formulation and execution of which he played a very active role. At a meeting in 1960 at the United Nations, for example, he removed one of his shoes and banged the table to show disapproval of comments by the British prime minister, Harold Macmillan. Khrushchev was also blunt as well as unyielding in refusing to relax controls over the satellite states in Eastern Europe, all of whom deeply resented domination by the Soviet Union. In 1956, when the Hungarians sought to assert their independence, he sent troops and tanks to crush the rebels. But it would be a mistake to depict Khrushchev as an unrelenting hard-liner in foreign affairs. In 1955, he evacuated a naval base in Finland, and, more important, he agreed to a peace treaty with Austria that provided for ending the occupation by the Soviet Union and the three Western powers and the withdrawal of all foreign troops from the country. In return, Austria vowed to remain neutral and to compensate the Soviet Union with goods for Austrian properties that the Russians abandoned.

For the rest, Khrushchev's foreign policy during the heyday of his period in power can be described as consisting of two different, even contradictory, tendencies. On the one hand, he pursued a forward policy in Berlin, the Middle East, Africa, and Latin America with the aim of sharply reducing the West's influence; on the other, he repeatedly sought to improve relations with the United States. Since in his mind capitalism was doomed and its replacement by communism was merely a matter of time, it seemed to him unnecessary to risk a military confrontation with the United States. So long as he pursued such a moderate policy, the Cold War remained a serious but bearable irritation for both sides. In the summer of 1962, however, for reasons that are still not clear, he embarked on what can only be characterized as a reckless and adventurous course that brought the Soviet Union and the United States to the brink of nuclear war.

In mid October an American reconnaissance plane discovered that the Soviets were installing launching pads in Cuba for medium range and intermediate range missiles, which meant that the United States would soon be susceptible to an atomic attack from these sites. The most plausible explanation for this daring Soviet move is that Khrushchev planned to use the missiles as a bargaining chip in upcoming negotiations over a peace treaty for Germany. The Soviet Union would offer to withdraw the newly installed weapons in Cuba in return for an American commitment not to place nuclear weapons in Germany. Apparently, Khrushchev also hoped to secure a promise from President John F. Kennedy that the United States would agree to a nuclear-free zone in the Pacific. To Khrushchev, the shipment of missiles to Cuba, which had embraced communism in 1959, did not seem to be unreasonably provocative. After all, the United States had placed nuclear weapons in Turkey, which was closer to Russia than Cuba was to the United States. Khrushchev had also persuaded himself that Kennedy was too weak a person to take resolute action, and that he would be especially cautious because congressional elections were to take place early in November.

The Soviet leader miscalculated badly. Kennedy took several measures to make clear that he would not accept Soviet missiles in Cuba: he asked Congress for authorization to call up military reservists and then, on 16 October, he put Cuba under a 'quarantine', which was in effect a blockade. Kennedy made it clear that American warships would search Soviet vessels bound for Cuba and would not permit any that carried offensive weapons to dock in Cuban ports. He also indicated that if the nuclear weapons already on Cuban soil were not removed quickly the United States would take military action against them. The initial reaction of the Soviet leadership to Kennedy's threats was alarming: they put their country on military alert and for a couple of days a nuclear war seemed to be a real possibility.

On 25 October, Khrushchev retreated, telling Kennedy that he would withdraw the missiles in return for an American promise not to invade Cuba, which, the Soviet leader now said, was what he had wanted to achieve all along.

War had been averted, but politically the entire escapade was a disaster for Khrushchev. To his critics at home, who had for some time bemoaned his erratic behavior, the Cuban adventure was yet another example of his 'harebrained schemes'. Over the previous four years he had come up with one reform after another and the results were mixed at best. Although he had been instrumental in dismantling much of the Gulag and in restraining the security forces, the police still maintained close surveillance over the population and at times arbitrarily arrested citizens guilty of no more than expressing dissatisfaction with the state of affairs. Khrushchev's economic reforms had also not yielded the results that people had expected. True, the population was better fed and such consumer goods as television sets and refrigerators were now more widely available. It has been estimated that during Khrushchev's years in power the production of consumer goods rose by some sixty percent. Moreover, the launching of the satellite *Sputnik* in 1957 and Yuri Gagarin's flight into space, the first manned orbit of the globe, enhanced the prestige of Russia. But there was still much grumbling about shortages of consumer goods, about their poor quality, and generally about the standard of living, which remained low. In 1963, an unexpectedly poor harvest caused considerable hardship for many citizens. And there was another reason for growing disillusionment with Khrushchev: his tendency, despite his criticisms of Stalin, to create a new cult of personality centered on himself. His photographs appeared endlessly in the press, and with increasing frequency books would include a preface lauding his achievements as the country's great leader. It is said that he was thoroughly pleased when his grandson asked him, 'Who are you? The Tsar?'

His colleagues in the Presidium and the Central Committee, however, were not pleased and early in 1964 they hatched another conspiracy to oust him. The prime movers were a former and a present head of the KGB (security police), A. Shelepin and V. Semichastny. Though many details are still unclear, we know that on 13 October 1964 officials in Moscow sent a message to Khrushchev, who was vacationing in the Crimea, asking him to return immediately to the capital to attend a meeting of the Presidium. On his arrival, he immediately realized that several people who owed their high positions to his benevolence had turned against him and that he would be sacked. As he had done seven years earlier, he insisted that only the Central Committee had the authority to dismiss him, but this time the plotters had anticipated his demand. The entire Central Committee had been summoned and at its meeting on 14 October M. A. Suslov, the party ideologist and one of the more senior members of the Presidium, formally charged Khrushchev with fifteen errors, among them recklessness in foreign affairs, mistreatment of colleagues, failures in economic policy, and dictatorial conduct. The committee voted unanimously to strip him of all his offices. Khrushchev tried to fight back, but, sensing the hopelessness of his position, he gave up, declaiming abjectly that 'I've got what I deserved.' He was allowed to retire on a pension that permitted him to live comfortably.

ERA OF STAGNATION

The dignitaries selected as Khrushchev's successor Leonid Brezhnev, a man no one had believed destined to assume the highest political position in the Soviet Union. The conspirators settled on Brezhnev only because they thought that choosing him would avoid controversy by concealing the fact that Shelepin, generally presumed to have the inside track to succeed Khrushchev, had been a central figure in the conspiracy. To everyone's surprise, Brezhnev quickly demonstrated the political skills necessary not only to outwit his rivals but to hold on to the highest post for eighteen years.

Brezhnev's career had not been distinguished. He was a typical *apparatchik* (party functionary) with a gift for remaining in the good graces of his superiors. He joined the Communist Party in 1932 at the age of twenty-six and steadily moved up the ranks. Khrushchev, then party leader in the Ukraine, especially appreciated Brezhnev's loyalty and secured rapid promotions for him. During the Second World War he served ably as a commissar on the southern and Ukrainian fronts, and in 1950 he became first secretary of the party in Moldavia, where he distinguished himself by ruthlessly suppressing the 'bourgeois nationalism' of the local population. In 1952, Stalin appointed him to the Presidium, and as an ardent champion of the virgin lands campaign Brezhnev achieved prominence in the early 1960s. Neither particularly intelligent nor effective as a public speaker, Brezhnev was a cheerful and charming man who acquired a special skill for planning agendas for meetings and ensuring that proposals would be accepted with a minimum of controversy. But he was also a vain man who would punish subordinates who did not praise him adequately by dispatching them to obscure and undesirable posts. Convinced, as he put it, that 'nobody lives just on his wages', he was unashamedly corrupt. He enjoyed high living and had a special weakness for big foreign limousines, which he collected assiduously. Foreign dignitaries who visited him frequently gave him one as a gift, and he derived childlike pleasure from sitting at the wheel of one of his cars at his various government retreats. A joke circulating in the 1970s nicely captures the public attitude towards the country's leader. Brezhnev took his aging mother on a tour of the lavish country homes where he kept his cars and lived luxuriously. She remained silent until the frustrated Brezhnev finally asked her point blank what she thought of all his comforts. 'It's very nice,' she responded, 'but what will happen when the communists come back to power?'

Soon after Brezhnev died in 1982, his eighteen-year rule came to be known very aptly as the 'era of stagnation'. Still trying to overcome the painful legacy of Stalinist repression and to achieve a decent standard of living for the people, the country could hardly afford a prolonged period with no marked economic and political progress. Brezhnev did not reintroduce mass terror, but after a few months in office he stopped criticizing the cult of personality, urged a more favorable assessment of Stalin's 'achievements', and adopted a hard line towards all dissent, which nevertheless continued to increase. When the government refused to sanction the publication of controversial works of literature, dissident authors, who during previous periods of severe repression kept their work secret by writing 'for the drawer', turned to *samizdat* (self-publishing). They would reproduce their writings by making carbon copies of them or by using mimeograph machines and then distribute them by hand. In a celebrated trial in the fall of 1965, the authors A. D. Siniavsky and Yu. Daniel were sentenced to, respectively, seven and five years in prison for having secretly circulated works that disparaged the official rules on how literature should portray Soviet life and for having satirized Stalin's terror. Alexander Solzhenitsyn, already famous for his depiction of the labor camps, protested the censorship and increasing repression, but to no avail. Eventually, Siniavsky and Daniel were allowed to emigrate, and in 1974 Solzhenitsyn was unceremoniously expelled from the Soviet Union.

One of the more cruel punishments of dissidents meted out with some frequency during Brezhnev's regime was their enforced placement in psychiatric wards. This practice had apparently been used at times by Stalin, and after the Gulag had been almost completely dismantled it again appealed to the authorities as an effective way of dealing with alleged troublemakers. A few men with medical degrees could be found to examine dissidents and diagnose them as suffering from such ailments as 'psychomotor excitement', 'sluggish schizophrenia', or even 'reformist delusions'. During a twenty-year period from 1962 to 1983, some five hundred citizens, many of them human rights activists, were detained in psychiatric hospitals. That the security police remained a force to be reckoned with is also demonstrated by the statistics that in 1973 the KGB employed 500,000 people and by 1986 the number had risen to 700,000.

In foreign policy, Brezhnev used a sledgehammer rather than a scalpel. He was not as bombastic and provocative as Khrushchev and he sought to maintain formally good relations – *détente* – with the United States. But he did not hesitate to use force to defend what he considered to be the vital interests of the Soviet Union. In 1968, when communist reformers took over the government of Czechoslovakia and proceeded to establish 'socialism with a human face', Brezhnev vacillated for a few months and then sent powerful forces to crush the liberal movement. Then he enunciated the 'Brezhnev doctrine', notable not so much for what it said but for the boldness with which he formulated it. Brezhnev declared that whenever the Soviet Union believed developments in a socialist state threatened its interests it had the right to intervene militarily. The pronouncement of the doctrine inevitably chilled relations between the USSR and the West and put a damper on reformist tendencies in Eastern Europe as well as in the Soviet Union itself.

Eleven years later, in 1979, Brezhnev made his most aggressive move in foreign affairs. He ordered the invasion of Afghanistan, which was undergoing a civil war that Soviet leaders feared the socialist regime might lose to Muslim fundamentalists. In a sense, then, the invasion was an application of the Brezhnev doctrine, even though Afghanistan was not part of the Soviet bloc. But the intervention proved to be a major blunder. The Afghans put up fierce resistance, the terrain was treacherous, and many Soviet troops fought sluggishly because they could not understand why they were in the country in the first place. The invasion also cooled relations between the USSR and the West, and in particular with the United States. As a sign of disapproval of the invasion, President Jimmy Carter prohibited Americans from participating in the Olympic Games in Moscow in 1980. In 1988, after a futile war of over eight years that had produced a stalemate, the Soviet troops withdrew from Afghanistan without having achieved their stated goals.

Long before that humiliating retreat, the Soviet Union was in the throes of a serious domestic crisis, the result of an economic slowdown and the incompetence of the political leadership. Ever since 1966, the government had exuberantly claimed that the country had entered the stage of 'mature socialism', but the data about economic developments indicated that the drive to improve the standard of living remained stalled. For one thing, the government maintained a huge military expenditure, some ten and a half to eleven and a half percent of the gross national product. Moreover, labor productivity, which had been low for many years, continued to lag behind that of other industrialized countries. In the period from 1951 to 1965, for example, the rate of increase in productivity amounted to between forty and fifty percent of that of American workers. In 1963, each miner in the United States produced fourteen tons of coal per day, whereas their Russian counterpart produced 2.1 tons per day, even though the level of mechanization was about the same.

There were several reasons for the poor showing of the Soviet economy. The central planners in Moscow determined the prices of all goods, but they made their decisions arbitrarily without taking into account the laws of supply and demand or the actual cost of producing goods. Some goods and services were absurdly cheap and therefore required heavy subsidies, which, in turn, prevented the planners from making the most rational allocation of resources. Also, the price of many items remained unchanged despite inflation, which the authorities for ideological reasons simply refused to acknowledge. Pay scales, also centrally determined, did not provide incentives for workers to exert themselves to maximize output. To understand the workers' attitude, one need only consider the lot of an unskilled worker, who in 1964 earned sixty rubles a month, a sum that could buy two pairs of shoes and nothing else. A witticism attributed to Eastern European workers also accurately describes the attitude of Soviet laborers: 'You [the government] pretend to pay us, we pretend to work.'

The agricultural sector was similarly stagnant in the 1970s. Investments in capital stock increased by no less than 160 percent in the years from 1965 to 1980, whereas total output went up by only about twenty percent. One reason for this disappointing development was the poor quality of agricultural machines. In western Siberia, for instance, only fifteen percent of milking machines were in working order. In other parts of the country, machines were obsolete and often broke down. Even when they did work properly they were inefficient. Throughout the USSR there was such a shortage of trucks and trains with refrigerators that a substantial amount of the agricultural yield perished before reaching the markets. In 1981, a Soviet newspaper reported that each year about 620,000 tons of fertilizer were lost in transit because of poor facilities or simple negligence.

Other features of Soviet society signaled stagnation. The rate of population growth slowed markedly. The annual rate of increase in the 1950s, 1.8 percent, had declined by more than half by the 1980s, to 0.8 percent. During the decade from 1969 to 1979, life expectancy fell from 69.3 years to 67.7 years. The health-care system was for most people woefully inadequate, but that was not the only reason for these declines. Alcoholism, a perennial problem in the Russian Empire, remained widespread in the Soviet Union. In Leningrad alone, in 1979, over eleven percent of the population was arrested for being inebriated in public. It has been estimated that in 1980 some fifty thousand people died from alcoholism and that eight to nine percent of the country's national income was lost because of alcohol abuse. The rate of absenteeism at factories and offices on Mondays of workers recovering from a weekend of excessive drinking was alarmingly high.

In a centralized political structure, reform measures to address these problems could come only from the top, but by the mid 1970s the Soviet leadership was incapable of taking any initiatives. Brezhnev had visibly deteriorated physically and, as is now known, suffered from some debilitating nervous ailments. Several strokes had impaired his gait as well as his diction; quite often he was incoherent. Instead of heeding the advice of respectable doctors, he turned to a quack who plied him with medicines that only worsened his condition. But he gave no thought to retiring. On the contrary, he encouraged a new cult of personality, which lauded him as the *vozhd*, a title previously accorded to Stalin. He collected one medal after another and was even awarded the Lenin Prize for Literature for his memoirs, which had been written by a hired hand. In 1977, he also took the initiative in drafting a new constitution, which would give him the honor of having replaced the outworn Stalin constitution of 1936. The new document proclaimed the attainment of a 'mature socialist society', but did not introduce any significant changes in the country's political system. It was clearly designed to massage Brezhnev's ego.

For about twelve months, beginning late in 1981, Brezhnev's condition was so precarious that he rarely appeared in public and yet no action was taken to remove him from office. The members of the Politburo, who knew of Brezhnev's infirmity, could have voted to oust him, but they were too timid. The most plausible explanation for their irresponsible behavior – Brezhnev, after all, had his hand on the nuclear button – is that they deeply distrusted each other and feared loss of power and privileges if any other person became first secretary. So it was not until Brezhnev's death on 10 November that the Politburo chose a new leader, Iu. V. Andropov, for many years the head of the KGB.

In some respects the choice seemed to be a good one. Andropov was a highly intelligent person with extensive experience in public affairs. Although quite cynical and determined to maintain the Soviet system of rule, he understood that the country had taken several wrong turns and that major reforms were essential. He vowed to end corruption and to reestablish discipline in society, and made extensive personnel changes to bring into the top echelons of government people who were honest and energetic. But he was too old (sixty-nine) and too ill to lead a campaign for reform. He suffered from a serious kidney ailment and barely six months after taking office he often had to miss important meetings. He died in February 1984, having served as general secretary for less than sixteen months. Now the Politburo returned to form and chose the seventy-two-year-old

K. U. Chernenko as their leader. Chernenko was in every respect a mediocrity and he was ill with emphysema. He died in March 1985 without any memorable achievement during his brief tenure in the highest office in the land.

ERA OF REFORM

For about a decade the USSR had essentially been rudderless, and for many people within the country and abroad the government had become an object of derision. No doubt for that reason, but also because it had become evident that dynamic leadership was needed to deal with the nation's economic decline and political disarray, the Politburo now selected as general secretary M. S. Gorbachev, who was relatively young (fifty-four), intelligent, very engaging, experienced in public affairs, and ambitious and energetic. Equally important, he seemed to be far more open-minded than most Soviet officials and understood, as did few others in the upper reaches of the government, that the country was in trouble and needed to be revitalized.

Although Gorbachev had belonged to the top echelon of the Communist Party for some eighteen years, not many people suspected that he was the kind of person who would lead the Soviet Union in a fundamentally new direction. He was, as the historian Robert Service put it, a 'brilliant dissimulator'; in public he toed the party line but in private conversations with his family and closest friends he had, ever since his days as a student at Moscow State University from 1950 to 1955, expressed dissatisfaction with the state of affairs in his country, though he had only the vaguest notion of how to improve conditions. Given his personal experiences, his caution was not surprising. Born in 1931 in southern Russia into a family whose roots as peasants stretched back for many decades, he was well aware of the horrors of Stalinism. One of his godfathers had been arrested during the collectivization drive of the early 1930s, several members of his own family were victims of repression, and about

a third of the inhabitants of Privolne, the village in which he was
born, died in the early 1930s directly as a result of Stalin's policies. As a youngster, Gorbachev worked diligently in the fields,
for which he was awarded the Order of the Red Banner of Labor
in 1949. But he was also an excellent student and was admitted into the prestigious Faculty of Jurisprudence at Moscow
State University, from which he graduated with very high grades.
Legal work, however, did not interest him and after a few days
in the office of the Stavropol procurator's office he embarked
on a career in politics. An indefatigable and efficient worker,
his promotions came rapidly. By 1970, he was the leader of the
Stavropol region party organization, and in 1978 he moved to
Moscow to become first secretary of the Central Committee of
the Communist Party with the specific charge of heading the
Agricultural Department and the various ministries dealing with
agricultural affairs. In this position he attended the sessions of
the Politburo though he could not vote. At forty-seven, he was
the youngest man in the top leadership of the country.

Immediately after Chernenko's death, the members of the
Politburo unanimously voted for Gorbachev as general secretary of the party and therefore the nation's leader. But there
is little doubt that had the Politburo members suspected that
Gorbachev had a strong, pragmatic bent and that he was determined to improve conditions even if it meant adopting ever more
far-reaching reforms, they would never have voted for him to lead
the Communist Party. By 1985, he was known to be relatively
open-minded, but his colleagues took him at his word when he
proclaimed that he was committed to Marxism-Leninism. To be
fair to Gorbachev, he was sincere in his expressions of loyalty to
party dogmas. In 1985, he had no idea how difficult it would be
to introduce reform. Nor did he himself know at the time how far
he would be willing to go to achieve his goals.

The six years of Gorbachev's rule were an extraordinarily
confusing period during which the public mood in the Soviet
Union alternated between optimism, anxiety, and frustration.
Well-wishers and critics of communism throughout the world

waited with bated breath for the latest pronouncements from the Kremlin. For both sides, one issue, posed in two forms, was paramount. Could communism reform itself, in the process becoming democratic, without abandoning socialism? Or was the rot in the communist regime so deep rooted that the entire system had to be abandoned before a more efficient and decent order could be created? These are questions that will preoccupy scholars for many years to come and it is not likely that they will reach a consensus, because the issues Gorbachev confronted were so complex. At critical points during his period in power Gorbachev himself was at a loss on where he wished to lead his country, as is clear from his response late in 1990 to a reporter's question of whether he was moving to the right. 'Actually,' he responded, 'I'm going around in circles.' Part of the problem was that every time he took an initiative to spur the economy, conditions deteriorated further. The advice he received from politicians and experts was contradictory, adding to the pervasive confusion: people on the right warned him that he was going too far and that his reformist policies were bound to produce chaos; people on the left berated him for not going far enough and warned him that if he did not introduce radical changes quickly he would lose the goodwill and support of the people, most of whom allegedly yearned for bold initiatives.

Moreover, despite his intelligence and political savvy, Gorbachev seems not to have been familiar with a basic rule of politics, first formulated by Alexis de Tocqueville, 'that the most dangerous moment for a bad government is generally that in which it sets about reform'. It did not occur to him that his reforms might unleash a chain reaction in Soviet society that he would not be able to control. Thus, he was surprised that his proposals, especially when they became more radical, triggered protest movements among the national minorities and in Eastern Europe, movements that played a major role in the break-up of the Soviet Union. Then there were unexpected disasters, such as the nuclear reactor meltdown in Chernobyl in April 1986 and the earthquakes in Armenia in 1988, both of which the

government mishandled, further eroding confidence in its competence. Finally, Gorbachev had to contend with personal rivalries
and betrayals, factors that are often overlooked by historians but
that can have a powerful impact on the course of events. Given
all these intractable problems, it seems as though Gorbachev
was destined to fail and the Soviet Union was bound to collapse.
But that would be too simplistic a reading of the country's history
from 1985 to 1991. A complicated interplay of factors accounts
for the final outcome, which no one could have foreseen when
Gorbachev began his period of rule.

Gorbachev's first initiative was moderate but also ill-advised.
Following in Andropov's footsteps, he launched a campaign
against alcoholism with a two-fold aim: to boost economic
productivity and to overcome a social problem that had reached
serious dimensions. The government sharply reduced the output
of liquor, ordered the police to enforce the prohibition of the
production of vodka at home (*samogon*), imposed restrictions on
the sale of alcohol at restaurants, and generally waged a campaign
to discourage the drinking of spirits. These measures did lead to
a decline in the consumption of liquor and to an improvement in
public health. But these positive achievements were outweighed
by deleterious consequences. A great many people addicted to
liquor resorted to such industrial products as methylated spirits
and anti-freeze to produce liquor, which was of inferior quality and often harmful. The government did not understand that
alcoholism is a symptom, not a cause, of personal malaise, and
that it can be effectively combated only by a long and sophisticated program of therapy and counseling. It also turned out that
by reducing the production of alcohol the government lost no
less than 28 billion rubles in income within three years, which it
could ill afford at a time of economic decline. And the campaign
against alcoholism did not stimulate an increase in productivity.
Within three years the campaign was quietly dropped.

Gorbachev's initiatives in political and cultural affairs were
more promising and certainly more enduring. In 1986, as he
began his move towards the left, he adopted the policy of

glasnost, a hazy term that literally means 'publicity' or 'openness' but that soon acquired a variety of meanings. Initially, Gorbachev seems to have had in mind little more than that the government would be more forthcoming and self-critical in issuing information. But it did not take long for that cautious approach to be abandoned in favor of official toleration of the dissemination of information and opinions on a wide range of issues. By 1988, newspapers, journals, and television were dealing with subjects that had been taboo for decades, such as the Stalinist terror, censorship, the degradation of the environment, corruption, crime, the failings of the health services, and the intrigues at the highest levels of authority. Works of fiction, including those of writers who had been forced to emigrate, were now freely published, and films could deal with the seamier aspects of Soviet life. Scholars who did not toe the party line could publish their works even if they went so far as to criticize Lenin, who was still revered by Gorbachev and his colleagues. In December 1986, Gorbachev personally invited Andrei Sakharov, a Nobel Prize winning scientist who had been exiled to Gorky for his human rights activities, to return to Moscow, where he soon became the leader of the democratic movement. As a result of *glasnost*, cultural and political life in the Soviet Union underwent a fundamental change, and the public's enthusiasm for the change appeared to be boundless.

Glasnost was actually part of a larger reform enterprise that Gorbachev dubbed *perestroika* (reconstruction), which too was never clearly defined. When he first used the term, in May 1985, he merely said, 'Obviously, we all of us must undergo reconstruction, all of us . . . Everyone must adopt new approaches and understand that no other path is available to us.' Alexander Yakovlev, a loyal and highly intelligent supporter of Gorbachev, viewed *perestroika* in moral terms, as a movement to inspire citizens to become creative and responsible people. However, within short order, the term became a watchword, a catch-all for the transformation of Soviet society. Devoid of specific meaning, it could be used to justify a wide range of economic, social, and political changes. As Gorbachev moved from timid reforms to moderate and then to radical reforms, he defended all of them in the name of *perestroika*.

ECONOMIC CRISIS

The most pressing problem for Gorbachev was the economy, which continued to deteriorate after he assumed leadership of the Soviet Union. In both industry and agriculture, output declined steadily. The farms did not produce enough food and about one-fifth of what is referred to as 'caloric intake' had to be imported, this at a time of growing budget deficits. Industry's failure to keep up with the technological advances that were sharply increasing productivity in the West not only adversely affected the country's standard of living but also raised fears in the government that their country was falling hopelessly behind the West in military strength.

In 1990, during Gorbachev's fifth year in office, the economic crisis deepened dramatically. Within one year the net national product declined by nine percent. Prices rose precipitately, some staple products such as milk, tea, coffee, and soap were hard to find, and in numerous regions the authorities introduced a system of rationing. In a desperate attempt to stimulate productivity, Gorbachev adopted a measure to allow workers to elect their own managers, but this backfired because the new managers, beholden to their employees, raised wages sharply, and that, in turn, caused further inflation. The government also tried a variety of other economic reforms, such as permitting a private (capitalist) sector to develop in services and small-scale industry and relaxing central control over wages, but these strategies too did not work, in part because many officials who opposed Gorbachev's program simply ignored them. Gorbachev then began to speak of establishing a 'socialist market economy', a self-contradictory notion whose meaning he failed to explain and which did not have any practical consequences.

Gorbachev sought the advice of highly competent economists, and almost invariably they recommended that the government abandon centralized control of the economy, as well as the restraints on ownership of private property and private initiative. In September 1990, a commission under the direction of the respected economist Stanislav Shatalin presented to the government a detailed list of economic reforms, known as the '500 Days Plan', to turn the country away from socialism and establish a system of free enterprise. The project even included the wording of twenty-one legal acts that were to be passed by the legislature to provide the basic regulations for the new economy. No one can be sure that Shatalin's plan would have worked, but it was widely regarded as the country's best hope for overcoming the economic crisis that threatened to turn into a catastrophe. Gorbachev seemed to favor the plan and the chances of adoption were promising, but, as so often when he had to reach a major decision, he got cold feet. Probably, he was not prepared for so sharp a retreat from his ideological commitments; he still regarded himself as a Marxist-Leninist and expressed his support for 'socialism with a human face'. It may also be that he feared that Shatalin's measures were simply too radical and would encounter so much resistance that they would only make matters worse. He now turned sharply to the right and dismissed several of his most dedicated, reform-minded supporters. In his public pronouncements he reverted to stale communist phraseology.

Gorbachev's inability to revive the economy undermined his other achievements, which were impressive. At no previous time in the history of the USSR did the people enjoy as much freedom as they did in the late 1980s. Equally important, a whole series of political institutions were established that appeared to be the bedrock of a genuine democratic order. Gorbachev had moved gradually, step by step, but in the political sphere he was bold and courageous. He created a new political structure that gave the people a greater voice in national affairs. A Congress of People's Deputies consisting of 2,250 members was elected and was to meet annually, serving as a check on the authority of the executive part of the government. The congress would elect a Supreme Soviet of 542 representatives, which would meet twice a year and serve as a legislature operating more or less like a parliament in Western countries. But only two-thirds of the Congress of People's Deputies were to be elected directly by the people. One-third of its members were to be chosen by 'social organizations' such as trade unions and the Communist Party. The Supreme Soviet would elect the chairman, who, it was assumed, would also be the general secretary of the Communist Party, the post that Gorbachev occupied. According to Article 6 of the constitution of 1976, the Communist Party was 'the nucleus of the political system and of all state and public organizations', and Gorbachev was not prepared to strip the party completely of that status. He remained committed to the Soviet Union as a workers' state in which the communists would enjoy important political privileges.

Still, the meetings of the Congress of People's Deputies over a two-week period in late May and early June 1989 were greeted with enormous excitement throughout the country. To be sure, the elections were not 'democratic' in the Western sense of the word. Not only were so many seats set aside for special organizations, but in over twenty percent of the constituencies only one name appeared on the ballot and in other areas there were irregularities that assured victory for Communist Party candidates. Not surprisingly, the conservatives – that is, party activists opposed to Gorbachev – won a solid majority of the seats. On the other hand, close to ninety percent of the eligible voters went to the polls, and more than a few Communist Party officials failed to be elected. A substantial number of the deputies were reformers, among them the now revered Andrei Sakharov, and, most important, the deliberations were broadcast on television. The people of the Soviet Union, and many outside the country, were riveted to their sets, amazed at the candor with which deputies questioned and criticized the leadership. There were extensive references to the brutal repressions during the Stalinist era, the activities of the security police, the ecological catastrophes, the

Nazi–Soviet Pact, not to mention the questions about the luxurious lifestyle of Gorbachev and other senior officials. Sakharov called for a fundamental political change: the Communist Party should no longer enjoy a monopoly of power. Gorbachev was elected to a new post, chairman of the Supreme Soviet, the leading position in the state; a title that was soon changed to 'president'. Gorbachev retained the post of general secretary of the Communist Party.

But his hope that the political reforms he had instituted, far-reaching as they were, would give him a breathing spell during which he would be able to revitalize the economy and restore stability would soon be dashed. The pressures on him from the left continued, and in March 1990 he took a leap forward in implementing a change that did nothing less than undermine the authority of the Communist Party. For some seventy-three years it had exercised power in the Soviet Union on its own, unencumbered by any checks. Now Article 6 of the constitution, which guaranteed that power to the party, was amended and power was placed in the hands of the state. In many ways, this was Gorbachev's crowning achievement, since it opened up the possibility of the Soviet Union evolving into a pluralistic democracy.

But by this time, Gorbachev was under siege, attacked savagely from the right and the left. The leader of the left was Boris Yeltsin, a flamboyant and impulsive politician who had made his mark as a hard-driving party official in Sverdlovsk (formerly and now again Ekaterinburg). In 1986, Gorbachev had brought Yeltsin to the capital where, as first secretary of the Moscow Party City Committee, he proceeded to make a mark by dismissing numerous functionaries for corruption. Yeltsin also played the role of a populist, often traveling around the city by bus, visiting factories, offices, restaurants; on his endless tours he would ask citizens how services might be improved. His popularity rose quickly, and as that happened he became more daring and tactless in pressuring Gorbachev to adopt more radical reforms. In October 1987, Gorbachev fired Yeltsin, who also resigned from his position as candidate member of the Politburo. He now assumed the relatively minor post of deputy chairman of the State Construction Committee, and it seemed that his career had come to an ignominious end.

But Yeltsin was bent on rehabilitation, driven not only by ambition but also by a determination to avenge his defeat by Gorbachev. The two men became bitter rivals, and for the next four years the conflict between them played a central role in the demise of the Soviet Union. In mid 1988, at the Nineteenth Party Conference, Yeltsin unexpectedly announced his support for almost all of Gorbachev's program and humbly asked that he be reinstated as a party leader. After a sharp attack by the rightist Egor Ligachev, the conference delivered Yeltsin another humiliating defeat by voting not to restore him to his party post. Undaunted, Yeltsin decided to resurrect his political career by throwing in his lot with the democratic opposition to Gorbachev and by running (in the spring of 1990) for election to the People's Congress of the Russian Soviet Federal Socialist Republic (RSFSR), the largest constituent republic of the Soviet Union, a move that signified a shift in his political allegiance from the Soviet Union to Russia. Within a few months Yeltsin was elected speaker of the Russian Supreme Soviet and a year later, in June 1991, he won election as president of Russia. He now had his own power base and, according to reliable polls, was considerably more popular in the Soviet Union than Gorbachev.

POLITICAL COLLAPSE

In the meantime, the Soviet empire had started to unravel, a process that tested to the utmost Gorbachev's skills and his commitment to peaceful reform. Gorbachev was thoroughly dedicated to the preservation of both the Soviet Union and socialism and he made every effort on behalf of both causes. To his credit, however, it must be said that he refused to apply massive force to maintain the empire or to retain power for himself. He still had the necessary forces under his command and occasionally he came close to launching a crackdown but in the end he held back. His restraint will surely be recalled by historians as one of his most admirable traits as a leader.

Beginning in 1989, the countries in the Eastern Bloc – Poland, East Germany, Bulgaria, Romania, Hungary, and Czechoslovakia – which were formally independent but in effect were vassal states of the Soviet Union, broke away, declared their independence, and discarded communism without encountering any forceful attempt by the Russians to restrain them. But that was not all. Since 1987, nationalist movements had become increasingly assertive within various republics of the USSR. At first, they demanded autonomy, but soon they escalated their demands and called for virtual independence. In November 1988, for example, the Estonian Supreme Soviet announced that it had the authority to veto laws enacted in Moscow. Two months later, Lithuania officially protested the presence of Soviet military forces on its territory. Both these states declared that Russian would no longer be the official state language. Within another year, nationalist movements demanding autonomy or more far-reaching self-government had spread to virtually every region of the country, including republics culturally and linguistically close to the Russians, such as Ukraine and Belorussia. To prevent the disintegration of the country, Gorbachev in April 1991 initiated a rapprochement with Yeltsin to secure his support for a new Union Treaty that would grant the constituent republics greater autonomy than heretofore in economic and political affairs but still retain the Soviet Union as a unified state. A formal treaty between the republics establishing the new arrangement was to be signed on 20 August.

Infuriated, hard-liners in the leadership of the Communist Party swung into action. First, they attacked Gorbachev so vehemently that he offered to resign as general secretary. Only the entreaties of his supporters led him to reconsider. But then the hard-liners made their most daring move: they initiated a coup to unseat Gorbachev. The events surrounding the plot would make a perfect storyline for a comic opera. Even the prologue to the coup is mind-boggling. In mid 1991, James Baker, the American secretary of state, warned Gorbachev that a coup was imminent, but he cavalierly ignored the information. He could not believe that the men he had outfoxed politically were capable of toppling him. In August he went for a rest to his dacha in the village of Foros on the Black Sea.

On 18 August, he unexpectedly received a visit from four senior officials, who had arranged to have all of Gorbachev's telephone lines inactivated. Without wasting time on formalities, the four men asked Gorbachev to give up power to the vice president, G. Yanaev, who would immediately proclaim an emergency to allow the authorities to restore order and, it was assumed, cancel the Union Treaty. Then Gorbachev would resume his position as head of state. The president rejected the plan and his defiance paid off because the conspirators were incredibly incompetent and cowardly to boot. They had neglected to arrest any of the leaders likely to oppose their scheme and they made no attempt to take control of the television stations or to guard against street protests. The press conference they held to inform the nation of their action was a fiasco. Far from being presidential, Yanaev was a nervous wreck who could not stop fidgeting with his fingers. Another of the conspirators, Valentin Pavlov, was too drunk to show up at the press conference. The government's first public appearance did not inspire confidence in the plotters' ability to run the country, let alone restore order at a time of crisis.

For Yeltsin, the coup was a golden opportunity to demonstrate his courage as well as his commitment to fundamental reform. In an unforgettable gesture, he climbed atop a tank outside the White House, the building that housed the Supreme Soviet of the RSFSR and had become the headquarters of the resistance to the coup, and before a large crowd vowed to defeat the conspirators. Yeltsin immediately became a national hero. Then the army delivered a fatal blow to the conspirators by refusing to support them. By midday of 21 August, just three days after it had started, the coup had fizzled out.

On his return to Moscow, Gorbachev made several major mistakes that played into Yeltsin's hands. He refused to criticize the Communist Party even though a number of its leaders had either joined the coup or had given their blessing to it. Many of them now resigned from their positions, but Gorbachev surprisingly replaced them with other people who were anathema to the people who had stood with Yeltsin at the White House. Inevitably, Yeltsin's prestige soared and he knew how to make the most of his chances. He treated Gorbachev with contempt, vowed support for a market economy, declared the independence of Russia from the Soviet Union, and recognized the independence of the other republics. The Soviet Union disintegrated into fifteen separate states, a development that two years earlier hardly any informed person anywhere would have believed possible.

To appreciate the historical significance of the Soviet Union's collapse, it is worth considering the fate of other powerful empires. The Roman Empire, the Spanish Empire, the British Empire all disappeared, but all of them lasted much longer than the Soviet empire; they declined gradually over a period of decades if not centuries. And all of them left powerful imprints on the lands they had dominated. The Roman Empire, for example, lasted roughly from 27 BC until AD 476, some five hundred years, and its period of decline took about 140 years. In the east, 'Roman' rule survived until 1453. Its legacy in law, art, and literature is too well known to require further comment. The Spanish Empire existed roughly from the late fifteenth century until the seventeenth century, and its cultural and political impact on the Americas was very pronounced and is still highly visible. The British Empire lasted from the seventeenth until the twentieth century and disintegrated gradually over a period of many decades. Its cultural and political influence was, of course, enormous.

By contrast, the Soviet empire – so different politically, economically, socially, and culturally from imperial Russia as to constitute a new polity – lasted only seventy-four years and the Soviet Union's domination of Eastern Europe a mere forty-five years. The Soviet legacy was deep discontent in the former communist states, passionate hatred among the subject peoples for the Russians, and violent ethnic conflict. And it is now clear that the successor states to the Soviet Union have retained few, if any, traces of the communist system in economics, politics, or culture. How can we account for this? How did it happen that a huge empire, one that appeared to be enormously powerful, dissolved within just six years after the government initiated reform, and left so few positive traces? Boris Yeltsin in 1992 made a statement that suggests an answer. 'The world can sigh in relief. The idol of communism, which spread everywhere social strife, animosity, and unparalleled brutality, which instilled fear in humanity, has collapsed.' A historian might legitimately refine Yeltsin's statement by suggesting that communism failed because it was from its inception a utopian and thus unattainable idea that was incompetently implemented by ruthless ideologues.

THE PRESIDENCY OF BORIS N. YELTSIN

As president of the newly independent Russian Federation, Yeltsin set himself a task so prodigious and complicated that in hindsight one can legitimately doubt whether he ever had a realistic chance of succeeding. He planned to transform Russia in short order from an authoritarian state, in which the economy was centrally owned and regulated, into a democracy, in which private enterprise predominated. This was to be achieved in a country without deeply rooted traditions of popular government, without the legal and economic institutions that are the backbone of capitalism, and without cadres of citizens familiar with the principles of democracy or the practices of capitalism. No country had ever undergone a transition within a brief period of time from authoritarian collectivism to free enterprise and popular rule, and although there were numerous plans on how to proceed no one could point to relevant precedents.

Even under the best of circumstances the chances of success would have been dubious, but conditions in Russia in 1991 were fraught with intractable problems. Probably the most serious were the failings of the political leadership. It was not simply that Yeltsin lacked experience in coping with the tasks at hand. He was an extremely erratic man apparently without firm convictions. At one time a loyal communist, he flitted from enthusiasm for reform to populism; then he repudiated communism entirely and proclaimed his support for democracy and a market economy. But once in power he convinced himself that the Russian people wanted a strong ruler. He now became increasingly authoritarian, going so far as to assume the role of 'father of the nation', and acting like 'Tsar Boris'. To the surprise of even some of his closest associates, he would refer to himself in the third person as 'the president' and issue terse orders in the manner of a monarch or dictator. Yeltsin was also a troubled man who suffered from deep depressions, during which he would disappear from public view for weeks at a time. Addicted to alcohol, he would occasionally be seen in public unable to walk in a straight line. And there were protracted periods when Yeltsin was so seriously ill that he could not perform his official functions. Struck down by several heart attacks, he underwent a quintuple coronary bypass operation late in 1996. During these periods of indisposition no one was legally empowered to take his place, since the constitution contained no provision on who was to govern when the president was incapacitated. The warring factions in his entourage, eager to protect their privileged positions, would unite in clever but not altogether successful attempts to conceal the president's infirmity.

Most of the time the factions were at loggerheads on how to deal with the rapidly declining economy, the creation of new political and social institutions, and the increasingly strident demands for independence of minority populations such as the Chechens. A brilliant political tactician, Yeltsin endlessly engaged in intrigues and sought to play off one group against another before reaching a decision, but this mode of governing proved to be ineffective because it often led to inaction by the government on critical economic and political issues.

Yeltsin's most pressing challenge was the economy, which had been stagnating for many years and had been a major stumbling block for Gorbachev. Determined to avoid his predecessor's indecisiveness, Yeltsin adopted the radical proposals – known as 'shock therapy' – of his newly appointed minister of economics and finance, Yegor Gaidar. The idea was to introduce quickly and suddenly a series of fundamental reforms that would in short order abolish the socialist economy and replace it with one operating on the basis of the market mechanism. Yeltsin was persuaded of the plan's feasibility and likened Gaidar to a physician who treated a paralyzed patient by dragging him off the bed and forcing him to walk. On 1 January 1992, the government announced that, as of 2 January, price controls would be lifted, allowing the market to determine prices of goods. Gaidar warned that there would be some inflation; he estimated that prices might rise as much as one hundred percent. His analysis was deeply flawed: in two months prices went up at least ten-fold. But that was not all. Industrial production fell sharply, the value of the ruble declined dramatically, and unemployment rose at a rapid pace.

There were short periods of economic recovery since the Gaidar reform. For example, 1996 is considered a good year because the rate of inflation was only about twenty-two percent. But all in all, the lot of the Russian people since 1992 has been grim. A few statistics tell the tale. In late 1992, for example, one-third of the country's 148 million citizens lived below the poverty line. Millions of working people – according to one reliable estimate, about three-quarters of them – did not receive their pay on time and sometimes the delay ran to months. Many residents in cities managed to feed themselves only because they had small plots of land on which they grew potatoes and vegetables. In large parts of the country, barter in goods was the normal mode of trading. Russia's system of health care was in a shambles, its dysfunctionality causing widespread hardships among low-income citizens. In lifting price controls, Gaidar and

Yeltsin undertook a necessary reform, but they did it without adequate preparation. A free market cannot operate without the prior existence of a legal order, an efficient banking system, a stock market, and a public that is accustomed to reasonably fair competition. None of these prerequisites prevailed in Russia, and this doomed the government's initiative.

The second aspect of Gaidar's economic program, privatization, did not fare any better. Again, his reasoning was sound, but the implementation of his reform was deeply flawed. From October 1992 the government, under the direction of Anatoly Chubais, a skilled and ruthless administrator, provided vouchers, each worth ten thousand rubles, to citizens for the acquisition of state enterprises. But at a time of high inflation, ten thousand rubles quickly became a paltry sum, and, in any case, the average citizen knew precious little about stocks or the running of a factory or business. Moreover, the entire process of privatization was shot through with corruption and as a consequence relatively small groups of former managers of Soviet enterprises became owners of huge enterprises and, occasionally, of enormous conglomerates. A nation that only a few years earlier had prided itself on not having a class of capitalist exploiters now had such a class, and many of the rich made a vulgar display of their wealth.

There is no doubt, however, that privatization fundamentally and quickly changed the Russian economic system. Within four months approximately one-third of all commercial and service establishments were in private hands, and the total number of businesses that were privately owned came to almost a million. Two years later, in 1994, private enterprises in Russia employed close to forty percent of the workforce, an amazingly rapid change in the country's economy. Stores were now stocked with quality goods as they had never been under communism. The main beneficiaries of the privatization of government enterprises came to be known as the 'oligarchs' because they exercised enormous influence over government policy. Some of them occupied senior positions in the Yeltsin government or his entourage.

Deputies in the two parliamentary chambers, the Supreme Soviet and the Congress of People's Deputies, vigorously criticized the government's economic program. The speaker of the Supreme Soviet, Ruslan Khasbulatov, was initially a strong supporter of Yeltsin, but soon became estranged from him, partly because he did not like the president's policies but also because he himself aspired to Russia's presidency. Under the Soviet system such open rivalry between a legislative leader and the executive would have been unthinkable. But now that Russia had a parliamentary system of sorts, the challenge for political leaders was to establish an effective working relationship between the executive and legislative branches. That is never easy, but it was especially difficult in Russia, which had no tradition of a balance of power between the two branches of government. Nor was there a tradition of independent political parties with clear-cut programs that could impart a degree of coherence and discipline to the deliberations in the legislative body. Although the various groups in the parliament, none of which ever enjoyed a majority in the chamber, proclaimed adherence to specific programs and represented specific social or economic interests, they were for the most part loose associations that for all intents and purposes represented the views of their leaders. Moreover, individual members of the chamber switched loyalties quite easily, further complicating the legislative process.

POLITICAL TENSIONS

A perennial problem for Yeltsin's governments throughout the nine years of his presidency was to obtain a majority for their legislative proposals. By inclination, and because he faced so many crises, Yeltsin wished to govern by decree. In October 1991, the Congress of People's Deputies of Russia had in fact granted him emergency powers to enact his economic measures by decree, but once the impact of the reforms became evident the legislature had second thoughts. By mid 1992, it would no longer give the president carte blanche and turned down one after another of the government's reform measures. The stage was set for a confrontation that ended in a terrible setback for the evolution of democratic institutions in Russia.

The conflict between the parliament and the president lasted for about a year. To end the gridlock, Yeltsin in September 1993 took the drastic step of ordering the dissolution of the legislature. He also indicated that in the meantime he would rule on his own and that an election of a new legislature would be held in December, at which time there would also be a referendum on a new constitution drafted by the authorities. Presidential Decree No. 1440, which proclaimed these measures, brought the conflict to a head. Only hours after the publication of the decree, the parliament in effect dismissed Yeltsin from his post by electing Aleksandr Rutskoi as president of the Russian Federation. Rutskoi was the vice president, but ever since early 1992 he had vigorously opposed Yeltsin's policies, and because of his fame as a military hero, and his charisma, the opposition, composed of communists and ultra-nationalists, embraced him as a man who could lead the struggle against the president. To safeguard Rutskoi's election, the parliamentary leaders convened an emergency session of the Tenth Congress of the People's Deputies and directed their civilian supporters to take up arms in defense of the White House.

Yeltsin responded by declaring a state of emergency in Moscow and by ordering military forces, including tanks, to surround the building. Fighting began on 2 October, and two days later tanks fired into the building, causing extensive damage and numerous casualties. Within hours, the people holed up in the White House surrendered. Rutskoi and other political leaders were imprisoned. It was a momentous event that tarnished the reputation of both Yeltsin and the opposition, both of whom had displayed a recklessness that had seriously harmed the country. As a leading historian of the Yeltsin period, Lilia Shevtsova, noted, the clash 'destroyed the long-standing taboo against the use of brute force in political struggles in Moscow'.[1]

The government now drafted a new constitution, which was adopted in a referendum in December. Although it provided for a bicameral legislature, the State Duma and the Federation Council, it clearly shifted the balance of power in favor of the president, who became what many called a 'superpresident' with an enhanced authority that in some ways resembled that of the tsars. According to the constitution, the president not only was to act as head of state and as the guarantor of the Fundamental Laws, but also was to appoint the prime minister and all other ministers. The prime minister had to be approved by the State Duma, but if it rejected the president's choice three times and voted no confidence in the government twice within a three-month period, the president could dissolve the legislature. At the same time, it was exceedingly difficult to oust the president. That could be done only if the chief executive could be proven to have committed high treason or some other crime, and even then the charges against him required the affirmative vote of two-thirds of both legislative chambers, the Supreme Court, and the Constitutional Court. And all the steps for the president's removal had to be completed within the short period of ninety days from the moment that the charges were first voted by the Duma.

Despite his victory in securing approval for the constitution, Yeltsin could not rest easy, for in the vote for deputies in the new legislature he suffered a bad defeat. Of the 450 seats in the State Duma, the bloc led by the communist Gennady Zyuganov commanded 103 and the ultra-nationalist and right-wing Liberal Democratic Party of Russia, under the erratic and eccentric Vladimir Zhirinovsky, had captured 64 seats. Yegor Gaidar's party, Russia's Choice, the movement most inclined to support Yeltsin, won only 66 seats. Of the remaining two hundred or so deputies, over 120 considered themselves independents and the rest were divided among four other parties. With such a complicated distribution of seats, it was not likely that the government would find the legislative support it needed for effective government.

Nor would the government readily find political support in dealing with a particularly recalcitrant problem in the northern

Caucasus, the attempt by the autonomous republic of Chechnya, home to about 1.2 million people, to achieve independence. Deeply committed to the Sunni branch of Islam, the Chechens have a long history, dating back to the nineteenth century, of resistance to Russian domination. In 1991, Yeltsin's government installed General Dzhokhar Dudayev, who had been an officer in the Soviet army, as leader of the Chechen republic on the assumption that he would remain loyal to the Russian Federation. But he quickly announced his support for independence, which he formally declared in November 1991. At first, Yeltsin did not react to Dudayev's move, perhaps because he was preoccupied with other matters. But late in 1994, the president decided to stop Chechnya's drift to independence. The Russian Federation was not a multinational state to the same extent as the Soviet Union, but eighteen percent of the population was non-Slavic. If the Chechens were permitted to establish a separate state, on what basis would the government be able to prevent other republics from following suit? In eight regions of the Russian Federation, movements for autonomy or independence were becoming increasingly vocal. But Chechnya was important to Russia for yet another reason. A pipeline was to be built through the region to carry large quantities of oil from the Caspian fields to the Black Sea port of Novorossiisk, and Russia expected to earn millions of dollars from this arrangement. Already in desperate straits financially, the government was not prepared to jeopardize that income.

Late in November 1994, a small group of volunteers organized by the Russian security forces marched towards Grozny, the capital of Chechnya, expecting to oust Dudayev in a matter of days. It was only the first of many miscalculations of the Russian government and military commanders. The Chechens quickly routed the volunteers, a drubbing that Yeltsin took as a personal insult. On 2 December, the Russians began what would turn out to be a bloody six-year conflict (with some pauses) that caused horrendous suffering among the Chechens. On two occasions Grozny was subjected to long series of air attacks and to invasion by Russian troops. It is estimated that during the first two years alone sixty thousand Chechens lost their lives and much of the capital was reduced to rubble. But the Russians also endured many casualties – about 25,000 – and, to the shock of many citizens, the army was exposed as an undisciplined, ill-equipped force that could not defeat a small country that officials denigrated as a haven for bandits and terrorists.

A fair number of Chechens were in fact engaged in criminal activities of various kinds, and on several occasions Chechen guerillas committed atrocities that aroused passionate condemnation in Russia. For example, on 14 June 1995, some two hundred guerillas seized control of a hospital in southern Russia, over a hundred miles from Chechnya, and, after killing twenty police officers, held two thousand patients as hostages. When Russian soldiers tried to storm the hospital, the Chechens managed to repel the attacks, in part because they used patients, including pregnant women, as shields. Only after the prime minister, V. Chernomyrdin, appeared on the scene did the Russians and the guerillas reach an agreement for the hostages' release. By that time the total number of deaths on both sides was 120. The war ended in August 1996, when General A. Lebed signed an agreement with the Chechens granting them 'political autonomy', a concept so vague that many commentators predicted, correctly, that the conflict would be resumed in one way or another. Outside Russia, but even more so within the country, the Chechen war provoked widespread condemnation of Yeltsin and his government. In a public opinion poll in January 1996, only eighteen percent of the respondents expressed willingness to vote for him even if the opponent was Zyuganov, leader of the unreconstructed communists, who was favored by thirty-three percent of potential voters. Yeltsin's political career appeared to have come to an end.

But the man was more resilient than anyone thought. In mid 1996, he defeated Zyuganov in a second-round, run-off election despite unfavorable polls, a new bout with near-fatal illness, and an economy still in deep decline. During the first six months of that year the government had managed to collect only sixty percent of due taxes, inflation had escalated, government employees had endured long delays in receiving their salaries, and the gross national product had fallen by another four percent. It cannot be said that Yeltsin's electoral comeback was an edifying event that reflected well on Russian democracy. He won because a small group of wealthy oligarchs spent huge amounts of money on his election campaign, the media controlled by the president's supporters publicized vague charges that the communists planned to tamper with the election, and many people still recoiled at the idea of having a communist as leader. A commonly heard opinion was that 'the president is a liar, but the communists are far worse.' Zyuganov won 40.31 percent of the vote and Yeltsin held on to the presidency by a slight majority, 53.82 percent.

THE PRESIDENCY OF VLADIMIR PUTIN

For the next three years Russia continued to muddle through, but only barely. In August 1998, the country teetered on the brink of financial collapse after the government, violating its own promises, suddenly devalued the ruble by fifty percent and defaulted on its debts. Yeltsin's health took another turn for the worse and for long stretches of time he could not carry out his presidential functions. Charges that people in his entourage and family were illegally enriching themselves further eroded public confidence in the government and the entire political system.

In August 1999, Yeltsin made yet another ministerial change that surprised everyone. He named Vladimir Putin, an unknown bureaucrat, as prime minister, the fifth person to occupy that post in seventeen months. Forty-seven years old, Putin had spent most of his adult life working for the security services and for several years he had served as a spy in East Germany. After the collapse of the Soviet Union he returned to his place of birth, St. Petersburg, where he held a senior administrative post in the

local administration under the reformist Anatoly Sobchak, rising
to the position of deputy mayor. He began to work for President
Yeltsin in 1996 and quickly joined Yeltsin's inner circle, known as
the 'family'. At the time he became prime minister, not much was
known about his political views or his political skills. 'Far from
charismatic,' one report noted, 'he has an expressionless mask-
like face, rarely smiles, and speaks softly.' By all accounts, he
made a conscious effort not to identify with any particular political group. He was on friendly terms with liberal reformers, but
he was also a passionate patriot determined to restore Russia's
prestige, and one of his first public pronouncements stressed
his intention to deal harshly with Chechnya, where fighting had
resumed. On Russia's future course, Putin was highly eclectic.
He favored a market economy but at the same time insisted
that the economy must be adapted to Russian conditions. 'We
can count on a worthy future,' he declared, 'only if we manage
to naturally combine the principles of a market economy with
Russia's realities.' Moreover, he said that the state would have to
be 'strong' and 'paternalistic'. The question of whether this would
benefit the country seemed irrelevant to him. The traditions of
Russia simply could not be cast aside. '[They] exist and remain
dominant for now. This should be taken into account, especially
in social policy.' Russia, Putin also insisted, would not in the
foreseeable future – or ever – resemble the United States or the
United Kingdom. 'Russian democracy', he has said, 'will never
parrot the West's liberal model,' and he contended that in Russia
'a strong state is a guarantee of freedom, not a threat to it.'

On 31 December 1999, Yeltsin made another startling
announcement. He resigned and appointed Putin acting president, giving him a clear advantage in the election scheduled for
March 2000, three months before the end of Yeltsin's term. The
president's health no doubt played a role in this sudden resignation, but there was also much speculation that Putin promised
not to investigate Yeltsin's family or entourage for corruption.

Putin was easily elected president and has since placed his
stamp on Russian politics. Early in 2001, the outlook for Russia

did not appear promising. The ghastly condition of the economy was highlighted in a series of articles in the *New York Times* on the state of the national health system. Every year, about twenty thousand cancer patients were dying because they could not afford to purchase the necessary medicines, and another 200,000 people suffering from diabetes could not afford insulin. Life expectancy, which is widely regarded as a 'barometer of a society's health', declined every month during 1999 and the average for men and women was 65.9 years, ten years lower than in the United States. Over the previous decade, death rates had climbed about one-third and it was estimated that, if the trend continued, in fifty years the total population of Russia could decline from 145.6 million to 121 million. The economy had stabilized but at a very low level of productivity. Much of it was still in ruins, a large percentage of the population still lived in poverty, and there were no signs of a serious reform campaign to stimulate productivity.

The political outlook was equally bleak, and many experts in Russian affairs feared that the new president would not be a champion of reform. A product of the most sinister Soviet institution, the security police, Putin did not appear to have shed his distrust of liberal democracy and in some respects seemed to revert to Soviet-style conduct. For example, after an explosion on 12 August 2000 killed all 118 men on board the nuclear submarine *Kursk*, the Russian admiralty, unwilling to acknowledge mistakes by Russians, blamed the accident on a collision with a foreign vessel, even though two retired Russian commanders insisted that a collision could not have caused the damage. Putin's government also tried in various ways to intimidate two national television channels that had the temerity to criticize the authorities. Perhaps most ominously, the government sought to increase its power by reducing that of regional leaders. Putin established seven new regional administrations, each one headed by a former general of the KGB or the army, to assume control over the outlying regions of the country.

Still, the fear, often voiced by liberals in Russia and by foreign commentators, that Putin planned to turn back the clock and reestablish a Soviet style of rule, has proven to be exaggerated. In fact, for several years it was hard to fathom Putin's long-range goals; he seemed to exemplify Winston Churchill's famous quip: 'Russia is a riddle wrapped in a mystery inside an enigma.' However, after he had completed two four-year terms in office there was little reason to retain the hopes of the 1990s that Russia would be transformed into a liberal democracy in the near future. Certainly, the Russian people no longer believe that their country is moving towards that goal. In fact, there is deep-seated discouragement with national trends, as was demonstrated in a public opinion poll in 2006: seventy-one percent regretted the collapse of communism and only twenty-two percent expressed no nostalgia for the Soviet Union. Most people accepted with equanimity the autocratic political system established by Yeltsin in 1993, often described as a 'superpresidency', under which the president was about as power-ful as the last monarch, who ruled from 1906 to 1917.

A major reason for the increasing acceptance by the Russian people of authoritarian rule was the violence that erupted between late August and early September 1999 in Moscow, Volgodonsk, and Buinaksk (in the Dagestan Republic). Chechen separatists bombed a series of apartment blocks in those cities and in the process killed hundreds of civilians. Putin now seized the oppor-tunity to flaunt his toughness and determination to restore order; he endeared himself to ordinary citizens craving safety by vowing to 'kick the shit' out of Chechen terrorists. Within weeks, the Russian army reentered Chechnya en masse, and after a singu-larly bloody war that lasted eight months the region was pacified and the virtual independence that Chechnya had achieved in 1996 was rescinded. But the costs were high. For several weeks, Russian troops laid siege to Grozny, the capital of Chechnya, and when they finally entered the city, on 2 February 2000, they found a devastated area that a United Nations report described as 'the most destroyed city on earth'. The Russians, too, suffered heavy losses, although reliable statistics are hard to come by.

Toughness became a constant theme of Putin's rule, enabling him to assume the role of protector of the people, many of whom felt threatened by violence and a breakdown of public order. In September 2004, when terrorists seized a school in Beslan, a town of 35,000 people in the Republic of North Ossetia-Alania, he ordered Russian security forces to attack the building even though 1,200 adults and children were held hostage. In the bloody melee, 334 civilians (among them 186 children) died, but Putin's government could claim to have preserved the prestige of the state by crushing the forces of disorder. Citizens (including many intellectuals) who support the government invariably emphasize their yearning for order and stability.

Although liberal democrats found the events in Chechnya alarming, there was some reason to believe that these harsh actions did not fully reflect Putin's conception of how Russia should be ruled or his vision of Russia's future. Early in his presidency, he sought to portray himself in various ways as a modernizer, as a man devoted to reform. For example, he placed flowers on the grave of Andrei Sakharov during a ceremony honoring the distinguished physicist, who during the 1970s and 1980s had courageously taken up the cause of the dissidents and had become a champion of civil rights and democracy. Putin also advocated – or paid lip service to – certain progressive ideas: he suggested that the power of the oligarchs was excessive and harmful to society, he spoke of the need to deregulate the economy, he called for reform of the notoriously inefficient and corrupt bureaucracy, and, perhaps most significantly, he urged the elimination of corruption. Corruption, as has been acknowledged by many senior officials in Russia, is not the preserve of a small group of miscreants but is firmly embedded in the country as a way of life, and as such it constitutes a major deterrent to the development of an efficient economy. According to a study by independent researchers, reported in the newspaper *Vedomosti* (The Record) on 6 February 2008, corruption is most widespread in departments administering the collection of taxes, the enforcement of the law, the handling of public health services, the adjudication of property disputes, and in the judicial system in general. The amounts of money to be paid for favors are very high: to be nominated by a party for a seat in the State Duma costs between two and five million dollars, the introduction of a legislative proposal in the Duma requires payment of a fee of $250,000, and anyone interested in obtaining a purchase order from a state agency must agree to hand over twenty percent of the order's total value. It has been estimated that the annual value of bribes runs to 240 billion dollars; about half the people in Russia consider corruption to be the single most important barrier to economic growth. In a speech to the State Council on 8 February 2008, Putin acknowledged that these statistics were accurate. 'One cannot start one's business,' he said. 'People have to give bribes in every controlling institution – fire prevention, environmental services, medical permissions – you need to go to all of them, and it's just terrible.' But his administration made no serious efforts to uproot corruption.

Especially appealing to Russian liberals and to Western specialists in Russian affairs was Putin's avowed interest, also articulated early in his presidency, in improving relations with the West. From 2000 until 2003, he made numerous gestures towards the West, and some commentators became convinced that Russia was at last bringing to a close a trend begun by Tsar Peter the Great, a champion of Westernization. In 2000, Putin went so far as to suggest that Russia might even welcome integration into the structure of NATO. A year later, in October 2001, he gave a speech in fluent German in the Bundestag in which he urged an end to the distrust that still remained from the Cold War era and called for greater cooperation, economically and politically, between Russia and Europe. Finally, after the terrorist attacks on the World Trade Center in New York, Putin expressed full sympathy for the victims of the assault and vowed to cooperate with the West in its war on terrorism.

But the embrace of the West was short-lived. Many among the elite in Russia were not prepared to accept the permanent relegation of their country to that of a minor power on the world stage. Still smarting from the break-up of the Soviet Union in 1991, a growing number of the political class yearned for the reestablishment of their country as a superpower. Their slogan, gaining steadily in popular approval, is that 'Russia is a great power or it is nothing.' In April 2005, Putin indicated that he shared this sentiment when he declared that the collapse of the Soviet Union was 'the greatest geopolitical catastrophe' of the twentieth century.

An unexpected development in 2004, the sudden and steep rise in the price of oil – within four years the price of a barrel of crude oil rose from $25.00 to $100.00 – greatly improved the country's economy and immediately boosted the self-confidence and influence of the government in the international arena. In short order, Russia, the second largest exporter of oil, paid off all debts to foreign countries and amassed foreign currency reserves that were surpassed in volume by only two countries. So far, the government has done little to apply the vast oil profits to revital- izing and modernizing the overall economy, which remains in the doldrums despite the improvement of conditions for some citizens. But as a wealthy 'petrostate', Russia has been able to use its new-found wealth to flex its muscles and to intimidate such former Soviet republics as Ukraine and Georgia and even Western Europe by withholding oil deliveries or by sharply rais- ing the price of oil. Inevitably, their more assertive foreign policy soured relations with the West.

By the same token, some policies of the United States have had the effect of antagonizing the Russian authorities and the political elite. Although President George W. Bush at one time praised Putin as a 'straightforward and trustworthy' man whose 'soul' he could accurately gauge, and although he generally refrained from criticizing the Russian government's domestic policies, including the drift to authoritarianism, the warm rela- tionship between the two leaders did not last very long. For one thing, during his early period in the White House Bush did not bother to pay much attention to Russia, a slight that rankled the men in the Kremlin. But, in addition, important policy differ- ences between Russia and the United States emerged after 2001. To mention only some of the most serious ones, Russia's leaders vigorously opposed as unnecessarily provocative the expansion of NATO into Eastern Europe, resented Western support of democratic forces in Ukraine and Georgia, opposed the granting of independence to Kosovo, refused to support America's invasion of Iraq, and, finally, they strongly protested the placing of US missiles, allegedly for purely defensive purposes, in Poland and the Czech Republic. The differences between Russia and the West are not by any means insignificant, but it should also be noted that, for the Putin government, conflicts with the United States and the European Union have served a useful domestic purpose: they have given credibility to the Kremlin's warnings that the country faces determined enemies who can only be withstood if the people rally around the government. Still, it would be a mistake to speak of a full-scale return of the Cold War, if for no other reason than that Russia is still militarily weak and must therefore exercise a fair degree of caution in reasserting itself. At the same time, there can be no question that in the years from 2006 to 2009 Russia and the United States no longer viewed each other as friends committed to pursuing common interests in international affairs. This is not likely to change in the near future; their interests are now too divergent.

It is not only in foreign policy that the United States (as well as the West in general) and Russia increasingly drifted apart. The accelerating trend towards authoritarianism in Russia has alienated many citizens in democratic countries who at one time had welcomed the political and economic changes that occurred after the collapse of communism. The list of actions by the Putin government that undermined democratic principles in recent years is long and deeply troubling. A few examples will suffice to indicate the trend. In a move designed to weaken possible opposition to the existing order, the authorities in the fall of 2003 nationalized major parts of the huge oil company Yukos and arrested Mikhail Khodorkovsky, the main shareholder of the company and an outspoken critic of the Putin regime. After a trial for fraud and tax evasion that was a travesty of justice, he was sentenced to nine years in prison, and in addition the government took various steps to bring about the collapse of Yukos. Soon thereafter, other oligarchs were deprived of their roles in the political process and the government expanded its control over the economy. Several oligarchs, fearful of persecution, now live permanently outside of Russia.

These individuals, however, cannot assume that they are beyond the reach of Russian security officials, as was demonstrated in November 2006 in the ghastly affair of Alexander Litvinenko. Formerly a lieutenant colonel in the Federal Security Bureau, Litvinenko had emigrated to the United Kingdom, where the authorities granted him British citizenship. It is widely assumed that in a throwback to the practices of officials at the time of the Soviet Union, Russian agents killed him by plying him with radioactive polonium-210. The Kremlin denied all charges of complicity in the murder, but the evidence against the Russian authorities is very persuasive.

According to the constitution adopted under Yeltsin, a person may serve no more than two successive four-year terms as president, and as Putin approached the end of that period of service late in 2007 there was much speculation about his intentions. He was still relatively young (fifty-five) and it was clear that he savored his role as 'superpresident'. He had become an adept leader and he was convinced that he had both stabilized the country and placed it on a path to regaining its position as a power to be reckoned with. For some time, ever since 2002 in fact, a 'mini cult of personality' had been promoted. Under Yeltsin, the walls in various government offices had been adorned with portraits of artists and some of the more prominent tsars, but now they were covered with photographs of Putin. Would a man of such prestige and stature, who was widely regarded as a 'soft dictator', willingly surrender his exalted office? Late in 2007, Putin gave his answer, and it was both clever and devious. He announced that he would step down as president and that in the upcoming election in March 2008 he would support the forty-two-year-old Dmitri Medvedev, a relatively unknown official who occupied the post of First Deputy Prime Minister and who was not known for his independence. Designated by Putin for the presidency, he was certain to win the election, and, most commentators assumed, he would do the bidding of his mentor and benefactor, who announced that he planned to remain in a leading position in the government, almost certainly as prime minister.

And in a four-hour news conference on 14 February 2008, weeks before leaving his presidential office, Putin left no doubt in anyone's mind that as prime minister he expected to be the decisive leader of the nation. 'The President is the guarantor of the Constitution,' he said. 'He sets the main directions for internal and external policies. But the highest executive power in the country is the Russian government, led by the premier,' a post that he himself intended to occupy for at least four years. Mr Medvedev did not dispute Putin's gloss on the constitution even though for eight years the leader and main spokesman of the government had been President Putin, not his prime ministers.

Putin also let it be known that the basic policies of the years from 2000 to 2008 would not be altered. There was no reason to change them since, as he put it, during his stewardship of the presidency 'there have been no major failures.' He indicated that he would not abandon his quest to restore Russia's power and prestige, and repeated his intention to aim strategic missiles at the Czech Republic and Poland if those countries permitted the United States to install its missiles. It was also reasonable to assume that there would not be any significant change in the government's domestic program, which had included a steady erosion of individual freedom and civil liberties. The seriousness of that erosion was dramatized one day before the president's press conference. The *Moscow Times* of 13 February 2008 announced that the city authorities in St. Petersburg had shut down, allegedly for 'fire safety violations', the European University at Saint Petersburg, which is funded largely by Western foundations and is considered the leading independent institution of higher learning in the city. After declaring that politics had played no role in the authorities' action, the president of the university, Nikolai Vakhtin, complied with the city ordinance and stopped all classes, but at the same time he quietly sought to persuade officials to rescind the order of closure. Liberal opponents of the government, however, insisted that the university was being punished for its research in Russian politics, and, more specifically, for its acceptance of a grant from the European Union to study Russian elections. Attempts to obtain clarification from offices that oversee fire-safety regulations regarding the order to shut down the university proved futile: no government official was willing to comment on the matter. But Putin had let the cat out of the bag some months before the closure when he accused the university of 'being an agent of foreign meddling'. After worldwide protests against the government's action, the authorities permitted the university to reopen on 21 March.

Two other aspects of Putin's behavior at his last press conference as president deserve to be noted: his vulgarity and his disdain for the democratic process. When he was asked about reports in the West that he had amassed a huge fortune as president, he replied that journalists picked such 'rumors . . . from a nose and smeared [them] onto their papers'. When a French journalist raised doubts about the credibility of recent results of the parliamentary election in Chechnya, in which ninety-nine percent of the population participated in the vote and ninety-nine percent of all ballots were cast for the president's party, Putin turned to a state journalist from Chechnya to respond. The reporter did not hesitate to give the answer that Putin expected: 'These are absolutely realistic figures. Personally, all my acquaintances, including myself, voted for United Russia,' the party that scored the resounding victory.

The emergence in Russia of a political system that is now widely regarded as a 'managed democracy' can be traced back to certain statements and actions by Putin early in his presidency, whose significance was not fully understood at the time. Within weeks of his assumption of presidential power, Putin revealed that he regarded the state, by which he meant the executive branch, as the institution that can most effectively guarantee personal liberties and undertake initiatives to benefit society. 'The stronger the government,' he said, 'the stronger personal freedom . . . Democracy is a dictatorship of the law.' The meaning of this brief and somewhat opaque statement was suggested by Putin's conduct during the Andrei Babitsky affair in January 2000. Babitsky was a reporter who sent dispatches from Chechnya revealing the brutality of Russian soldiers in putting down local insurgents. On 16 January, Babitsky was arrested by Russian officials and was immediately accused by the government of being a supporter of Chechen rebels. A month later, the Russian authorities exchanged him for two Russian soldiers held captive by the rebels, clearly a move designed to gain credibility for their charge that Babitsky had engaged in treasonous activities in Chechnya. Since then, official pressure on journalists to toe the government's line has become more insidious. Within a few years no fewer than thirteen Russian reporters had been murdered, and in October 2006 an eminent and courageous critic of the government, Anna Politkovskaya, was found shot dead in the elevator of her apartment building. Although ten suspects have been arrested in connection with Politkovskaya's murder, few people familiar with the case believe that the actual murderer was ever in custody.

In addition, the government has sought to avoid criticism of its policies by exerting various forms of pressure on television stations: local governors or mayors 'advise' business executives not to place any advertisements with stations that are considered hostile to the authorities; officials suddenly and unexpectedly discover irregularities in a lease of a TV station, or violations of fire or sanitation codes; and, finally, the police carry out raids on newspapers to confiscate 'illegal software' and thus intimidate reporters. These measures to stifle freedom of speech, important as they are, do not exhaust the endeavors by the authorities to sustain the 'managed democracy'. At the same time, various steps have also been taken to centralize political power in the Kremlin and, what is more ominous, to prevent opponents from running for office. In 2004, Putin enhanced his power by abolishing the election of local governors and independent legislators; under the new procedures, governors were appointed by the central government, and in elections of legislators citizens could no longer vote for individual candidates but had to cast their ballots for a political party. Putin justified the changes as essential to promote 'national cohesion', which, he claimed, was necessary for the ongoing struggle against terrorism.

But democrats in Russia were not persuaded by the claim and denounced the new procedures as 'the beginning of a constitutional *coup d'état*' or a 'step towards dictatorship'. Then, in the run-up to the presidential election in March 2008, Putin's government invoked highly technical and specious reasons to prevent three men (among them the former world chess champion Garry Kasparov) from running for the office. This left only four very weak candidates in the race against the heavily favored Dmitri Medvedev. The final blow undermining confidence in the legitimacy of the electoral process in Russia was delivered by the international monitors who were to observe the vote and pass judgment on its fairness and honesty. They left the country after declaring that so many restrictions were imposed on their work that they could not possibly render an objective evaluation of the legitimacy of the election.

The results of the election confirmed Putin's prediction that Medvedev would win by an overwhelming margin because, as the president put it, the vast majority of Russians approved of his policies and achievements. Medvedev received slightly over seventy percent of all the votes, and almost seventy percent of all eligible Russians cast ballots. These statistics, virtually unheard of in national elections in Western democracies, inevitably raise further doubt about the fairness of the electoral process in Russia.

What, then, can we say about Yeltsin's legacy twenty-five years after he took the lead in destroying the Soviet Union and committed himself to establishing democracy and a free market in the newly independent Russian Federation? His actions were unquestionably revolutionary, as were his stated aims. But at this moment no simple answer to the question can be satisfactory for the simple reason that his policies were driven by contradictory impulses, and the same can be said of his successor. Yeltsin retained the democratic procedures that had been introduced during the last years of Gorbachev's tenure as general secretary of the Communist Party, but he did virtually nothing to create institutions that would perpetuate those procedures and impress upon the people the desirability of maintaining them. He did not establish the rule of law, the constitution drafted under his direction granted more power to the president than is healthy in a democracy, and he did not lend his support to the formation of independent political parties, which are one of the lifelines of democracies. Moreover, his toleration of corrupt officials undermined confidence in democracy, as did his frequent hints that the president might dispense with elections. On the other hand, it has become the rule in Russia that political struggles are to be decided by elections, although their imperfections are understandably disturbing to committed democrats. Moreover, despite the growing arbitrariness in recent years of the security police there has not been a reversion to the practices of the Soviet era, when vast numbers of people suspected of opposition to the existing order were sent to the Gulag or otherwise persecuted. The press and other media have come under severe pressure, but there is still more freedom of expression now than there was during the period from 1917 to about 1986. Russia certainly cannot be said to be a 'democracy' in the sense the word is understood in the West, but neither can the country's political system be characterized as totalitarian.

In foreign affairs, Yeltsin's legacy has also been ambiguous. Neither he nor initially his chosen successor, Putin, made any extensive efforts to force the other former Soviet republics to reunite with Russia, even though relations with Ukraine, Georgia, and Moldova were at times contentious. In relations with the West, and particularly the United States, there were some tense moments that grew more strident during the years 2007–9, but there were no major clashes, certainly none that could have led to military conflict. This is not an insignificant matter because

Russia, despite the decline in its armed forces, still has thousands of nuclear weapons and therefore cannot be discounted militarily.

The economy under Yeltsin underwent a radical change from a highly centralized structure, in which private property played a minimal role, to a decentralized one in which most enterprises are privately owned. But this transformation exacted a terrible price, steep economic decline. The output of goods plummeted, many people became impoverished, and in the late 1990s the morale of the nation reached a nadir. President Putin has not eliminated the free enterprise system but he has imposed more state control over the economy. The ultimate outcome of this process remains in doubt. In the meantime, the spectacular rise in the price of oil after 2004 produced a sharp and steady upward climb of the national economy, and the lot of sizable groups of Russians, especially those who live in the larger cities, has improved substantially. There is still much poverty in the country and some economists contend that on the whole the population of Russia is worse off now than it was in the early 1980s. Few of them dare to predict when the market economy will produce a standard of living in Russia comparable to that in the West.

In concluding this account of Russian history it seems appropriate to touch again on an issue that has frequently been a central concern of Russian political leaders and intellectuals and that was raised on the first page of chapter 1: is Russia part of the West or does it belong culturally to the East? Lilia Shevtsova, in my view the leading specialist on Yeltsin's presidency and on recent Russian history in general, offered a nuanced answer to the question in a book she published in 1999, before Putin's assumption of the presidential office. I believe that her answer accurately reflected the state of affairs at that time and remains valid today. The superpresidency created by Yeltsin, she argued

follows the country's historic Byzantine model of governance, in which all power is concentrated in a leader
– a czar, general secretary, president – who becomes the

symbol of the nation and its arbiter as well as its main
guarantor of stability. In contrast to the Western political
tradition, in which power is based on rational ideas and
institutions, the Byzantine tradition has always invested
power with something sacred, irrational, and personal.
The ruler was considered to be simultaneously the father
of the nation, omnipresent, and not responsible to any
other person or institution.

Stalin, Shevtsova continued, 'was the full embodiment of the
Byzantine tradition of irrationality, mystery, and contempt for
society'. Although 'the past still keeps Russia in its embrace',
and although it is too early to decide definitively whether the
country will be able to shake off that embrace, the changes in
the economic and political system of the country that followed
the collapse of communism suggest that 'Russia is gradually
understanding the need to finally close the Byzantine chapter in
its history.' True, in the seventeen years since Shevtsova wrote
these lines President Putin has steadily moved Russia back to
the Byzantine tradition. But it is not yet clear how long-lasting
his influence on Russian political culture will be. It will be some
time – perhaps decades – before we know whether the Western
traditions of freedom of the individual and private property,
which animated the upheaval in 1991, have struck deep roots in
Russia, providing the country with the preconditions for a stable
democracy and flourishing economy.

10

THE RISE AND RISE OF PUTIN

In some respects, the composition of an update for a book of history initially published at the turn of the millennium has proven more difficult than writing the original work, which covered a thousand years during which Russia underwent major changes in size, economy, and political system. It is extremely hard to write a detailed and accurate account of contemporary developments because the relevant documents, especially the ones drafted by senior government officials, are for the most part classified and therefore not readily available. Moreover, even when journalists and scholars have access to a wide range of information about current economic and political conditions, they are often unable to determine its significance. For example, early in the 1980s, many educated Russians were aware of the severe economic hardships endured by a large percentage of the Soviet population, but no one predicted that this would lead to the collapse of communism. It was widely assumed that the government would introduce reforms to improve the economy and avoid its disintegration.

More recently, very few students of British politics thought that the citizens of the United Kingdom were so disgruntled with the status quo that they would vote to leave the European Union. And even fewer experts on contemporary affairs predicted that discontent in the United States would prompt so many citizens to vote for Donald J. Trump and bring about his election as president.

I was afraid of falling into a similar trap. I would collect a vast amount of information on the recent history of Russia but would then be incapable of drawing correct conclusions about the government's intentions or likely success in implementing its policies. But after much soul-searching I decided to take the plunge because I sensed that many citizens in the West have a strong interest in succinct accounts of recent economic and political changes in Russia and in analyses of how those changes might affect domestic conditions and, more important, its relations with foreign countries.

It is not simply curiosity that drives these interests. Many people in Europe, the United States, and elsewhere fear that political trends in Russia are moving in a direction that could lead to a new cold war even though President Putin and President Trump have expressed interest in a rapprochement between their two countries. During the Cold War, from 1946 to 1991, there were occasions when a military conflict seemed likely but was avoided by astute statesmen determined to prevent the horrors endured by millions of people during World War II. Contemporary statesmen may not be skillful enough in diplomacy to follow their example.

MEDVEDEV-PUTIN

In May 2008, when Medvedev assumed the office of president, Russian liberals had reason to be pleased with the change in national leadership even though it was known, as indicated above, that Putin had pulled strings to secure the election of his successor and that he planned to play a dominant role in determining government policies.

For one thing, Putin had not violated the constitutional provision that no one may serve more than two consecutive terms of four years in the highest office of the land. Moreover, Medvedev was a lawyer and the son of educated parents who, as far as we know, had no 'background' in the Soviet police agencies, which played a critical role in politics from the moment the Bolsheviks seized power in 1917.

Before entering politics at the age of thirty-four, Medvedev had devoted himself to teaching law at the Saint Petersburg State University and to scholarly pursuits; in his publications he had projected, according to Steven Myers, the author of *The New Tsar: The Rise and Reign of Vladimir Putin*, the most authoritative biography of Russia's ruler, 'a gentler image of a Russian politician than Putin'. The new president had expressed approval of the rule of law and had advocated firm measures by the government to eliminate corruption. To committed liberals in Russia, as well as some statesmen in the West, it seemed that the dreams of 1991, when the Soviet Union collapsed, might at last be within reach. Russia, they thought, would begin to adopt policies that would lead to the transformation of the country into one resembling Western democracies.

But it soon became evident that Putin's departure from the presidential office was merely a formality. Immediately after Medvedev's inauguration, Putin assumed the position of prime minister and made clear his intention to retain the powers he had exercised for eight years. It is not known whether Medvedev had agreed to this arrangement before the election of 2008 or whether he was simply too weak to resist Putin's assertion of superiority. But to senior officials who were in regular contact with both of them, it became evident soon after the election that in their relationship the new president was subordinate. Medvedev continued to address the prime minister with the formal 'you' ('vy' in Russian) and Putin addressed the president with the informal 'ty'.

Many senior officials also knew that Putin examined drafts of speeches that Medvedev planned to deliver and that he altered them to reflect his views. During political crises the prime minister took pains to be on hand to make the critical decisions. For example, when Georgia unexpectedly and unwisely attacked South Ossetia during the night of 7 August 2008, in response to artillery fire emanating from that country, Putin rushed to

Moscow from Beijing to take charge of formulating a counter-response. The small country of South Ossetia (as well as Abkhazia) had been granted partial independence when the Soviet Union collapsed, but both were placed under the protection of the Russian Federation. Medvedev followed Putin's advice to send Russian forces into Georgia, a small and weak country, to beat back the invasion. Georgia had deployed an army of ten to eleven thousand soldiers and, once the military struggle began, it became clear that they could not match the better-equipped and better-trained Russian troops. After five days of fighting, the Georgians, who lost 170 soldiers and fourteen policemen, retreated from South Ossetia. Russian losses amounted to forty-eight soldiers. The people of the Russian Federation applauded the victory and Putin received most of the credit for it.

Many Russian citizens who followed politics now suspected that Putin's decision not to run for a third term out of respect for the constitution was a sham. That suspicion was reinforced well before Medvedev's term as president expired in 2012, when Putin announced that he would run again for the presidency. That decision, however, did not violate the constitution, which only prohibited the same person from serving for three consecutive terms.

Before the elections were held, two-thirds of the Duma passed an amendment to the constitution to extend future presidential terms to six years, a measure also approved by regional legislators. At about the same time, Medvedev announced that he would not run for a second term, assuring Putin an easy victory; he won the election with sixty-three percent of the vote, which suggests he could be in a position of power for a long while. If the four years of Medvedev's period in that office are credited to Putin – as they should be – by 2024 he will have served a total of twenty-four years as the leader of the country, equaling Stalin's period of rule.

As noted above, during his first few years as the effective leader of the government, Putin was not an advocate of democracy in the sense that he showed little interest in the rule of law.

But he was not an autocrat in the mold of Stalin or the tsars who had ruled the country until 1917, and he displayed a degree of pragmatism in domestic and international affairs.

Soon after his third term in office began in 2012, however, Putin revealed traits that suggested he would pursue a much more assertive course in foreign affairs than he had in the years from 2000 to 2008. He indicated that he was not interested in the 'reset' of relations towards greater amity with the United States that President Barack Obama proposed. No doubt there had been developments in Russia as well as on the international scene that prompted his new stance, and these will be touched upon below. But it also seems that as early as 2005 he had begun to change his views on some fundamental issues relating to politics and international affairs. He gradually abandoned pragmatism and became more rigid in his outlook – in effect, he adopted an ideology that several commentators have named *Putinism*. Just as Stalin by the 1930s committed himself to a set of economic and social policies and programs that many scholars have designated as Stalinism, so Putin championed a cluster of ideas that now carries his name, although, as will become clear, those ideas are not original.

ILYIN'S IDEOLOGY

In doing so, Putin borrowed from various writers and most notably from Ivan Ilyin, an author whose publications apparently caught the president's attention during his first term in office. Ilyin, who was born in 1883 in Moscow to an upper-class family, advocated authoritarian rule, fervent nationalism and deep hostility towards the West. He was an intellectual whose work and life can only be described as extraordinarily complicated – his ideas on some issues are so convoluted and unusual that one is tempted to call them weird. In a recent article in *Foreign Affairs*, Anton Barbashin and Hannah Thoburn offered the following assessment of Ilyin: 'Never a deep or clear thinker, he was not truly an academic or philosopher in the classical sense, but rather a publicist, a conspiracy theorist, and a Russian nationalist with a core of fascistic leanings.'[1]

His writings, amounting to twenty-three volumes, became popular among certain circles of the Russian intelligentsia several decades after he died (in 1954), in large measure because his ideas were lauded by the distinguished novelist Aleksandr Solzhenitsyn and by President Putin. Putin was so taken with the views of Ilyin that he played a role in the transfer of his remains in 2005 to the Donskoy Monastery in Moscow, where the president used his own money to pay for a new headstone for Ilyin in his final resting place.

It is not easy to summarize Ilyin's views because he tended to move in different directions. But he clung tenaciously to several convictions: he despised communism, revered the Russian people and Russian institutions of the pre-Soviet era, and passionately subscribed to the teachings of the Russian Orthodox Church. He considered democracy to be unsuitable for a country the size of Russia. He wanted its leaders to devote themselves to making, in his words, 'Russia great again', and he insisted that to achieve that goal the Russian people would have to 'believe in God and [that] this faith will strengthen their power . . . and make them strong enough to overcome themselves',[2] a contention that appealed to many Russian citizens even though it is not a prediction that is easily substantiated.

Ilyin admired Nazism for having put a hold on the 'Bolshevization of Germany', an achievement that he thought deserved the gratitude of all of Europe. Even though he lived in Germany during the 1930s, he never joined the Nazi Party, apparently because it was not a religious movement. Given this deep reservation about Nazism it is hard to understand why he was grateful to Hitler for having resisted the spread of communism.

PUTIN AND THE CHURCH

Putin's admiration for Ilyin's philosophy and especially for Ilyin's stress on the importance of religion marks a radical departure from communism by the president. Lenin, Stalin, and their successors in the years from 1917 to 1991 were atheists who disparaged all religions. (Gorbachev became a practicing Christian only after he left office.) Once Putin took over the reins of power, he demonstrated not only tolerance but also strong approval of the Russian Orthodox Church. He is the first ruler of Russia since 1917 to attend services on religious holidays and to exploit his alleged faith in Christianity to bolster his political aspirations.

As Andrew Higgins pointed out in the New York Times, Putin is determined to display 'Russia's might as a religious power, not just as a military one'. His government has offered to spend a hundred million dollars to establish a 'spiritual and cultural center' near the Eiffel Tower, a coveted section of Paris. The former French minister of culture Frédéric Mitterand suggested that the church be named 'St. Vladimirov' in honor of the Russian president. Attempts to establish an Orthodox church have also been made in the French city of Nice. Similarly, the leaders in the Kremlin have sought to extend Russia's religious influence in Moldova, formerly part of the Soviet Union.

In all the new churches the priests espouse social and political views that are in keeping with traditional doctrine. They regularly denounce homosexuality as well as 'any attempt to put individual rights above those of family, community or nation'.[3] Moreover, they make a point of rejecting the moral and political values of the West; in Moldova, they have spoken out strongly against all proposals for the government to join NATO.

Sergei Chapnin, a journalist and former editor of the official Journal of the Moscow Patriarchate, made the most explicit statement, reported in the New York Times in 2016, on the Russian Church's ties to Putin's government: 'The Church has become an instrument of the Russian state. It is used to extend and legitimize the interests of the Kremlin.' In short, President Putin's positive attitude towards the Orthodox Church is part and parcel of his determination to restore Russia's role as a world power. One of his most significant steps in advancing that goal has been his attempt to increase Russia's influence in Ukraine, and it is widely assumed that ultimately he intends to absorb the country into the Russian Federation.

UKRAINE

Ukraine is a large country to the west of Russia with a population of about 45 million people. It had been part of the Russian state ever since 1654 with two brief exceptions, during the final period of World War I and for two years after Hitler's invasion of the country in 1941. Ukraine maintains strong cultural affinities to Russia, but most of its citizens – about 67.5 percent – prefer to live in their own state, and at the time the Soviet Union collapsed, they opted for independence. They contend that their culture is unique even though the Ukrainian language is very similar to Russian. Close to thirty percent of the people speak Russian at home and with friends, and many among that minority want the country to revert to the Russian state.[4]

For Putin, reunification is highly desirable for two reasons. It would be a major step towards restoring the grandeur of Russia and it would prevent the West from enlarging its sphere of influence in Eastern Europe. Eight countries that fell under communist control in the post-World War II period have joined NATO, whose purpose ever since its creation in 1949 has been to safeguard countries committed to democracy and to prevent their domination by the Soviet Union and, after 1991, by the Russian Federation. Putin fears that Ukraine might also join that military alliance, which would further hinder his plans to increase Russia's – and his – influence in international affairs.

His goals did not seem to be beyond reach from 2012 to 2014, when Ukraine was floundering. The economy had declined sharply, as had the standard of living of most citizens;

corruption prevailed at all levels of society; and the divisions between citizens who wanted to remain in an independent country and those who yearned for reunification with Russia became increasingly intense. In February 2014, a revolution erupted and the pro-Russian president, Victor Yanukovich, was deposed and replaced in the interim by Oleksandr Valentynovych, who favored Ukraine's independence. For President Putin it seemed to be the ideal moment to launch a campaign to weaken the country and destabilize that independence.

Putin's first move, in February 2014, was to engineer the seizure of Crimea, a peninsula in southern Russia that had been handed over to the Ukraine in 1954 by the authorities in Moscow. At that time, the transfer seemed to be merely an administrative measure; Ukraine and Crimea enjoyed close cultural ties, and both areas formed integral parts of the Soviet Union. But with Ukraine an independent state, the union was anathema to Putin.

Without warning, a large contingent of well-armed Russian troops invaded Crimea early in the morning of 27 February 2014, and within hours seized the two airfields on the peninsula and numerous government buildings. Ukrainian troops were ordered by their government not to resist, and by nightfall Crimea was in the hands of the Russians. The invaders had removed the insignia from their uniforms, and officials in Moscow declared that neither they nor their troops had played any role in the military operation, a claim that few believed. The regional parliament in Crimea then held a meeting in secret and announced the following month that the local population would vote on a referendum to grant more autonomy to Crimea – in effect, to allow the people the right to secede from Ukraine and join Russia.

The entire military operation was shrouded in secrecy; even many of Putin's subordinates were surprised by the audacious maneuver. Political leaders in Europe and the United States were stunned and quickly imposed sanctions on numerous Russian officials who had been involved in planning the invasion; in addition, Russia was expelled from the 'Group of Eight' (G8), which meets annually to discuss issues of common concern, such as terrorism, global energy, global supply of food, and climate change. Angela Merkel, the German chancellor, who generally exercises restraint in her comments on foreign leaders, told then President Obama that in her view Putin was living 'in another world'. Obama did not disagree.

The referendum was held, as Myers put it, 'under the barrels of Russian guns' and yielded an overwhelming vote in favor of joining the Russian Federation. Putin announced the annexation of Crimea and Sevastopol, a Ukrainian city, parts of which had been leased to Russia to be used as a port for its navy. According to polls conducted in Russia, a vast majority of Russians hailed the bold seizure of foreign land, and Putin's approval rating rose dramatically, to over eighty-five percent.

For Putin, the annexation of Crimea was only the first step in his plan to unravel Ukraine. He encouraged Russian-speaking citizens in eastern Ukraine to launch attacks on local authorities to compel them to abandon their country and join the Russian Federation; he claimed that Ukrainian citizens well disposed towards Russia had initiated the violence. But there is over-whelming evidence that the Russian government had shipped weapons to the so-called separatists. Moreover, it is well established that Russian soldiers were sent to Ukraine – without wearing their uniforms – and that they played a major role in the ensuing military conflicts.[5]

Late in the summer of 2015, the fighting subsided as a result of an agreement to a cease-fire, which remained more or less intact for several months. Putin is widely assumed to have counted on the economic decline of Ukraine, which continued unabated, together with its severe social and political problems, to weaken the country to such an extent that a growing number of its citizens would demand closer ties with Russia.

In fact, local anger at the Russians deepened when information came to light about the 2014 downing of a Malaysian plane flying from Amsterdam to Kuala Lumpur. Everyone on board – 283 passengers and 15 crew – died in the crash. After careful examination of the evidence, an international committee stated categorically in 2016 that Russian officials, responding to a request from Ukrainian separatists, had sent them a surface-to-air missile known as Buk or SA-11 and it had been used to bring down the plane. A few hours after the plane crashed, the weapon was returned to Russia, making it difficult to pinpoint from where it had been fired. Nevertheless, the committee found ample evidence in support of its conclusion.

Before seeing the report, Dmitri S. Peskov, President Putin's spokesman, issued a statement disparaging 'speculation' about the incident. He was sure that if a missile had in fact been fired it must have originated in a territory other than Ukraine. And Putin himself also denied responsibility for the downing of the plane long before the report had even been drafted; he claimed that the accusation leveled at Russia was part and parcel of an elaborate strategy to besmirch the reputation of his country and to weaken him politically.

As noted above, the fighting between the separatists and Ukrainian loyalists had subsided towards the end of the summer in 2015. But a year later, the violence resumed and the number of casualties increased substantially. The reporter Andrew E. Kramer described in detail what he had observed in just one city, Avdiivka, in the province of Donetsk. In the period from 2014 to 2016, its population of 35,000 declined to about 17,500 because many citizens had fled from the violence. According to reliable estimates, during the first twenty-five months of fighting in various areas close to the Russian border, almost ten thousand people lost their lives. Kramer could not discern an end to the conflict in the foreseeable future.

Kramer's prediction proved to be accurate. On 1 February 2017, he reported that the war in Ukraine had escalated once again, apparently because Putin was confident that the newly elected president of the United States, Donald Trump, would not take any measures to punish the Russians for their aggressions. However, it seemed that the American government may be divided on this issue; it has issued mixed signals. It is true that President Trump frequently said that he is loath to criti-cize Russia, but Nikki R. Haley, the new US ambassador to the United Nations, declared in her first official statement: 'We do want to better our relations with Russia. However, the dire situ-ation in eastern Ukraine is one that demands clear and strong condemnation of Russian acts.'

Not surprisingly, the Ukrainian authorities were alarmed by the possibility of a change in US policy under Trump towards the conflict in their country, and they consequently vowed not to cave in to the invaders. Kramer again suggested that a prolonged military conflict was probably in the offing.

THE BALTIC STATES

Russia's invasion of Crimea has rattled the nerves of citizens in Latvia, Lithuania, and Estonia, three countries that had been part of the Soviet empire. By late 2016, there were increasing signs that Putin might be preparing to restore control over these coun-tries. In November, Russia deployed nuclear-capable Iskander ballistic missiles in Kaliningrad, a city located between Lithuania and Poland, for the apparent purpose of intimidating not only the Baltic states but also the West, which is committed to protecting that entire region. The Russian government claimed that there was no reason to fear the deployments, which were nothing more than 'routine drills'.

Neither the governments in the Baltics, the senior officials of NATO, nor the United States authorities were persuaded by the Kremlin's assurances. It is well known that Russian officials have made extensive efforts to discredit the Lithuanian govern-ment by suggesting that its leaders were preparing for some sort of military action. The Kremlin claimed, for example, that the Lithuanians had conducted military exercises with a ship that carried chemical weapons and that five people on the boat 'had died from the chemicals'. The Russians offered no evidence to support this charge.

On the contrary, the Lithuanian authorities are so concerned about the likelihood of an invasion by Russia that they have brought up to date a 'civil defense booklet' that gives their citizens detailed instructions on how to resist invaders. The booklet assures readers that it 'is most important that the civilians are aware and have a will to resist – when these elements are strong, an aggressor has difficulties in creating an environment for military invasion'. More important and more ominous, the United States and its NATO allies have stepped up military exercises in Eastern Europe and, according to the reporter Eric Schmitt, they planned to send 'battalions to each of the three Baltic states and Poland'.[6]

The tensions in Eastern Europe are so deep-rooted that Gorbachev, the man who led Russia at the time communism collapsed and who is a recipient of the Nobel Peace Prize, warned in January 2017: 'The world is preparing for war.'

SYRIA

In his quest to reestablish Russia as a world power, Putin has focused on expanding his country's influence in areas beyond Eastern Europe. In September 2015, he decided to send military aircraft to bolster Bashar al-Assad, the Syrian president who for five years has waged a brutal war against various groups determined to end his authoritarian rule. Putin claimed that Russian pilots had been ordered to unleash bombs only on terrorist organizations such as ISIS (the Islamic State of Iraq and Syria), but in fact most of the targets were Assad's opponents in the civil war, who are favored by the West. Russia's military intervention in Syria has led to a further deterioration of relations between Putin and the West.

President Obama and many of his advisers were convinced that Putin would be 'caught in a quagmire', but by early August 2016 it seemed to Michael Kofman, a specialist on the Middle East, that 'Russia has won the proxy war [in Syria], at least for now.' Russia's airstrikes, which have numbered ninety a day, and the four thousand Russian military men who serve in Syria, have inflicted far-reaching damage on the opposition to Assad. It is clear that Putin has gone far in achieving his goals in the Middle East. He has strengthened Assad's position, assured Russia of a naval base in the region, can test Russia's newest weapons without endangering Russian lives, and perhaps most important, he has demonstrated to the citizens of Russia that their country is once again a key player on the world scene.

The Russian foray into Syria succeeded in part because Putin pursued conflicting policies that tended to confuse foreign statesmen. In the summer of 2016, it seemed that he was on the verge of reaching an agreement with the United States to unleash joint attacks on Islamic State fighters who were besieging the city of Aleppo with its two million inhabitants. But a day after the announcement of the agreement, it turned out that Russia had secured the right to bomb Syrian rebels on its own from a base in Iran. Those rebels were struggling, with the encouragement of the United States and the West in general, to overthrow Assad. In short, Russia had adopted a two-fold strategy designed to support Assad but also to give the impression that it is helping his opponents. In the meantime, the agony of the Syrians has been horrendous. Over 470,000 people have lost their lives, 6.5 million have been displaced within Syria, and 5 million have fled the country.[7]

DOMESTIC TROUBLES

Although Putin is solidly entrenched in power, public expression of discontent has been growing in Russia in the form of a series of anti-government demonstrations. The principal causes of the unrest were the decline of the economy brought about mainly by the sharp drop in the price of oil, and the increasing drift towards harsh authoritarianism by the government, which relied on the support of a large number of officials trained in stifling opposition to decisions emanating from the Kremlin. It is estimated that more than twenty-five percent of the officials in senior government positions served at one time in the Committee for State Security (KGB, now known as FSB), an institution that trained its employees to implement the orders of the country's leaders at all costs.

That the police and judiciary were determined to take a hard line in dealing with critics of the president became clear even before Putin returned to the office in 2012.

Many of the street protests, which began in December 2011, were directed at the flawed and rigged electoral process. Russian and foreign journalists provided extensive coverage of the unrest and stressed the seriousness and dignified conduct of the people voicing their discontent. For example, the British journal *The Economist* published an article entitled 'A Russian Awakening' on a demonstration that had taken place on 4 December. It described an

> uplifting display of both dignity and indignation. Citizens were riled not only about the electoral fraud, but at being treated as imbeciles by their leader, Vladimir Putin. There was anger at the Kremlin, calls for "Russia without Putin" and against the ruling United Russia party ("the party of thieves and crooks"), but no aggression. The crowd contained not only liberals but communists, anarchists and some nationalists. But protesters were almost conspicuously polite towards each other.

Fearful of the spread of protests, in February 2012, the government called on its supporters to take to the streets – within a few days, about 130,000 marched in Moscow in support of Putin. But this did not put an end to the anti-government demonstrations. During that same month, approximately thirty thousand citizens marched again in the streets of Moscow, and soon the unrest spread to St. Petersburg and to Astrakhan, a city 790 miles from the capital. The police resorted to severe measures to clear the demonstrators from the streets; they arrested many and charged them with misdemeanors; judges imposed large fines on them. The last time Russia had witnessed such an outpouring of street demonstrations was in the early 1990s, at the time of the demise of communism.

The government's harshest response to peaceful expressions of protest occurred on 12 February 2012, when five young women, members of the Russian punk band Pussy Riot, entered the Cathedral of Christ the Saviour, the main Russian Orthodox church in Moscow, walked up to the altar, and sang a song critical of Putin. It was an unnecessarily provocative but rather amusing form of protest, and it can be argued that the women could have chosen a more appropriate place to voice their opposition to the government's conduct of affairs. But their imprudent behavior was hardly a crime that deserved extraordinarily severe punishment.

The police seized three of the singers and handed them over to the legal authorities, who charged them with 'hooliganism motivated by religious hatred'. All three were found guilty. The judge sentenced two of the singers to two years in prison and imposed a suspended sentence on the third. The criticism of the harsh penalties was so widespread that the two women were released after serving twenty-two months, not a very generous reduction of the sentence. Most probably, officials were willing, and even eager, to shorten the sentences because the Winter Olympics were to begin shortly in Sochi, Russia, and foreign media were about to show up to cover the sports festival. It seemed wise to remove a likely source of criticism by foreigners. Interestingly, at about the same time, Mikhail Khodorkovsky, mentioned above, was released after serving ten years of a sentence arbitrarily extended in 2010 for crimes most observers believe he had not committed.

The two singers visited the United States shortly after their release and, during a meeting with the editorial board of the *New York Times* early in February 2014, one of them, Maria, described the horrors of prison life in Russia: 'We were constantly watched . . . and the more they watch you, the harder your life is.' Maria's bandmate, Nadezhda, revealed that some inmates were forced to work twenty hours a day and that 'prisoners were sometimes locked outdoors, even in the cold and the rain for eight hours a day.' Upon their return to Russia the young women vowed to campaign for reform in Russia's prisons.

In large measure, Putin's popularity in the years from 2000 to 2008 can be attributed to the improvement in the economy, which was a direct result of the high price of oil, by far the country's most profitable product. Unexpectedly, in June 2014, the world-wide glut of oil caused a precipitous decline in its price, from $115 per barrel to $35. The dramatic downturn called for drastic changes in the economy, but the government made no effort to promote alternative sources of income or to reform the economy established in 1990. It still operates as a free market under the control of a small number of oligarchs who are beholden to the government for their success. The result is a society in which a very small number of people live luxuriously and the vast major-ity can barely make ends meet. In its Global Wealth Report, the bank Credit Suisse said, 'Russia has the highest level of wealth inequality in the world apart from small Caribbean nations with resident billionaires.' The historian Walter Laqueur expands on this in *Putinism: Russia and Its Future with the West*: 'About 110 Russian citizens are reported to control thirty-five percent of household wealth, largely comprising money made in the natural resources sector over the last twenty-five to thirty years. This has become not only a major political problem, but a very seri-ous economic issue.' According to Credit Suisse, the thirty-five percent of wealth that 110 Russian billionaires own is equivalent to $420 billion.[8] The privatization of the economy, begun in the 1990s, has failed to spread the country's wealth, and has not given rise to a sizable middle class.

Corruption is rampant and one reason for the wide disparity in income. To succeed in the economy a person must kowtow to the authorities in Moscow, and that includes generous distribu-tion of bribes; those who refuse to abide by these rules face the wrath of the rigged judicial system and often land in jail. A fair number of oligarchs – according to some estimates, half of them – have escaped Putin's control by sending their wealth abroad and by taking up residence in foreign countries. For many, London is the city of choice. Putin himself has taken advantage of this corrupt system; he is said to have amassed a fortune worth forty billion dollars. In 2014, the Organized Crime and Corruption Reporting Project awarded him the 'Person of the Year Award for furthering corruption and organized crime'.

RELATIONS WITH THE US

In 2016, President Putin's hostility towards the West took a new and unexpected turn. In the summer and fall of that year, when the Republican and Democratic candidates were campaigning in the election for the presidency, American intelligence agencies in Washington concluded, after extensive investigations, that they had 'high confidence' that the Russian government had sponsored efforts to obtain information harmful to senior officials of the Democratic Party; the aim of the Russians appeared to be to influence the outcome of the election.[9] The private emails of various campaign staff working for Hillary Clinton, the then Democratic candidate for president, were obtained and released by Wikileaks, an organization that publishes documents from anonymous sources, for the most part embarrassing to government authorities or institutions.

After Clinton's nomination, information was leaked, seemingly to weaken her campaign against the Republican candidate, Donald Trump. The finger of blame has been pointed at Putin; as Secretary of State, Clinton gradually became very critical of Putin's policies, and it did seem as if a Trump presidency would treat him with more respect. During the presidential campaign, Trump frequently made favorable comments about the Russian leader, and insisted that he would have no difficulty in reaching agreements with him on issues that had previously caused rifts between the United States and Russia.

When the initial rumours of Russian meddling in the American election appeared in the press, President Obama did not, at first, take any retaliatory measures.

But several weeks after the election, Obama decided he could no longer remain silent. A new study by all three American intelligence services (the Central Intelligence Agency, the National

Security Agency, and the Federal Bureau of Investigation) had concluded that there was no doubt about Russia's intervention in the election.[10] Their investigation pointed to hacking of leading US political officials by a Russian intelligence unit known as the GRU (the foreign military intelligence agency of the General Staff of the armed forces of the Russian Federation).

A few days after newspapers divulged the findings, a Moscow newspaper disclosed that Sergei Mikhailov, 'a senior officer of the Federal Security, or FSB', had been arrested, as had Ruslan Styanov, 'the head of computer incident response investigations at Kapersky Lab, which makes antivirus programs'. So far, all that is known about these arrests is that Mikhailov was charged with treason, the first time since the breakup of the Soviet Union that so senior an official of the FSB has been accused of such a serious a crime. Could it be that these two senior government officials were suspected of having leaked information to foreign, that is, American, agents? Or, as a reporter for the *New York Times* speculated, on 27 January 2017, were the arrests a 'goodwill gesture to the United States, which has penalized Russia for the electoral meddling'?

President Obama, whose term in office ended in January 2017, had imposed a series of penalties on Russia for hacking American computers. Obama ordered the ejection from the United States of thirty-five 'suspected Russian intelligence operatives' and imposed sanctions on four senior officers of the GRU. The president also ordered the closing of two waterfront estates in the US that Russian officials had used for 'intelligence activities'.

The response of the Russian government to the sanctions was interesting and once again demonstrated that Putin is a clever politician who knows how to turn a potential embarrassment into a public relations triumph. He rejected the advice of the Russian foreign minister, Sergei Lavrov, who urged the president to retaliate by expelling thirty-five US diplomats and closing two American facilities in Russia. Putin knew that Trump, soon to be the president of the United States, had criticized Obama's conduct of foreign policy and, as already noted, had a rather favorable opinion of Putin. And to demonstrate that he was a man of good intentions, the Russian president decided to apply the carrot rather than the stick. 'We will not create problems for the US diplomats,' he announced. 'We won't expel anyone. We won't forbid their families and children to use their usual recreation places during the New Year celebrations.' He also invited the children of US diplomats to various holiday functions at the Kremlin. He ended his response to Obama's sanctions by declaring: 'We will not resort to irresponsible "kitchen" diplomacy . . . We will not expel anyone.'[11]

PUTIN'S SUCCESS

Since 2000, Putin has been remarkably successful not only in holding on to power but also in increasing his sway as an authoritarian ruler. Russian and American journalists attribute his ability to retain his position as the country's absolute leader to three factors: he is extraordinarily clever in formulating policies that appeal to the masses; he has surrounded himself with officials too insecure to question his decisions; he has not hesitated to engage in 'targeted killings' of ambitious individuals he views as threats to his authority, and often his subordinates have carried out the murders abroad if the president's enemies have succeeded in escaping from Russia. According to Andrew Kramer, 'No other power employs murder as systematically and ruthlessly as Russia does against those seen as betraying its interests abroad.' In 2006, killings outside Russia of citizens considered traitors were given legal sanction by the national parliament.[12]

Several months after he was reelected president early in 2016, Putin faced a political challenge of sorts, the vote for a new Duma. The outcome of that election was important to the president because it may have a bearing on Russia's future domestic and foreign policies, although it should be noted that just about

THE RISE AND RISE OF PUTIN

all commentators on Russian affairs predicted that Putin's political dominance made it unlikely that he would lose his majority in the chamber of 450 representatives.

But the president took no chances. Initially, the elections were scheduled for December 2016, but he insisted they be held three months earlier, in September. Putin was still profoundly angry over the public display of disapproval of his rule in 2011 and 2012. So cynics would argue that this decision was to move the campaigning to August, when many citizens were on vacation and would therefore not be available for political demonstrations.

Ahead of the vote, Putin also persuaded the Duma to adopt legislation increasing the penalties for violations of the elaborate laws against dissent. In addition, legislators adopted a law broadening the latitude for agents of the FSB to use their weapons against protesters found to be violating existing laws against public displays of opposition to the government. More specifically, agents of the FSB were now permitted to shoot demonstrators 'without any warnings of their intention to use weapons, special means or physical force'.

It is not known whether these precautionary measures were effective in discouraging potential demonstrators. But we do know the elections proceeded without any significant unrest, and there were few reports of voting irregularities. Putin's party scored a decisive victory by winning 343 of 450 seats in the new Duma, an increase of 105, which is enough support to secure passage of amendments to the constitution. Four small parties, all of them supporters of Putin, won all but one of the remaining seats. Dmitry G. Gudkov, the only liberal in the outgoing parliament, was not reelected.

However, there was one indication that a sizable number of citizens were less than enthusiastic about the ruler in Moscow: 'turnout', according to a BBC report, 'was a record low of 47.8 percent.'[13] In Moscow and St. Petersburg, the two largest cities, only about thirty percent bothered to vote.

The low turnout could suggest widespread despair about the possibility of liberal change in the near future. But it should also be

kept in mind that any reservations about President Putin's leadership are overshadowed by admiration for his successes. Aleksandr
Gremin, a political journalist and editor of *Ponedel'nik*, offered
a plausible explanation for this: 'People liked what happened in
foreign policy in recent years; people like it that we can bomb
Syria. People like that the candidates in the US elections say
that Putin can influence the vote there. We feel that we are a
superpower again that reaches beyond its immediate borders.'[14] If
Gremin is right, which is very likely, as long as Putin is president
no fundamental change in government polices can be expected.

During his years as leader of Russia, President Putin has gone
from being an advocate of friendly relations with the West and
supporter of some modest democratic reforms to a champion of
Russia's greatness as a world power and the reestablishment of
an autocratic system of rule. If he has any lingering attachment
to the ideals of socialism as propounded by Lenin and Stalin,
which he probably had supported as a young man in the Soviet
Union's main security agency (KGB), he keeps that hidden.
Economically and socially, Russia is home to unbridled capitalism, a system that has greatly benefited Putin, who is reputed to
be a very rich man. The president has also discarded atheism and
secularism, cardinal principles of communism.

But he has not abandoned all of Stalin's political goals. He
is as determined as Stalin was in the post-World War II period
to expand Russia's influence in Europe and in other parts of the
world. Deep down, Putin appears to be a fervent believer in the
greatness of Russia and will resort to all means at his disposal to
revive the country as a superpower, even if that requires military
action. Of course, in doing so, he is also vastly increasing his own
power and stature, another goal to which he has devoted himself.
It is a risky goal, whose pursuit has already involved the country
in military conflict in Eastern Europe and the Middle East and
may eventually lead to a new cold war.

It boggles the mind to recall that only one century ago Russia
underwent a revolution designed to transform the autocratic

system of tsarism into a social and political order based on the principle of egalitarianism. Many Russians, including Putin, now recognize the critical flaws in the political and economic program of the Bolsheviks. In a fascinating article in the *New York Times*, the journalist Neil MacFarquhar pointed out that there is a fairly widespread sense that the country took a fundamentally wrong turn; the upheaval in 1917 'wrecked the country' because Lenin 'fomented appalling bloodshed and destroyed the Russian Orthodox Church, a pillar of Mr. Putin's support'. Even Putin, eager to preserve his position as dictator, 'loathes the very idea of revolution', and on one occasion said that 'we didn't need the world revolution.'[15] Consequently, he decided not to make any pronouncement on the centenary of the resignation of Tsar Nicholas II, which occurred on 15 March 1917, three days after the turmoil that led to Lenin's seizure of power.[16]

The official reason for ignoring the centenary of the 1917 revolution is that the Kremlin wanted to avoid domestic discord between those who still revere Lenin, and the liberals. 'We can't allow splits, animosity, insults and the bitterness of the past to be dragged into our lives today,' Putin warned.[17] But the liberals warn that a government that pays no attention to the vast inequality of income and that makes no effort to protect the civil rights of citizens should be concerned about an upheaval from below. To be sure, the likelihood of a successful revolution similar to that of 1917 in the foreseeable future is slight. But there are enough signs of discontent, such as protest marches, that have rattled the authorities in the Kremlin.

Does the fact that today's Russia bears little resemblance to the goal of the 1917 revolutionaries mean, as I suggested in the preface to this edition, that the dreams of Lenin and his colleagues were based on a misunderstanding of human nature or perhaps on wishful thinking? Could it be that the doctrines of Marx and the founders of Bolshevism were so unrealistic that they could never have been implemented? If that is the case, the history of communism may be a prime example of how a misreading of human beings can lead to unspeakable disasters.

NOTES

CHAPTER 1: THE BEGINNINGS

1. My discussion of the geography and economy of Russia refers to the Russian Empire down to 1917 and the Soviet Union to 1991. During the latter year the country split into fifteen separate states.
2. For a discussion of this school and its opponents, see Nicholas V. Riasanovsky, 'The Norman Theory of the Origin of the Russian State', *Russian Review*, 7 (1947), pp. 96–110.
3. B. D. Grekov, *Kiev Rus*, trans. Y. Sdobnikov (Moscow, 1959); V. V. Mavrodin, 'Osnovnie momenty razvitiia russkogo gosudarstva do XIII v' [The Fundamental Stages in the Development of the Russian State to the Eighteenth Century] *Vestnik Leningradskogo Universiteta*, 3 (1947), p. 84; S. V. Yuzhkov, *Istoriia gosudarstva i prava SSSR* [The History of the State and Law of the USSR] (Moscow, 1947), vol. 1.
4. V. O. Kliuchevsky, *A History of Russia*, trans. C. J. Hogarth (New York, 1960), vol. 1, pp. 239–93; M. N. Pokrovsky, *A History of Russia from the Earliest Times to the Rise of Commercial Capitalism*, trans. and ed. J. D. Clarkson and M. R. M. Griffith (New York, 1931), vol. 1.

CHAPTER 3: TIMES OF TROUBLES AND GRANDEUR, 1584–1725

1. Kliuchevsky, *A History of Russia*, vol. 3, p. 57.
2. V. I. Sergeevich, *Russkiia iuridecheskiia drevnosti* [Russian Legal Antiquities], 3 vols (St. Petersburg, 1900–3).
3. Jerome Blum, *Lord and Peasant in Russia from the Ninth to the Nineteenth Century* (Princeton, 1961), *passim*; Kliuchevsky, *A History of Russia*, vol. 2, pp. 219–41.
4. Exactly how much land the average peasant had is hard to determine. According to a study of twenty provinces, late in the eighteenth century

'each male peasant on obrok had an average of 13.5 desiatins [one desiatin equals 2.7 acres], including 4 desiatins of arable, and each male on barshchina had 10.6 desiatins, including three desiatins of arable.' Blum, *Lord and Peasant in Russia*, p. 528; see pp. 528–35 for more details.

CHAPTER 5: RUSSIA AS A GREAT POWER, 1801–55

1. Eugene V. Tarle, *Napoleon's Invasion of Russia, 1812* (London, 1942), p. 231.
2. Ibid., p. 393.
3. For more about the state peasants, about forty percent of the population at the time, see chapter 6, pp. 121–3.

CHAPTER 6: REFORM AND COUNTER-REFORM, 1861–94

1. For more on Russian serfdom, see chapter 3, pp. 57–8.
2. For more on the *mir*, see chapter 3, p. 57.
3. I. M. Aronson, *Troubled Waters. The Origins of the 1881 Anti-Jewish Pogroms in Russia* (Pittsburgh, 1990); John D. Klier and Shlomo Lambroza (eds), *Pogroms: Anti-Jewish Violence in Modern Russian History* (Cambridge, 1991); Louis Greenberg, *The Jews in Russia* (New Haven, 1951), vol. 2, pp. 19–26.

CHAPTER 7: REVOLUTIONARY RUSSIA, 1894–1917

1. Abraham Ascher, *P. A. Stolypin: The Search for Stability in Late Imperial Russia* (Stanford, CA, 2001), pp. 376–86; A. Ia. Avrekh, *Stolypin i tretiia duma* [Stolypin and the Third Duma] (Moscow, 1968), pp. 367–406; Richard Pipes, *The Russian Revolution* (New York, 1990), p. 190.
2. E. H. Carr, *The Bolshevik Revolution, 1917–1923* (New York, 1951–61), vol. 1, p. 115.

CHAPTER 8: THE SOVIET UNION UNDER LENIN AND STALIN

1. The Russian acronym for 'Chief Administration of Corrective-Labor Camps', a loose reference to the penal system under Stalin.
2. Robert Conquest, *The Great Terror: A Reassessment* (New York, 1990), pp. 484–89. For a different assessment of the number of victims, see J. Arch Getty and Roberta T. Manning (eds), *Stalinist Terror: New Perspectives* (Cambridge, 1993), pp. 11–13.

CHAPTER 9: REFORM, STAGNATION, COLLAPSE

1. Lilia Shevtsova, *Yeltsin's Russia: Myths and Reality* (Washington, 1999), p. 91.

CHAPTER 10: THE RISE AND RISE OF PUTIN

1. Anton Barbashin and Hannah Thoburn, 'Putin's Philosopher: Ivan Ilyin and the Ideology of Moscow's Rule', *Foreign Affairs*, 20 September 2015, https://www.foreignaffairs.com/articles/russian-federation/2015-09-20/putin's-philosopher.
2. Quoted in Iben Thranholm, 'Putin's Christian Vision', *Russia Insider*, 9 October 2014, http://russia-insider.com/en/culture/putins-christian-vision/ri436.
3. Andrew Higgins, 'Russia Mobilizes Faith to Extend its Influence', *New York Times*, 14 September 2016, pp. A1, A8.
4. Ukrainian census of 2001.
5. NATO's top military commander, General Philip M. Breedlove, is quoted confirming Russian weaponry and forces in Ukraine by David M. Herszenhorn, 'Fear Rises as Military Units Pour into Ukraine', *New York Times*, 13 November 2014, p. A5.
6. Eric Schmitt, 'U.S. Lending Support to Baltic States Fearing Russia', *New York Times*, 2 January 2017, p. A3.
7. Anne Barnard, 'Death Toll from Syria Now 470,000, Group Finds', *New York Times*, 2 January 2017, p. A3; *Guardian*, 10 February 2016; Priyanka Boghani, 'A Staggering New Death Toll for Syria's War – 470,000', *PBS Frontline*, 11 February 2016, http://www.pbs.org/wgbh/frontline/article/a-staggering-new-death-toll-for-syrias-war-470000/.
8. Credit Suisse Research Institute, Global Wealth Report 2013, p. 53; *Sydney Morning Herald*, 10 October 2013; Walter Laqueur, *Putinism: Russia and Its Future in the West* (New York, 2015), p. 178.
9. *New York Times*, 9 December 2016, p. A1.
10. David E. Sanger, 'Obama Strikes Back at Russia for Election Hacking', *New York Times*, 29 December 2016.
11. Neil MacFarquhar, 'Vladimir Putin Won't Expel U.S. Diplomats as Russian Foreign Minister Urged', *New York Times*, 30 December 2016.
12. Andrew Kramer, 'More Enemies of the Kremlin End Up Dead', *New York Times*, 21 August 2016, pp. A1, A6.
13. 'Russian Election: Big Victory for Putin-backed party, United Russia', *BBC News*, 19 September 2016, http://www.bbc.co.uk/news/world-europe-37403242.
14. Neil MacFarquhar, 'Kremlin Says it Wants a Spotless Election, But Locally It Is Marred', *New York Times*, 17 September 2016.
15. Neil MacFarquhar, '"Revolution? What Revolution?" Russia Asks 100 Years Later', *New York Times*, 10 March 2017, https://www.nytimes.com/2017/03/10/world/europe/russian-revolution-100-years-putin.html.
16. MacFarquhar, 'Revolution? What Revolution?'.
17. Howard Amos, 'Want to mark a revolution? Kremlin says you can count it out', *Associated Press*, 15 March 2017.

BIBLIOGRAPHY

GENERAL WORKS

Clarkson, J. D. *A History of Russia*. New York, 1969.
Florinsky, M. T. *Russia. A History and An Interpretation*, 2 vols. New York, 1955.
Freeze, G. L. (ed.) *Russia. A History*. New York, 1997.
Hosking, G. *Russia: People and Empire, 1552–1917*. Cambridge, MA, 1997.
—— *Russia and the Russians*. Cambridge, MA, 2001.
Kliuchevsky, V. O. *A History of Russia*, 5 vols, trans. C. J. Hogarth. New York, 1911–31, reissued 1960.
Pipes, R. E. *Russia under the Old Regime*. New York, 1974.
Raeff, M. (ed.) *Russian Intellectual History: An Anthology*. New York, 1966.
Riasanovsky, N. V. *A History of Russia*, 6th edn. New York, 1999.
Seton-Watson, H. *The Russian Empire, 1801–1917*. Oxford, 1967.
Vernadsky, G. *A History of Russia*, 5 vols. New Haven, 1943–69.

THE BEGINNINGS

Cross, S. H. and Sherbowitz, O. P. (eds and trans.) *The Primary Russian Chronicle, Laurentian Text*. Cambridge, MA, 1975.
Fedotov, G. P. *The Russian Religious Mind. Kievan Chrstianity. The 10th to the 13th Centuries*. Cambridge, MA, 1946.
Fennell, J. *The Crisis of Medieval Russia, 1200–1304*, 2 vols. London, 1983.
Franklin, S. and Shepard, J. *The Emergence of Rus, 750–1200*. London and New York, 1996.
Halperin, C. J. *Russia and the Golden Horde*. London, 1987.
Kaiser, D. H. *The Growth of the Law in Medieval Russia*. Princeton, 1980.
Levin, E. *Sex and Society in the World of the Orthodox Slavs, 900–1700*. Ithaca, NY, 1989.
Martin, J. *Medieval Russia, 980–1584*. Cambridge, 1995.

THE RISE OF MUSCOVITE RUSSIA

Alef, G. *Rulers and Nobles in Fifteenth-Century Muscovy*. London, 1983.
Crummey, R. O. *The Formation of Muscovy, 1300–1613*. London and New York, 1987.
Fennell, J. *Ivan the Great of Moscow*. London, 1963.
—— *The Emergence of Moscow, 1304–1359*. Berkeley and Los Angeles, 1968.
Kollmann, N. S. *Kinship and Politics. The Making of the Muscovite Political System, 1345–1547*. Stanford, CA, 1987.
Martin, J. *Treasury of the Land of Darkness*. Cambridge, 1986.
Platonov, S. F. *Ivan the Terrible*. Gulf Breeze, FL, 1974.
Presniakov, A. E. *The Tsardom of Muscovy*. Gulf Breeze, FL, 1978.

TIMES OF TROUBLES AND GRANDEUR, 1584–1725

Anisimov, E. V. *The Reforms of Peter the Great*, trans. and ed. J. T. Alexander. Armonk, NY, 1993.
Avrich, P. *Russian Rebels, 1600–1800*. New York, 1976.
Blum, J. *Lord and Peasant in Russia from the Ninth to the Nineteenth Century*. Princeton, 1983.
Crummey, R. O. *Aristocrats and Servitors: The Boyar Elite in Russia, 1613–1689*. Princeton, 1983.
Hellie, R. S. *Enserfment and Military Change in Muscovy*. Chicago, 1971.
Hughes, L. *Russia in the Age of Peter the Great*. New Haven and London, 1998.
Keep, J. L. H. *Soldiers of the Tsar: Army and Society in Russia, 1462–1874*. Oxford, 1985.
Platonov, S. F. *The Time of Troubles*, trans. J. T. Alexander. Lawrence, KS, 1970.
Raeff, M. (ed.) *Peter the Great: Reformer or Revolutionary?* Boston, 1963.
Sumner, B. H. *Peter the Great and the Emergence of Russia*. New York, 1966.
Wortman, R. S. *Scenarios of Power: Myth and Ceremony in Russian Monarchy*, vol. 1. Princeton, 1995.

DECLINE AND REVIVAL IN THE EIGHTEENTH CENTURY

De Madariaga, I. *Russia in the Age of Catherine the Great*. New Haven and London, 1981.
Dukes, P. *The Making of Russian Absolutism, 1613–1801*. London and New York, 1990.
Freeze, G. L. *The Russian Levites: Parish Clergy in the Eighteenth Century*. Cambridge, MA, 1977.
Fuller, W., Jr. *Strategy and Power in Russia, 1600–1914*. New York, 1992.
Hans, N. A. *History of Russian Educational Policy, 1701–1917*. London, 1931.
Johnson, W. H. E. *Russia's Educational Heritage*. Pittsburgh, 1950.

LeDonne, J. P. *Ruling Russia. Politics and Administration in the Age of Absolutism, 1762–1796*. Princeton, 1984.

Marker, G. J. *Publishing, Printing, and the Origins of Intellectual Life in Russia, 1700–1800*. Princeton, 1984.

McConnell, A. *A Russian* Philosophe: *Alexander Radishchev, 1749–1802*. The Hague, 1964.

Raeff, M. *Origins of the Russian Intelligentsia. The Eighteenth-Century Nobility*. New York, 1966.

—— *Imperial Russia, 1682–1825*. New York, 1971.

—— *The Well Ordered Police State*. New Haven, 1985.

RUSSIA AS A GREAT POWER, 1801–55

Berlin, I. *Russian Thinkers*. London, 1978.

Blackwell, W. L. *The Beginnings of Russian Industrialization, 1800–1860*. Princeton, 1968.

Lincoln, W. B. *In the Vanguard of Reform*. DeKalb, IL, 1982.

—— *Nicholas I, Emperor and Autocrat of all the Russias*. DeKalb, IL, 1989.

Malia, M. *Alexander Herzen and the Birth of Russian Socialism, 1812–1855*. Cambridge, MA, 1961.

Mazour, A. G. *The First Russian Revolution, 1825*. Berkeley, 1937.

McConnell, A. *Tsar Alexander I. Paternalistic Reformer*. New York, 1970.

Orlovsky, D. T. *The Limits of Reform: The Ministry of Internal Affairs in Imperial Russia, 1802–1881*. Cambridge, MA, 1981.

Raeff, M. *Michael Speransky: Statesman of Imperial Russia, 1772–1839*. The Hague, 1957.

—— *Political Ideas and Institutions in Imperial Russia*. Boulder, 1994.

Saunders, D. *Russia in the Age of Reaction and Reform, 1801–1881*. London and New York, 1992.

Stanislawski, M. *Tsar Nicholas I and the Jews*. Philadelphia, 1985.

Tarle, E. V. *Napoleon's Invasion of Russia, 1812*. London, 1942.

Walicki, A. *A History of Russian Thought from the Enlightenment to Marxism*. Stanford, CA, 1979.

Wortman, R. S. *Scenarios of Power: Myth and Ceremony in Russian Monarchy*, vol. 2. Princeton, 2000.

REFORM AND COUNTER-REFORM, 1861–94

Becker, S. *Nobility and Privilege in Late Imperial Russia*. DeKalb, IL, 1985.

Byrnes, R. F. *Pobedonostsev: His Life and Thought*. Bloomington, IN, 1968.

Eklof, B. *Russian Peasant Schools*. Berkeley, 1986.

Emmons, T. *The Russian Landed Gentry and the Peasant Emancipation of 1861*. Cambridge, 1968.

Field, D. *The End of Serfdom: Nobility and Bureaucracy in Russia, 1855–1861*. Cambridge, MA, 1968.

Lincoln, W. B. *The Great Reforms*. DeKalb, IL, 1990.

Mosse, W. E. *An Economic History of Russia, 1856–1914*. New York, 1892.

Robinson, G. T. *Rural Russia under the Old Regime*. New York, 1932.

Rogger, H. *Russia in the Age of Modernisation and Revolution, 1881–1917*. London and New York, 1983.

—— *Jewish Policies and Right-Wing Politics in Imperial Russia*. Berkeley, 1986.

Starr, S. F. *Decentralization and Self-Government in Russia, 1830–1870*. Princeton, 1972.

Stites, R. *The Women's Liberation Movement in Russia: Feminism, Nihilism, and Bolshevism, 1860–1930*. Princeton, 1978.

Suny, R. G. *The Making of the Georgian Nation: From Prehistory to Soviet Rule*. Bloomington, IN, 1988.

Vuccinich, W. S. (ed.) *The Peasant in Nineteenth Century Russia*. Stanford, CA, 1968.

Zelnik, R. E. *Labor and Society in Tsarist Russia: The Factory Workers of St. Petersburg, 1855–1870*. Stanford, CA, 1971.

REVOLUTIONARY RUSSIA, 1894–1917

Ascher, A. *The Russian Revolution of 1905*, 2 vols. Stanford, CA, 1988–92.

—— *P.A. Stolypin: The Search for Stability in Late Imperial Russia*. Stanford, CA, 2001.

Avrich, P. *The Russian Anarchists*. Princeton, 1967.

Bonnell, V. E. *Roots of Rebellion: Workers' Politics and Organizations in St. Petersburg and Moscow, 1900-1914*. Berkeley, 1983.

Brooks, J. *When Russia Learned to Read: Literacy and Popular Culture, 1861–1917*. Princeton, 1985.

Bushnell, J. *Mutiny amid Repression: Russian Soldiers in the Revolution of 1905–1906*. Bloomington, IN, 1985.

Carr, E. H. *The Bolshevik Revolution, 1917–1923*, 3 vols. New York, 1951–61.

Chamberlin, W. H. *The Russian Revolution, 1917–1921*, 2 vols. New York, 1960.

Daly, J. W. *Autocracy under Siege: Security Police and Opposition in Russia, 1866–1905*. DeKalb, IL, 1988.

Engelstein, L. *Moscow, 1905*. Stanford, CA, 1982.

—— *The Keys to Happiness: Sex and the Search for Modernity in Fin-de-Siècle Russia*. Ithaca, NY, 1992.

Figes, O. *Peasant Russia Civil War: The Volga Countryside in Revolution 1917–1921*. Oxford, 1989.

—— *A People's Tragedy: The Russian Revolution: 1891–1924*. New York, 1997.

Frankel, J. *Prophecy and Politics: Socialism, Nationalism, and the Russian Jews, 1862–1917*. Cambridge, 1981.

Galai, S. *The Liberation Movement in Russia, 1900–1905*. Cambridge, 1973.

Getzler, I. *Martov: A Political Biography of a Russian Social Democrat*. Cambridge, 1967.

Haimson, L. *The Russian Marxists and the Origins of Bolshevism*. Cambridge, 1955.

Hosking, G. *The Russian Constitutional Experiment: Government and Duma, 1907–1914*. Cambridge, 1973.

Keep, J. L. H. *The Rise of Social Democracy in Russia*. Oxford, 1963.

—— *The Russian Revolution: A Study in Mass Mobilization*. New York, 1976.

Lampert, E. *Sons against Fathers: Studies in Russian Radicalism and Revolution*. Oxford, 1965.

Lieven, D. C. B. *Russia and the Origins of the First World War*. New York, 1983.

—— *Russia's Rulers under the Old Regime*. New Haven, 1989.

—— *Nicholas II: Twilight of the Empire*. New York, 1994.

Manning, R. T. *The Crisis of the Old Order in Russia*. Princeton, 1982.

Mendelsohn, E. *Class Struggle in the Pale: The Formative Years of the Jewish Workers' Movement in Tsarist Russia*. Cambridge, 1970.

Miller, M. S. *The Economic Development of Russia, 1905–1914*, 2nd edn. London, 1967.

Neuberger, J. *Hooliganism: Crime, Culture, and Power in St. Petersburg, 1900–1914*. Berkeley, 1995.

Pipes, R. E. *The Russian Revolution*. New York, 1991.

Rieber, A. J. *Merchants and Entrepreneurs in Imperial Russia*. Chapel Hill, NC, 1982.

Robbins, R. G., Jr. *The Tsar's Viceroys*. Ithaca, NY, 1987.

Venturi, F. *Roots of Revolution: A History of the Populist and Socialist Movements in Nineteenth-Century Russia*. New York, 1960.

Von Laue, T. H. *Sergei Witte and the Industrialization of Russia*. New York, 1963.

Wcislo, F. W. *Reforming Rural Russia*. Princeton, 1990.

Weeks, T. R. *Nation and State in Late Imperial Russia: Nationalism and Russification on the Western Frontier, 1863–1914*. DeKalb, IL, 1996.

Weissman, N. B. *Reform in Tsarist Russia*. New Brunswick, NJ, 1981.

Wildman, A. K. *The End of the Russian Imperial Army*, 2 vols. Princeton, 1980–7.

Wolfe, B. D. *Three Who Made a Revolution: A Biographical History of Lenin, Trotsky, and Stalin*. New York, 1948.

Wortman, R. S. *The Crisis of Russian Populism*. Cambridge, 1967.

Wynn, C. *Workers, Strikes, and Pogroms*. Princeton, 1992.

THE SOVIET UNION UNDER LENIN AND STALIN

Avrich, P. *Kronstadt 1921*. Princeton, 1970.

Cohen, S. F. *Bukharin and the Bolshevik Revolution*. New York, 1971.

Conquest, R. *The Great Terror: A Reassessment*. New York, 1990.

Dallin, A. *German Rule in Russia, 1941–1945*. London, 1957.

Fainsod, M. *How Russia Is Ruled*, rev. edn. Cambridge, MA, 1963.

Fitzpatrick, S. *Education and Social Mobility in the Soviet Union, 1921–1934*. Cambridge, 1979.

—— *Stalin's Peasants: Resistance and Survival in the Russian Village after Collectivization*. Oxford, 1994.

—— *Everyday Stalinism: Ordinary Life in Extraordinary Times: Russia in the 1930s*. New York, 1999.

Getty, J. A. *Origins of the Great Purges*. Cambridge, 1985.

Hosking, G. *The First Socialist Society: A History of the Soviet Union from Within*. Cambridge, MA, 1993.

Kotkin, S. *Magnetic Mountain: Stalinism as a Civilization*. Berkeley, 1995.

Lewin, M. *Russian Peasants and Soviet Power: A Study of Collectivization*. New York, 1975.

Malia, M. *The Soviet Tragedy: A History of Socialism in Russia, 1917–1991*. New York, 1994.

Nove, A. *An Economic History of the USSR*, 3rd edn. London, 1990.

Pipes, R. E. *The Formation of the Soviet Union: Communism and Nationalism, 1917–1923*. Cambridge, MA, 1964.

—— *Russia under the Bolshevik Regime*. New York, 1994.

Schapiro, L. *The Origins of the Communist Autocracy*. London, 1955.

—— *The Communist Party of the Soviet Union*. London, 1960.

Service, R. *A History of Twentieth-Century Russia*. Cambridge, MA, 1997.

—— *Lenin*, 3 vols. London, 1985–95.

Stokesbury, J. L. *A Short History of World War II*. New York, 1980.

Suny, R. G. *The Baku Commune, 1917–18: Class and Nationality in the Russian Revolution*. Princeton, 1972.

Tucker, R. C. *Stalin as a Revolutionary, 1879–1929*. New York, 1975.

—— *Stalin in Power: The Revolution from Above, 1928–1941*. New York, 1990.

Ulam, A. *The Bolsheviks: The Intellectual and Political History of the Triumph of Communism in Russia*. New York, 1965.

—— *Expansion and Coexistence: The History of Soviet Foreign Policy, 1917–67*. New York, 1968.

Viola, L. *Peasant Rebels under Stalin: Collectivization and the Culture of Peasant Resistance*. New York, 1996.

Von Hagen, M. L. *Soldiers in the Proletarian Dictatorship*. Ithaca, NY, 1991.

REFORM, STAGNATION, COLLAPSE

Aron, L. *Yeltsin: A Revolutionary Life*. New York, 2000.

Aslund, A. *Gorbachev's Struggle for Economic Reform*. Ithaca, NY, 1991.

—— *How Russia Became a Market Economy*. Washington, 1995.

Bialer, S. *Stalin's Successors*. Cambridge, 1980.

Brown, A. *The Gorbachev Factor*. Oxford, 1997.

Goldman, M. I. *USSR in Crisis: The Failure of an Economic System*. New York, 1983.

Gorbachev, M. S. *Perestroika: New Thinking for Our Country and the World*. New York and London, 1987.

Hosking, G. *The Awakening of the Soviet Union*. Cambridge, MA, 1991.

Keep, J. L. H. *Last of the Empires: A History of the Soviet Union, 1945–1991*. Oxford, 1995.

McCauley, M. *The Soviet Union since 1917*. London and New York, 1981.

—— *Nikita Khrushchev*. London, 1991.

Remnick, D. *Lenin's Tomb: The Last Days of the Soviet Empire*. New York, 1993.

Shatz, M. S. *Soviet Dissent in Historical Perspective*. New York, 1980.

Shevtsova, L. *Yeltsin's Russia: Myths and Reality*. Washington, 1999.

Suny, R. G. *The Revenge of the Past*. Stanford, CA, 1994.

Yeltsin, B. *Against the Grain*. London, 1990.

THE RISE AND RISE OF PUTIN

Laqueur, W. *Putinism: Russia and Its Future with the West*, New York, 2015.

Myers, S. L. *The New Tsar: The Rise and Reign of Vladimir Putin*, New York, 2015.

INDEX